THE BRITISH SPY NOVEL
Styles in Treachery

LPL

By the same author

Literary Commentary:
The Art of Ernest Hemingway
George Orwell
Arthur Koestler
Aldous Huxley
Graham Greene
Tomorrow Revealed
Six Novelists Look at Society
J.B. Priestley

Fiction:
Cat on Hot Bricks
Rain and the River
A Land Fit for Eros *(with J.B. Pick)*

Literary History:
Sex in Literature: I, Introductory Survey
Sex in Literature: II, The Classical Experience
Sex in Literature: III, The Medieval Experience
Sex in Literature: IV, High Noon: The 17th & 18th Centuries

JOHN
RIVERR

THE BRITISH SPY NOVEL

Styles in Treachery

JOHN ATKINS

CALDER · LONDON
UN PRESS · NEW YORK

First published in Great Britain in 1984 by
John Calder (Publishers) Limited
18 Brewer Street, London W1R 4AS
and in the United States of America by
Riverrun Press Inc.
175 Fifth Avenue, New York City 10010

British Library Cataloguing in Publication Data
Atkins, John, *1916–*
    The British spy novel.
    1. Spy stories, English—History and criticism
    I. Title
    823'.0872   PR830.S65

ISBN 0-7145-3997-X
Library of Congress Catalogue Card Number 84-42650

SUBSIDISED BY THE
Arts Council
OF GREAT BRITAIN

Printed in Great Britain by Photobooks (Brist

ACKNOWLEDGEMENTS

Among writers, I owe much to the encouragement of Len Deighton and Warren Tute. I am also grateful to my friend, John Pick, for introducing me to the work of Lionel Davidson and to my son-in-law, Mark Jones, for bringing that underrated writer Manning Coles (perhaps I should say 'writers', it's a partnership!) to my attention. I am also indebted to the following: Robert Easton, for giving me information about that mysterious writer, Max Brand; Sir Hugh Greene, for suggesting ways through the maze created by William Le Queux and E. Phillips Oppenheim; Bob Evans, for supplying me with photocopies of critical work in American magazines; and the Crime Writers Association and their secretary, Marian Babson, for allowing me to see their 1968 pamphlet, 'Intelligence'.

I would like to thank the following authors, publishers and agents for permission to quote from the novels indicated. Marcel d'Agneau and Arlington Books, *Eeny, Meeny, Miny, Mole*. Eric Ambler and William Heinemann Ltd., *The Light of Day*. Blond & Briggs for Alan Williams's *Gentleman Traitor*. Jonathan Clowes Ltd. for *Goodbye to an Old Friend* by Brian Freemantle. William Collins, Sons & Co. Ltd. for Desmond Bagley's *The Freedom Trap*. Len Deighton and Jonathan Cape Ltd., *Yesterday's Spy, Billion-Dollar Brain*. J.M Dent & Sons Ltd. for Warren Tute's *The Tarnham Connection*. John Farquharson Ltd. for *Yesterday's Enemy, The Hard Sell* and *The Hardliners* by William Haggard. Brian Freemantle and Jonathan Cape Ltd., *Face Me When You Walk Away* and *Charlie Muffin*. Glidrose Productions Ltd. for Ian Fleming's *Moonraker, From Russia With Love, Dr No, Thunderball, For Your Eyes Only, You Only Live Twice, Casino Royale*, and *The Man With the Golden Gun*. Victor Gollancz Ltd. for *Other Paths to Glory, October Man, War Game* and *Tomorrow's Ghost* by Anthony Price and *The Anti-Death League* by Kingsley Amis. Hodder & Stoughton Ltd. for *Uncommon Danger* and *Journey Into Fear* by Eric Ambler and *No. 70, Berlin* by William Le Queux. John Le Carré and William Heinemann Ltd., *The Looking Glass War*. The Trustees of the Estate of the late Colonel H.C.

McNeile for *Temple Tower* by Sapper. Robert Markham (Kingsley Amis) and Jonathan Cape Ltd., *Colonel Sun.* Campbell Thomson & McLaughlin Ltd., for *The Schirmer Inheritance* and the Introduction from *To Catch a Spy* by Eric Ambler. The Rt. Hon. Lord Tweedsmuir CBE for John Buchan's *Greenmantle* and *The Courts of the Morning*. Weidenfeld (Publishers) Ltd., for *The Spy Who Sat and Waited* by R. Wright Campbell.

And especial thanks to Agnes Rook whose suggestions and advice were so invaluable while getting this book ready for the press.

CONTENTS

PREFACE

First we need a definition of the subject: espionage. If we look in the accepted first source, the *Encyclopaedia Britannica*, we will be directed to 'Intelligence and Counterintelligence'. This is what it says:

> Covert sources of intelligence are more dramatic, falling into three major classifications: aerial and space reconnaissance, electronic 'eavesdropping', and the secret agent working at the classic spy trade. Broadly speaking, the value of each as a source of crucial information is probably in descending order as listed. This is because a photographic report constitutes 'hard' intelligence, whereas the report of a secret agent may be speculative, difficult to prove, and therefore 'soft'.

It is the software that provides the drama in this instance and makes it such a suitable subject for fiction. The author of this article is naturally not concerned with the fictional aspect but he cannot resist a snide comment which is, nevertheless, undeniable. 'Of writers of spy fiction it has accurately been said, "Never have so many been misled by so few." '

It has even become fashionable in some quarters to speak of our period as the Age of the Spy. Spying is a very old trade, historically either the first or the second, but it does seem likely that the amount of wealth and effort invested in espionage is greater today than ever before. Alfred Hitchcock, who made a collection of spy stories which he called *Sinister Spies*, wrote in his introduction, which he nattily entitled 'Spies and Otherwise', that contemporary life is so complicated and new developments take place so quickly that each nation feels it is necessary to know what all the other nations are up to. He may have got this idea from Eric Ambler. He adds that 'the international spy has multiplied a thousand fold. Scientists or street sweepers may act as spies, for money, for patriotism, for adventure. Women, with their eye for detail and their acting ability, make excellent spies.' In these few words Hitchcock pinpoints many of the matters that will concern anyone who studies spy fiction. As a rough test of the nation's awareness of the spying activity that is going on all the time, how many people today would be puzzled by the initials CIA, KGB, MI5 and MI6? Not everyone will know what they stand for but most will have a very good idea of what the organizations do.

That the spy writers have made a considerable impact on the public is the reason why I am writing this book. Nothing will illustrate this better than the reaction of *The Times* to the escape of George Blake. It may be recalled that he was committed to Wormwood Scrubs in 1961. He pleaded guilty to five offences against the Official Secrets Act. None of the details could be published or even discussed in open court. He had worked continuously for the Russians for nine years. His information had not been scientific but it was very important and rendered much of Britain's defence strategy completely useless. Or so we were told.

He escaped on 22 October 1966. He had been taken off the 'escape list'. It was assumed that he had passed all the information that might be useful to the Russians, for whom he would be no longer useful. He had been sentenced to forty-two years, the longest in British history. At the time of his escape some other spies were also serving long sentences: Peter and Helen Kroger (twenty years), Frank Bossard (twenty-one years) and William Vassall (eighteen years). A pot of chrysanthemums was found against the wall where Blake was believed to have escaped.

Lord Hailsham, then Mr Hogg, Conservative member for St Marylebone, proposed a vote of censure on the Home Secretary, Roy Jenkins. The question was whether a spy was of any value after he had escaped. Lord Hailsham said it was 'rather innocent to believe that a dedicated enemy of his country who had been ten years or more in the security service could be of no use at all when he took refuge behind the Iron Curtain, either as a matter of consultation on organization of the matters on which he had been previously employed or the methods of interrogation to which he had been subjected. All that must have told Blake a good deal about methods of interrogation employed by the counter-espionage service, and it would be of the highest use in training agents from the other side.'

And now, this is how *The Times* reacted to the news on 31 October:

> Theories about the real story behind the escape continue to pour forth and now fall into three main groups. The choice between them depends as much as anything on personal

predilections in the fictional world of crime and spies.

For the Fleming set there is the theory that Blake had a two-way radio in Wormwood Scrubs and messages were sent in to him from outside prison. Supporting evidence for this is that work in the prison radio shop was stopped last week after a search . . .

The Le Carré enthusiasts see it rather differently. To them the escape is quite clearly a plot by the British Secret Service, and Blake will now act as a double (or whatever the number is) agent. The main defect in this theory is that it presupposes the Home Secretary would be willing to take the risk of placing his head on the block because of the escape.

Defective or not, there were spy fiction writers who later showed themselves ready to accept this theory. As for the third one, it was based on Agatha Christie (who has written spy novels but is not considered primarily a spy writer), and it centred on the pot of pink chrysanthemums.

Behind the Novel

How accurate is spy fiction? It is impossible to give a positive answer because there are so many writers covering such a wide range of knowledge and imagination. The usual charge is that it is over-sensational. I would like to point out that not so long ago a British Ambassador in Moscow went to bed with a chamber maid. A real Ambassador, not a fictional Warren Tute-Len Deighton Ambassador!

One of the accepted truths of spy lore is that British Intelligence is extremely efficient and probably the best in the world. Philby rejected this in his book. Between the wars, the intelligence service had enjoyed a mythical prestige; but this myth had little substance (*My Silent War*, 1968). Compton Mackenzie makes a mocking reference to the myth in his *Water on the Brain*, 1933. But it used to be stated with monotonous frequency in spy novels, especially by foreigners, as if to emphasize the validity of the statement. Blenkiron, Buchan's American, said it and so does General Vozdvishensky of the Soviet Foreign Ministry in Fleming's *From Russia With Love*:

Their Security Service is excellent. England, being an island, has great security advantages and their so-called MI5 employs men with good education and good brains. The Secret Service is still better. They have notable successes. In certain types of operation, we are constantly finding that they have been there before us. Their agents are good. They pay them little money—only a thousand or two thousand roubles a month—but they serve with devotion. Yet these agents have no special privileges in England, no relief from taxation and no special shops such as we have, from which they can buy cheap goods. Their social standing abroad is not high, and their wives have to pass as the wives of secretaries. They are rarely awarded a decoration until they retire. And yet these men and women continue to do this dangerous work. It is curious. It is perhaps the Public School and University tradition. The love of adventure. But still it is odd that they play this game so well, for they are not natural conspirators.

There are one or two very odd points here, although one soon discovers that Fleming's work is full of anomalies. First of all, there is the habit, dating back at least to Oppenheim, of calling the British Service English. This is all the more surprising in view of the fact that Bond himself is not English. He is half Scottish, Hannay wholly so. Then it comes as a shock to hear the Public School and University (meaning, of course, Oxbridge) tradition praised when recent history encourages us to regard it as a weak link. And it is doubtful if any high-up Soviet official would regard it as strange that English wives should be employed as secretaries when some of the most eminent Soviet agents masquerade as doormen and chauffeurs.

But there is another circumstance which is held to militate against the excellence of the British Service, and it is one that is being increasingly noted by spy writers. Britain is no longer a great world power. No matter how efficient the Service may be, it is not likely to be anything like as influential as the CIA or KGB. It has in fact been relegated to another division where its main rival (or colleague) will be another service that is sometimes called 'the most efficient in the world'—the Israeli Mossad. This decline in status worries Altmann, the Austrian double agent in Freemantle's *The November Man*, who is wondering where to defect to. 'He dismissed England immediately: they still had what was possibly the most efficient secret service in the world, but it was small, without the scope of either Washington or Moscow.'

Incidentally, if the British have rivals in the Secret Service stakes it is apparently the Russians. During the nineteenth century in particular the Russian spy was feared and respected. (Today he is feared but not always respected.) Gerald Morgan, writing in the *Contemporary Review* for November 1969, claims that the Russians have a 'remarkable bent for espionage' and attributes it to their contact with the Mongols, who ruled partly by intrigue. He says that throughout their history they have loathed defections ('A glimpse of Russian Nineteenth Century Espionage'). Ronald Seth, in his unsatisfactory *Encyclopaedia of Espionage*, says that Russian espionage is the most feared spying organization in the world after the British Secret Service, and adds that MI6 is 'the most secret intelligence service in the world'—whatever that means, except that it is a superlative.

It was stressed at the time of the Blake trial and later escape that his activities had caused irreparable damage to British security. One often hears statements of this kind and is tempted to wonder if it is anything more than hyperbole. Robert Cecil, in a valuable article entitled 'Legends Spies Tell' in *Encounter* (April 1978) doubts if the damage caused by spies is ever quite as great as is frequently claimed. His argument was that the usefulness of Burgess and Maclean to the Russians ceased with their defection. Whatever information they may have carried in their heads would have soon lost its value. The main damage was to Anglo-American relations and in particular to the confidence between the counter-espionage services of the two countries. Certainly the 'excellence' and 'efficiency' of the British service must have been put in doubt. But on the other hand, the Americans suffered losses nearly as sensational. And, of course, it is difficult to estimate the damage done by an agent before he defects.

In this study I draw a good deal of attention to the general murkiness of the spy situation. How can we possibly, for instance, evaluate the work of the double agent? Ideally it is a 100-0 division, with each side believing it possesses the 100. This can never be true. Supposing it is 50-50, then no-one benefits and the agent might just as well not exist. The breakdown is more likely to be in the region of 75-25, but *cui bono*? Cecil writes of Maclean that 'his double life had induced in him something of a split mind.' The day he disappeared he left 'a concise and accurate record of a visit paid to him on 25 May by the Argentine Minister-Counsellor, who had raised an intricate point connected with current trade negotiations.' So much for the professional. But what of the amateur, the innocent who is drawn into espionage against his will or even his knowing? Davidson's *The Night of Wenceslas* gives a good idea of bewilderment in the trade.

The Attraction of Spy Fiction

To begin with, espionage is a constant. It has been with us for a long time and presumably will continue for as long as the world is divided into sovereign states and human beings remain suspicious and envious. Spy fiction was late in arriving for reasons which I submit to the reader later in this study. Anyone who is interested in this aspect of espionage could not do better than read Michael Burn's *The Debatable Land*, subtitled A Study of the Motives of Spies in Two Ages. The two ages are the Elizabethan and our own. He compares the personnel and motives of two sets of spies. For our own time he pays especial attention to Philby, whom he holds in contempt. All the characteristics of modern espionage were to be found among the spies who worked for Cecil and Walsingham: there were codes and ciphers, 'cover', informers, double agents; false information was planted, and a known spy was allowed to carry on to further incriminate himself and bring in more information; there was blackmail, spying on your own man and, in extremis killing him. 'Little in these aspects has altered save the original source of inspiration and the names.'

This does not explain the flood of spy literature since the last World War, however. Deighton puts forward an ingenious theory in *Spy Story*. Is the vogue for espionage stories and for espionage itself just a way of continuing the atmosphere of military bonhomie and comradeship which many found so congenial? (One might reach the same conclusion on reading Le Carré's *The Looking-Glass War*.) In the Deighton novel Armstrong is more or less hi-jacked to the Hebrides to join Toliver's group who are planning to meet and bring in a defecting Russian admiral. He finds the atmosphere distasteful. 'They weren't satisfied just to create a self-congratulatory, and exclusively masculine, society, they were attempting to recreate one that existed only in their wishful thoughts. The I've-been-here-before feeling that all this was giving me had come undiluted from old

British war films, especially those about Colditz.' They even use the out-dated slang of the period: 'Good show, Mason.'

We certainly cannot ignore the mystery element, a sure winner in story-telling, even in the mainstream novel. (Who is Tom Jones's mother? Why was Pip left money?) The mystery in spy fiction is of a specialized kind: *Something is going on—but what?* This aspect at its purest is to be found in the first masterpiece in the genre, *The Riddle of the Sands*, and followed up with Price's *Other Paths to Glory.* Then there is a subsidiary question which is frequently exploited: *We know what is going on—but how?* If the crime story is Whodunit, the spy story (in fact, the political thriller) is Howdunit.

The individual agent is in danger today. He cannot think as quickly as a computer nor move as quickly as a radio wave. So is there a future to spying and, it follows, the spy story?—a question that already agitates the minds of the more thoughtful. So far as the story is concerned there is always the historical approach, as already exploited by Dennis Wheatley. But there are meeting grounds for the various genres, and space fiction will surely accommodate the spy. Robert Sheckley, a science fiction writer, assumes in his story 'Citizen in Space' (in the Hitchcock collection) that after, say, 1991 a man will be judged by the number and quality of spies he has attending him. The hero was an 18-D Suspect—it was the same classification as that of the Vice-President—and this entitled him to part-time sur-veillance. He was dissatisfied with the Spy allotted to him and went to the Senate Investigations Committee to ask why he couldn't have a *trained* Spy, like his friends.

There are some who are already predicting the end of the spy novel. One of these is P.D. James who celebrated the Fiftieth Anniversary of the Collins Crime Club with an article in *Now!* entitled 'The Magical Mystery Tour' (3–10 April, 1980). Now Ms James writes detective fiction and her forecast seems to me to have as much impartiality as that of a soccer player foreseeing the collapse of rugger or a Worcester Pearmain grower celebrating the end of the Golden Delicious. After making some sensible comments on developments in the crime novel and noting the end of hanging and the new importance of treachery and failure (which should have warned her to tread carefully) she writes:

> Will the spy thriller, today's dominant genre, hold its pre-
> eminence? Personally, I think not, if only because its present

practitioners, notably Graham Greene, John Le Carré and
Anthony Price have done it as well as it is capable of being
done.

This seems to be a particularly inept observation. There are many
critics and readers who think Conan Doyle wrote the detective story
as well as it was possible to write it, but the genre continued to
flourish. Perhaps *because* of Doyle.

Variety of Spy Fiction

I suppose it is in the nature of the critic to look for peaks and troughs
in his material. There are Great Periods and Blue Periods and Periods
of Decadence. Those few critics who have turned their attention to
spy fiction are no exception. Myron J. Smith composed an Annotated
Guide to Spy Fiction, 1937–75, which he called *Cloak-and-Dagger
Bibliography*. For this relatively short period (though it probably did
contain the bulk of spy fiction) Smith lists 1675 titles. It is true that
they are American as well as British, plus a few translations from
other languages, but the majority appear to be British in origin—and
Smith does say, in his introduction, that they are, on the whole, the
best. Remember, Fleming's Russian said the British make good spies.
They also seem to make good spy writers. Smith makes an interesting
comment in a note on Le Carré: 'After Le Carré, the cuteness, by and
large, went out of spy fiction (and movie) business and probably
contributed in no small degree to its decline in vogue.' I should never
have thought of calling the spy story 'cute' but possibly my
Americanization has not gone far enough. But has there been a
decline? Smith must be referring to the greater realism (and lesser
romanticism) of the genre. Le Carré and Deighton have usually been
held responsible for the sordidness that has characterized recent
novels, just as before them Greene (a powerful influence) had been
held responsible for increased sordidness in the tone of mainstream
novels.

Certainly these writers (and others) introduced a change of tone
which I, for one, welcomed. There are signs of a reaction against the
realist spy writer though it is hard to believe that the average reader
wants a return to scrambling over the heather (and anyway, he still
gets that from Household) or uttering patriotic tosh in the

Chancelleries of Europe. I think the change is much more likely to be the result of a familiar development in literature which does not depend on thought at all but merely on reaction. It is what Kingsley Amis, in an essay called 'The Cockney's Homer', calls 'dropping writers'. He refers to a 'restlessness, a tendency to drop a writer once he becomes established and to turn their talent-detectors elsewhere.' Ever since I have taken an interest in current writing and its public reception I have seen this happening. The critic (or intellectual) heaps praise on a new writer and then recoils in disgust when the *hoi polloi* follow suit. It happened with John Fowles; Le Carré has ceased to be the darling of the fashionable mob; and I think it is time Ian MacEwan started thinking about his future.

The range between good and bad is possibly greater in spy-fi than in any other genre, though that is not a matter I would care to be dogmatic about. It gives scope to an enormous variety of subject-matter. At one end we have blondes and automatics and invisible inks and poisoned drinks and underwater death struggles; at the other end we have political discussions and Marxist dialectic and historical hypotheses and 'plateau' thinking; and all of these things can be mixed up in medleys which can be fascinating or idiotic. It might be possible to judge the general level of a genre by the writing which comes out of it, about it. Merry's *Anatomy of the Spy Thriller* is excellent. With *Clubland Heroes*, a work vastly different in approach and character, it forms the classic canon of criticism arising out of the spy thriller. The use of 'spy' in this study is strained—'subversive' or 'conspiracy' would be more accurate. In fact, it is impossible to distinguish between these forms; if it were possible, it would be futile. Espionage necessarily leads to counter-espionage, which is another way of saying that stealing plans necessarily leads to catching thieves. Merry's aim is to illustrate 'the universality of popular literature and the atemporality of its appeal', beginning with the fairy tale and going right through to Deighton and Le Carré. Now and again his prejudices break through. For example, he believes that Forsyth's *The Day of the Jackal* may represent the ultimate in this field. 'It will be hard for the spy thriller to surpass the concentrated economy of violence achieved in Forsyth's book, and this is a further sense in which he may have constructed the model example of the genre.' He points out that this novel does not contain a single joke, whereas Deighton appears to build his novels around a constant succession of sarcastic riposte and wisecracks.

But to return to *The Day of the Jackal*, which is certainly the most impressive product of the Documentary Fiction School, though Deighton's *Bomber* runs it very close. It is a genre which has a special appeal to the writer on espionage, and in fact there is considerable overlap. Forsyth is writing about conspiracy, not espionage. (There is a single mention of Philby, whose personality looms over the whole field and cannot be ignored.) The political documentary novel also has an unavoidable structural weakness, clearly exhibited by *The Jackal*: as we know that de Gaulle was not assassinated, it is clear that the assassin's aim cannot be accomplished. (Compare this with Fleming's *Casino Royale*, where the end is affected by technical considerations).

There is no more impressive picture of a professional killer in the whole of spy-cum-conspiracy literature. The anonymity of the would-be assassin strengthens the portrait. He is referred to by his code-name, The Jackal, and then by a series of aliases. Even when we think we know who he is we discover on the last page that this was yet another alias. Forsyth also manages to inject precise detail without resorting to snobbery. Unlike Fleming, he can tell us the Jackal smokes without mentioning a brand only obtainable in Bond Street. The police are not represented as muddle-headed fools, although some of the rural police bumble and lick their pencils in the established manner of detective fiction. The security organizations, both French and British, are frequently outwitted but not because they are stupid. It is because the Jackal has planned his project brilliantly.

One last point before embarking. It is a common practice among mainstream novelists to try their hand at genres once the particular genre is obviously attracting readers. It happened with science fiction and it has happened and is still happening with spy literature. To take one example, that sturdy old campaigner of fiction, J.B. Priestley, joined the ranks. The title of the novel is *The Shapes of Sleep* and one feels that the author's heart is not in the espionage. It is told satirically—one feels Priestley is mocking every spy writer who ever put pen to paper—and this is why it fails to satisfy. In general it is true to say that any hack can write a better spy novel than any genius, if the former believes in the rubbish he is writing and the latter cannot. The spy novel is sufficiently outrageous in itself; the world of espionage may be a reflection of the real world but it is a distorted one. Ben Sterndale, an honest newspaperman who is down on his luck, thinks 'this whole world of propaganda and secret services, espionage and counter-espionage, is nothing but dreary and dirty lunacy. To hell with it—and all the men who spend other people's money on it!' Ben ends with some vintage Priestley-preaching. 'We'll hush-hush and top secret ourselves off the face of the earth soon if we don't stop behaving like hypnotized sheep.' Le Carré and Greene make us see the idiocy and the sordidness without the ranting. It helps belief.

The Plan

A few words about my procedure in this book. A sheer analytic approach is death and an attempted synthetic approach is confusion. Chronology is important but not all-important. In describing any complex movement or organization it is necessary, if one is to approach the feel of truth, to proceed by a series of associations, links, cause-and-effects, which together form a mesh rather than a line. This is shockingly metaphorical but only because a point is reached where linguistic imperfection allows no alternative.

I start with Childers and *The Riddle of the Sands*. It is a fortunate accident that the genre virtually started with a minor masterpiece. Buchan follows because Buchan believed in the value of what he was doing and happened to write good traditional English. He was, therefore, a model for those many writers who desire a model. Oppenheim and Le Queux are jokes. It is fashionable to sneer at them but no sneer will eradicate them. Bulldog Drummond was a disaster and we should be ashamed of ourselves if we are not ashamed of him. But Valentine Williams and his endearing Clubfoot, practically forgotten though they are, do something to redeem the balance. So far it is all personality. But now we move to the fearful pomposity of the early spy story, the insistence that civilization would collapse if the naval plans were not recovered. And then: Fleming. I do not pretend that Fleming is a genius but I cannot deny that he is the most successful (in terms of sales) spy writer there has ever been. I give him three chapters: one on himself, one on his Bond and the third on the most astonishing aspect of all his industry—the amount of punishment Bond could soak up without any obvious ill-effects.

After that I turn to more technical matters: how espionage and conspiracy are carried out on the fictional page. I relate this to the 'real' background, and then discuss the determination of spies and spy writers to refer to their activity as a Game. Ethics and motives lead me inevitably to Somerset Maugham; the logic may not be obvious but I think most spy writers would accept it. And now we are back with personalities: Le Carré (two chapters for the man who made the spy novel respectable) and Greene, who made it impossible to distinguish between the novel and the spy novel. Who is the Enemy? Not an easy question. What about Tradition, Public School spies—and contemptuous Grammar School Types? And then Deighton, who in some ways has come to meet us from the future, like another Asimov. Different writers pointing in different directions. And finally, attempts at the virtually impossible—satirizing what is in itself a kind of satire.

1: THE BEGINNING

Robert Erskine Childers, 1870-1922, was always a bit of a mystery man to his colleagues among the clerks in the House of Commons. His closest friend was Basil Williams who once remarked: 'Few realized that the unobtrusive little man with the glasses and the sciatic limp was leading a double life. He let none of us know—until the information tumbled out one day, quite by chance—that his weekends were spent in the Thames estuary, sailing single-handed a scrubby little yacht.' It seems a very satisfactory image for the spy writer, especially the progenitor of the genre. It also fed the mistrust which later led to his execution. He made six voyages of discovery through the narrow sand-locked channels of the Frisian islands to the open Baltic. The first was the hardest, a long haul across the North Sea in August 1897. Somewhere along the line he invented the spy novel as we know it today.

The Spy's Trade

One feels that Carruthers, the hero of *The Riddle of the Sands* (1903), or his creator Childers knew far more about the contemporary world, especially the political world, than Bond or Fleming ever did. Scattered through the book is a good deal of informed and intelligent comment. We are told that Carruthers and his companion had frequent and detailed conversations about 'the burning question of Germany'. Carruthers used to outline to a willing listener the growth of German power: 'Our great trade rivals of the present, our great naval rivals of the future.' Britain, with her 'delicate network of empire', was at risk. Davies is quick to catch on. 'And we aren't ready for her; we don't look her way. We have no naval base in the North Sea, and no North Sea fleet. Our best battleships are too deep in draught for North Sea work. And, to crown all, we were asses enough to give her Heligoland, which commands the North Sea coast.'

Davies had a small library of books about sea power. Mahan was a strong influence, especially his *Influence of Sea Power*. In his Preface the author says that the important facts discovered in the course of the cruise had been communicated to 'the proper authorities' who, after both delay and 'dignified credulity', due perhaps to 'the pitiful inadequacy of their own secret service', had made use of them to avert a great national danger. A postscript tells us that while the book was in the press a Committee of National Defence had been set up and a site on the Forth had been selected for a new North Sea naval base.

The book had a utilitarian purpose. It was also deeply concerned with international morality, an edifice that has crumbled considerably since its time. Carruthers could not at first believe that Dollmann had tried to murder Davies. 'It was incredible that the murder of a young Englishman should be connived at in modern days by a friendly and civilized government!' In more modern days it is no longer incredible. Nothing illustrates so starkly the immense change that has taken place during this century in international morality. We can go further: 'civilized' governments have been known to put their own spies to death once their usefulness has been exhausted.

Everyone agreed, eighty years ago, that spying was a dirty trade. Childers helped to change all that. To the decent young yachtsmen of his book, as yet uncorrupted by the post-1918 world, there is something extremely disreputable and degrading about espionage. Davies was prepared to reveal any dirty tricks the Germans might be up to in the channels between and around the islands off the German North Sea coast, but he was not prepared to spy on their naval defences. This was an idea he 'dreaded and distrusted'. He had to change his mind; he found justification in the fact that the 'enemy' was a traitor. Dollmann was British! He *had* to be unmasked. There had to be an adjustment of opinion. Spies were 'dirty though necessary tools'. Carruthers and Davies were convinced that Dollmann had been spying in England. It was this that finally made the difference. One feels that his activities in Germany were distasteful but permissible. Dollmann was compounding his treachery to a degree that was unacceptable.

Childers could make this mental leap in his attitude to spying. So far as women were concerned (and fictional spies have been greatly concerned) he remained a staunch Victorian. In his Foreword to the Penguin edition of *Riddle* Geoffrey Household says the only fault of the book is 'its shadowy heroine, Dollmann's daughter.' Childers wrote: 'I was weak enough to spatchcock a girl into it and now I find her a horrible nuisance.' It was at the insistence of his publisher. Fleming, of course, was never to find the spatchcocking a nuisance. Davies is surely one of the most inept lovers in the whole of English literature, and that's saying something. The mere thought of Clara causes him to blush and mumble extravagantly; at the end of the story it is true she is in his arms, but how she got there is one of the biggest mysteries of the novel. Seventy years later she would have lain across the gunwale a dozen times by then, or wherever modern marine-spies lay their victims. One other thing about Clara. Apart from her personal relationship with Davies, she is very much a riddle in herself. Did she know what her father was up to? Did she know his past history? It remains possible, right to the end, that she is not really such a nice girl as she appears to be.

Significance of the 'Riddle'

The Riddle of the Sands, subtitled A Record of Secret Service, is usually and rightly referred to as the first modern espionage novel, and sometimes as the best, though the latter judgment may be part of a familiar cliché: 'first and best'. The story is told by Carruthers from his diary and Davies's log, edited by an unnamed third person—and this must be Childers, as author. Because it has always been classified as a spy story it hasn't had the recognition it deserves. Its description of unfamiliar material, at first sight not at all likely to stimulate interest except among a few yachtsmen, is excellent. *The Times Literary Supplement* review of 14 August 1903 says the 'whole story can scarcely be understood by any but practical navigators.' 'The wearied critic of fiction' is outworn with 'shoals, sands, channels and "glances at the chart."' After uncomplimentary references to the sex interest the reviewer concludes that 'the book must stand, not as a novel, but as a sketch in naval geography, with adventures, incomprehensible to the landsman, thrown in.'

The reviewer, quite understandably, didn't know what he was handling. Classification very often destroys a proper judgment. If *Riddle* is treated as a spy story or an adventure yarn about boats, it will not receive the consideration it deserves as a novel. The characterization, especially of Davies, is controlled and consistent. Carruthers loathes discomfort, in an unadventurous way, and displays great charm when the need arises. Davies, on the other hand, is gauche and at times boorish, but he is humanly presented and is not treated as a kind of mechanical contrast to Carruthers. The writing is taut and the reader is credited with intelligence and powers of concentration.

Household says that Childers's intention was 'propaganda disguised as fiction'. It certainly takes its time in introducing the espionage theme but it was written in a leisurely age. For the first seven chapters there is nothing more agonising than a few Dutch boys throwing stones and mud at foreign yachts. The first forced note comes when Carruthers asks: 'Was I never to be at an end of the puzzles which Davies presented to me?', and this is forced because there have in fact been very few puzzles indeed, and what there are have been quite unsensational. Davies is really way ahead of all of us, readers as well as Carruthers, and it is easy to take his statement that 'I had come to the conclusion that *that chap was a spy*' with a pinch of salt.

The whole concept of spying, as applied to this novel, is rather curious. For who was the spy, Dollmann or Davies? Davies has twigged that Dollmann is an Englishman, which makes his classification as a spy even more difficult to sustain, unless he is to be regarded as spying for his native land, for he operates in German waters and along a stretch of German sea-coast. In fact, it is finally revealed that it is Carruthers and his friend who are the spies, not Dollmann, and this gives the development of the novel as a whole a remarkable and extremely unconventional twist.

The major blemish in the novel is its apparent lack of plausible motivation. Without Davies's almost manic distrust of Dollmann the mystery does not even exist. Davies is convinced that Dollmann tried to murder him (lure him to his death would be the accurate way of expressing it) and the reader is as reluctant as Carruthers to take this seriously at first. It is part of the excellence of the narrative that we are slowly and inexorably persuaded that something is wrong. But still, it is difficult to see what or who Dollmann is spying on and then we finally realize that it is not he who is spying. Unless we are to believe that it is the German authorities who are suspicious of their own warships and their own mudflats, Dollmann cannot be a spy. And in fact he is not, he is a traitor, and what appears to be a blemish is not one after all. It is a very well sustained piece of writing.

I have made much of this point because of the overwhelming conviction at the time that spying was dirty work and was only indulged in by scoundrels. We call *Riddle* the first of the spy novels not because it was the first chronologically to take espionage as its subject but because it was the first to do so seriously and plausibly. There had been spy stories before this and Carruthers had a low opinion of them. Davies once asked him if he looked like a spy. The idea was laughable. 'I figured to myself one of those romantic gentlemen that one reads of in sixpenny magazines, with a Kodak in his tie-pin, a sketch-book in the lining of his coat, and a selection of disguises in his hand luggage. Little disposed for merriment as I was, I could not help smiling, too.'

It is possible that Childers had read E.P. Oppenheim's *Mysterious Mr Sabin*, which appeared five years before his own novel and was re-issued in 1899. In a few pages we are told that Wolfenden retires to his room at midnight in a state of great dejection, having just been rejected by Hélène, Mr Sabin's beautiful niece, who cannot hide her hatred of England. Between two and three o'clock he is disturbed by his supposedly mad father, a retired Admiral, who says there is an intruder in the library. His own door had been locked but he had escaped through the window. They arrive just in time to see a table strewn with papers and the figure of a man escaping as the light is turned out. The Admiral fires. There is a flurry of skirts and a woman passes Wolfenden. He realizes from her perfume who she is and lets her go. A dead servant is found—but he had not been shot. Not only are the rascals trying to provoke a war between England and Germany, they are also plotting to restore the French monarchy. Hélène is a Bourbon.

Riddle must have come as a relief after this sort of thing. Household points out that Carruthers and Davies were amateur spies. They have an early, one might say pristine, view of espionage, with few complications. The sixpenny spies may have had their concealed cameras; their successors of the post-World War II period would certainly outbid them in that direction. Bond would have felt naked with such miserable aids. Carruthers and Davies were simple patriots. They consoled themselves with the thought that spying was necessary because 'the man's an Englishman, and if he's in Germany he's a traitor to us, and we as Englishmen have a right to expose him. If we can't do it without spying we've a right to spy, at our own risk—.' It was patriotic spying, not professional. Their favourite maxim would have horrified Bond. 'When in doubt, tell the truth', says Carruthers and Davies comments, 'It's a rum thing how often it pays in this spying business.'

Childers didn't realize the significance of what he was doing. He wrote to his friend Williams about the story he was working on in 1901. 'It's a yachting story, with a purpose, suggested by a cruise I once took in German waters. I discovered a scheme of invasion directed against England.' He called it as 'being in the nature of a detective story'. Then follows the remark about spatchcocking the girl.

Buchan liked it but simply saw it as an adventure story—'the best story of adventure published in the last quarter of a century . . . as for the characters, I think they are the most fully realized of any adventure story that I have met', which in view of TLS is not very convincing, but was if the statement was narrowed to spy-fiction. Eventually the importance of *Riddle* was held to be political. His warnings began to be taken seriously in Whitehall and Childers was relieved to find Fisher at the Admiralty in sympathy with his ideas. It was only half a century later, when espionage began to be treated as a serious literary theme, that the novel came to be seen as a landmark.

Other Lines

One must always have reservations about using terms like 'first' and 'best' to describe *Riddle* because of Kipling's *Kim*, which appeared two years before the other book in 1901. The reason is because *Kim* is so much more than a spy novel whereas *Riddle*, despite its merits, cannot bear comparison as literary fiction. Very gradually Kim realizes he is being used in some great intrigue, first through his friendship with the Pathan horse-dealer, Mahbub Ali, and then by Colonel Creighton and others when they discover his mental alertness and deep knowledge of the Indian people and their ways. Mahbub Ali was registered in one of the books of the Indian Survey Department as C.25.1.B. His information was checked by statements from R.17 and M.4. They supplied the vast mass of 'information received' on which the Indian Government acted.

As the novel proceeds the reader encounters situations and mental attitudes which belong recognizably to spy fiction. Espionage activity is referred to as the Great Game. Kim realizes that where the Great Game is concerned, he is on his own. E.23, whom Kim saved from certain death by his expertise in disguise, said: 'We of the Game are beyond protection. If we die, we die. Our names are blotted from the book. That is all.' He is always in danger. 'If he spits, or sneezes, or sits down other as the people do whom he watches, he may be slain.' Every modern fictional agent will recognize the situation. Was there not once a spy who forfeited his life in France because he put the tea in after the milk? The Great Game never ceases, 'day and night, throughout India.'

One advantage of the Secret Service was that it had no audit. It was starved of funds, but at least the funds were administered by a few men who did not call for vouchers or present itemized accounts. Bond could imagine no other way. When Kim managed to get hold of the baggage belonging to the Russian spies, he decided to keep only the letters and the maps. They were the objects of the spies' trade. Nothing else should be taken—that would be stealing and Kim was aware that Sahibs did not steal. This was an early phase of espionage. Modern professional Sahibs must steal to confuse the enemy.

Like generations of spies to follow, Kim and his colleagues had to use passwords. Hurree Babu says that if Kim is ever in 'a dam'-tight place' he should say, 'I am Son of the Charm'. This means he may be a member of the *Sat Bhai*, the Seven Brothers, which is Hindi *and* Tantric. The foolish natives will always hesitate before killing a man who says he belongs to a specific organization. But if a trader comes and asks him if he wishes to buy precious stones he should reply, 'Do I look like a man who buys precious stones?' The other says, 'Even veree poor man can buy a turquoise of *tarkeean* (vegetable curry)'. Then Kim is to say, 'Let me see the *tarkeean*' and the other says, 'It was cooked by a woman, and perhaps it is bad for your caste.' Kim now says, 'There is no caste when men go to—look for *tarkeean*.' In the whole of this exchange the pause between the words 'to' and 'look' is critically important. This is all Hurree Babu's invention.

At the time there were in fact two areas, geographically, in which spy fiction might expand. One was the North-West frontier, where Russia was the enemy. The other area, exploited by Childers, was closer to home. The enemy was Germany and was to grow in menace as the Russian threat subsided—that is, until war and politics once again changed the lines of tension. Buchan wrote a spy story *The Half-Hearted* (1900), based on the Frontier but as the century proceeded this category petered out. There were occasional attempts to revive it, but they were hampered by having to be historical and never contemporary. *The Lotus and the Wind* by John Masters appeared in 1953 but the action took place in 1879-82, partly coinciding with the

Third Afghan War. It gives a clear summary of the agent's job in a story which is good in parts and hamfisted in the rest.

Hayling briefly outlines what is expected of him. 'The task of the ordinary agent is to live in a place, travel about a bit, keep his eyes and ears open, and report. He does not deduce or infer, he just sees and tells. And he never sees much.' Familiar aspects of the Great Game necessarily exhibit themselves. There is the double agent. 'Half the agents in Asia work for both parties to any quarrel—and both the parties know it. What's more, each party knows just about every agent of the other party.' Wherever double agents are used, misleading information will be passed. 'Agents are seldom arrested in time of peace. Once they are known, each side uses them to channel misleading information to the other side.'

These novels are about agents, officially employed. The spies of *Riddle* were amateurs. The idea of professional espionage horrified them. Nearly all spy fiction is contemporary. For that reason it is taken much more seriously than the historical exploits described in, for example, books by Baroness Orczy. *The Scarlet Pimpernel* was published in 1913 and was set in the French Revolution. The enemy were neither Germans nor Russians but French. It is not strictly speaking a spy novel at all, yet it is immersed in an atmosphere of espionage. Chauvelin, the accredited agent of the French Republic at the Court of St James (he is not styled Ambassador, any more than the Libyan representative was in 1983), has an 'army of spies' at his beck and call. One of the major changes between Then and Now (whether Then be the England of Sir Percy Blakeney or that of Baroness Orczy) lies in the degree of acceptable violence. When Sir Andrew hears that Chauvelin is still in Dover, he suggests way-laying him and running his sword through him. Marguerite, Lady Blakeney (who is nevertheless French) is horrified: 'Nay! Sir Andrew, do not jest! Alas! I have often since last night caught myself wishing for that friend's death. But what you suggest is impossible! The laws of this country do not permit of murder!' Later, when the Pimpernel is in danger yet has Chauvelin at his mercy, he escapes not by attacking him but by offering him a pinch of snuff—which is in fact pepper. In both these situations the modern adventurer would have killed without hesitation.

Marguerite is in fact recruited by Chauvelin to discover and inform him of the identity of the Scarlet Pimpernel. It turns out to be her husband. Chauvelin is able to do this because he has discovered that

Marguerite's brother, Armand St Just, is helping aristocrats to escape. Marguerite is placed in what the author calls an 'either-or' situation—she must sacrifice either her brother or her husband. It is a classic example, mythological in its neatness, of the blackmail situation which has caused so many people to embark on a career of fictional espionage.

Baroness Orczy did in fact write a fully-fledged spy novel, called *A Spy of Napoleon* (1934), which I mention here because it belongs to a small group of historical espionage fiction which lies outside the mainstream of this genre. The adventure writers of Orczy's generation have been generally condemned but not always justifiably. This novel is by no means as inferior as a modern critic might expect. It is certainly much better than the Pimpernel stories, by which the author is generally known. The background is informed, the element of romantic coincidence is not too obtrusive, and her portrait of M. Toulon, Chief of the *Cabinet Secret*, is comparable with similar portraits by later (and supposedly superior) writers. The action takes place during the last two years of Napoleon III's reign. The secret police had ramifications in every city. It was believed that Toulon hoped for the re-establishment of a Ministry of Police, with himself as the new Fouché. At the same time France was suffering from a spy-scare, accompanied by suicides of officers who had been selling military secrets (especially the details of a new gun) to Germans. There were two good reasons for this activity: firstly, the growing unpopularity of the dynasty, and a widespread desire that it should be brought to an end; and secondly, greed. There were many people in influential positions who realized that they had a commodity for which considerable sums would be paid. The spies' main field of operations lay in Switzerland, as was to occur in the First World War as for example in Maugham's *Ashenden*. (Conrad in *Under Western Eyes* also made Switzerland the centre of international conspiracy.) Information could be brought in and passed on with relatively little danger—unless the spy could be inveigled out of the country, as we see in both this novel and at least one of Maugham's stories.

One other popular writer who manipulated the spy theme with considerable expertise was Dennis Wheatley. His seven Roger Brook novels are set in the time of the first Napoleon. (When the enemy is French the novel must be historical.) Brook managed to become a confidant of Napoleon. It is ironical to think that the model for this character was probably Karl Schulmeister, a French spy who was appointed Chief of Intelligence to Napoleon's antagonist, the Austrian Marshal Mack. Wheatley was despised by superior critics as a romantic pulp writer. It is to his credit that he never wrote a novel, whether historical or occult, without first doing his homework. But apart from accuracy, he was also relatively realistic. He is certainly more realistic than Fleming ever was, despite his romantic themes and Fleming's apparent concern for detail. Briefly, Wheatley recognizes the physical limitations of his characters. Fleming presents us with superman. Wheatley is credible where Fleming, and even Deighton, is not.

The Sultan's Daughter (1963) is one of the seven Brook novels, whose plausibility probably decreases if one reads them in series. In itself it is a splendid adventure story and can also serve as a common man's Guide to the period immediately preceding Napoleon's *coup d'état*. Brook is the son of a British admiral who has spent most of his childhood in France. (This solves the language problem, so often ignored by spy writers.) He is a spy for Pitt and also a close intimate of Napoleon. Although he is on excellent terms with Bonaparte and all the members of his entourage, he has no scruples whatsoever about passing information to the British. It is another classic case of early espionage morality: the sole consideration is King and Country. Fact and fiction are inextricably mixed. (This mode is being employed increasingly in the modern spy novel.) There are references to other characters in fiction—for example, Brook sent some of his despatches by members of Sir Percy Blakeney's League of the Scarlet Pimpernel. (Again, modern spy fiction frequently makes in-group cross-references, especially to James Bond.) The foreign spy's vulnerability is illustrated when Brook is wounded and loses consciousness in the company of his friend Talleyrand, and in his delirium raves in English. There is also an instance of passing false information to the enemy—in other words, Brook is at one time employed as a double agent.

But now we will return to the main line of spy fiction, which was to be absolutely contemporary and obsessively concerned with the contemporary enemy: Germany.

2: JOHN BUCHAN

A personal success story. Born a 'son of the manse', he died in 1940 as the first Lord Tweedsmuir, Governor-General of Canada. His main literary reputation rests on *The Thirty-Nine Steps* (1915) and two other Richard Hannay novels, *Greenmantle* (1916) and *Mr Standfast*, (1919) referred to as a trilogy. The third cannot be accurately called a spy novel but all three are conspiracy novels. The first, and favourite, was serialized in the summer of 1915 in *Blackwood's* over the initials 'H. de V.' and book publication followed in October. It was an immediate success and sold 25,000 copies between 19 October and 31 December. (These figures may sound small today but they were considered very healthy at the time.) He was in great demand as a lecturer on the war but reports began to refer to him as 'the famous novelist and war correspondent.' Although at one stage he was engaged in Intelligence work, *Steps* was written earlier during an illness. He didn't rank the book very highly, and called it a 'shocker' and tales of this general type 'precipitous yarns'. Like Childers, he had little idea of the vogue he was encouraging. There has never been any detailed description of the work he did for Intelligence (which might have had some bearing on the later novels). 'His work was of far too confidential a nature, was far too intimately linked with the work of the Secret Service, for even posterity to be told much about it' writes Arthur Turner, one of his biographers—rather unctuously, I fear. By the time Janet Adam Smith came to write her account (1965) *Steps* had sold well over a million copies in English and had been translated into Persian, Arabic, Czech, Swedish, Spanish, French, German, Dutch and Danish. The combined sales of editions published by Hodder & Stoughton up to 1960 numbered 355,000. *Greenmantle* actually topped this figure with 368,000, yet inexplicably remains less well-known. Smith confirms that Buchan always deprecated this side of his work. 'Any enthusiasm about his thrillers would be met by some deprecatory remark to the effect that only the young and simple-minded could like them.' There is actually much to be said for this point of view. They do not really constitute adult reading.

He wrote serious biographies and books about public affairs. Like most writers of this type he thought they were his best. In fact, his studies of Montrose, Scott, Julius Caesar and Cromwell are certainly not negligible. He probably felt that in this kind of work he could give stronger expression to his belief that our civilization is contained beneath a very thin veneer. He was so convinced of this that he could not keep it out of his fiction, even the 'precipitous yarns'. His great hero Hannay (who is rightly knighted by a grateful monarch) is a solid and respectable citizen who is drawn into adventure accidentally (the only good spies are still amateurs) and is hunted by the police! The moral is that solidity and respectability are no defence against the powers of evil and disorder. This feeling of inner defencelessness had been communicated as early as 1902 in a collection of stories called *The Watcher by the Threshold*. It is also central to *The Power-House* (1916). Leithen, even in the heart of London, realizes his vulnerability.

Buchan's father was a Calvinist minister whose theological teaching he managed to discard, but he never lost his sense of the ever-present reality of evil, and its power to break through into the most prudent and sheltered of lives. In his thrillers evil is felt as the power of unreason, disorder or destruction, which may crack the thin crust of civilization and morality. He is not alone in this. Charles Russell, in Haggard's *A Cool Day For Killing*, considers the increase of torture as a means of extracting information. 'It was a barbarian regression, increasing daily in its use. The skin of civilization was thin enough in any case, and this was the ugliest crack of his sixty years.' Buchan felt this deeply and made it the subject of addresses to the General Assembly of the Church of Scotland in 1933 and to the University of Toronto in 1936. In his book on Augustus he compared the crisis in the Roman world with that of our own day. 'Once again the crust of civilization has worn thin, and beneath can be heard the muttering of primeval fires. Once again many accepted principles of government have been overthrown, and the world has become a laboratory where immature and feverish minds experiment with unknown forces.' This outlook has become familiar to us—Keynes recognized it and William Golding has charted it. It was implicit in much of Aldous Huxley and Bertrand Russell. But Buchan was one of the first to recognize it.

Richard Hannay

It is customary to look for models for Buchan's characters. Hannay is said to have been based on Ironside, a soldier whom Buchan first met in South Africa. He was six foot four inches and known as 'Tiny', and he spoke fourteen languages, including Cape Dutch or *taal*. He had fought through the Boer War, escorted Smuts to the Peace Conference at Vereeniging, and had done intelligence work in South-West Africa. (Hannay in *Greenmantle* knew 'all about Damaraland'.) Disguised as a Boer transport driver, Ironside accompanied the German military expedition against the Hereros. For this he was awarded a German military medal before disappearing back to British South Africa. In 1914 he was the first British officer in uniform to land in France and he spent the whole war on the Western Front until 1918, when he commanded the Allied expedition to Archangel. Like Hannay, he never worried much about comfort, and like Blenkiron (another of Buchan's band of heroes), when he wanted to think out a problem he would sit and play patience. It will be seen at once that this model for England's most famous spy (barring James Bond) was far removed in experience from either Carruthers or Smiley.

The model for Sandy Arbuthnot (who joined Hannay in *Greenmantle*) was supposedly Aubrey Herbert. He had travelled in Albania, Greece, Turkey and Arabia, making friends 'with the most extraordinary heroes and ruffians, facing danger and discomfort with a zest that never failed, revelling in life' we are told by his friend, St John Lucas (letter to *Spectator*, 6 October 1923). He was an aristocrat who looked like a tramp, a master of languages, a champion of minority views; he was short-sighted and was said to have got into the B.E.F. in 1914 by putting on khaki and joining a battalion of the Irish Guards as it came out of Wellington Barracks, a tale I would love to believe. He was invited by the Albanians of America to command the regiment they raised.

It comes as no surprise to learn that Hannay had great skill in disguise. Richard Usborne compiled a list in *Clubland Heroes*. Hannay had played the role of milkman, roadmender and chauffeur in *The Thirty-Nine Steps*; Cornelis Brandt, Richard Hanau and an American in *Greenmantle*; Cornelius Brand (*sic*), Archibald McCaskie (a traveller in religious books), a movie producer, Private Tompkins, Joseph Zimmer (a swiss) and Graf von Schwabing's chauffeur in *The Three Hostages*. He spoke English with a colonial accent, Highland and lowland Scots, good German, good French, excellent Dutch and Portuguese fairly well, 'the guttural tongue of the Grisons' and at least two South African *taals* (Shangaan and Sesutu).

Hannay and his friends were very definitely amateur heroes. He always declared himself reluctant to tackle the jobs the authorities (either a government department or the police) landed him with. In *Steps* he adopts the pose of the bored man who finds England tame and unexciting and thinks nostalgically of his native South Africa. 'It struck me that Albania was the sort of place that might keep a man from yawning'—he probably got that idea from Arbuthnot. When we first meet him Hannay has neither knowledge of or connection with the worlds of crime and espionage.

When he meets the Literary Innkeeper he tells him the story of his life (slightly embroidered) and says he can make a novel of it. But he actually brings it up to date, telling a complete stranger of the Portland Place murder, and adds: 'You're looking for adventure; well, you've found it here. The devils are after me and the police are after them. It's a race that I mean to win.' This is the primal innocence of the spy story, before Bond and Smiley come on the scene. The way he parts with Scudder's important little book, containing the clues, when he changes clothes with Mr Turnbull, is likewise barely credible. Fortunately everyone else is equally careless. In *Mr Standfast* Hannay is very nearly apprehended by the deputy-lieutenant of the county, who has instructions to watch out for him. He escapes by spinning a yarn which causes the other to look puzzled and then put him up for the night! Espionage situations in those days were superbly casual.

Yet although Hannay seems incredibly naive and simple-minded to the modern reader (and, we must remember, his opponents were equally so), he did not see the struggle as entirely one of patriotism. 'I had got out of the way', he says in *Greenmantle*, 'of regarding the thing as a struggle between armies and nations. I hardly bothered to think where my sympathies lay. First and foremost it was a contest between the four of us and a crazy woman, and this personal antagonism made the strife of armies only a dimly felt background.' This remark is worth noting for it places Hannay in the context of the adventure thriller. The crazy woman was Hilda von Einem. Each of the great fictional agents has his personal enemy—Sherlock Holmes had Professor Moriarty, the little known Okewood had the redoubtable Clubfoot, and James Bond would have his Blofeld—and it seems likely that it is basically the personal struggle which captured the public interest rather than the patriotic dimension. The personal element has been so overlaid in histories and accounts of Hannay that his admiration for his enemies, especially when they become really menacing, is usually overlooked. He actually admired Hilda von Einem for despising him. 'It was not the first, or the last, time Hannay's "sportsmanship" drifted over the edge into a sort of masochism, a desire to be mastered. This is a noticeable streak in Hannay's character, but I don't think Buchan noticed it', writes the percipient Richard Usborne, who certainly did.

Spying, 1914-24

Blenkiron the American speaking: 'You Britishers haven't any notion how wide-awake your Intelligence Service is. I reckon it's easy the best of all the belligerents. You never talked about it in peace time, and you shunned the theatrical ways of the Teuton. But you had the wires laid good and sure. I calculate there isn't much that happens in any corner of the earth that you don't know within twenty-four hours.' *Greenmantle*, (1916.) And very gratifying. But it was, in a way, common knowledge. Yet Hannay wasn't always consistent. He said he believed the best way to baffle the enemy was by not disguising (they expect disguise), which tallied with Blenkiron's view, even if Hannay owed the idea to the South African Pienaar. But, as we have already seen, Hannay was an expert in disguise when he felt the occasion called for it. And Sandy Arbuthnot could be positively theatrical, despite Blenkiron. For instance, he once posed as the leader of some religious dancing maniacs. 'A tall man dressed in skins, with bare legs and sandal-shod feet. A wisp of scarlet cloth clung to his shoulders, and, drawn over his head down close to his eyes, was a skull-cap of some kind of pelt with the tail waving behind it. He capered like a wild animal, keeping up a strange high monotone that fairly gave me the creeps.'

The clues which lead Hannay to his quarry are often mysterious words written on scraps of paper or even overheard. Sometimes verse was employed. When Scudder talked to Hannay he mentioned a few things which Hannay recalled after his murder, and they all turned out to be clues. This neatness of raw material, this convenient tameness of phenomena, is another familiar feature of early spy-writing. Here we have the name of a woman, a Black Stone, a man with a lisp, and an old man with a young voice who could hood his eyes like a hawk. In Scudder's note-book he sees that some nouns are frequently repeated and suspects that they involve a cipher. In *Greenmantle* the method is even more obtrusive. Bullivant hands Hannay a slip of paper with the words *Kasredin*, *cancer* and *v.I.* written on it. The key to the mystery lies in them as certainly as the solution of a crossword puzzle belongs to the numbered clues. In *Mr Standfast* the mystery words are overheard in a conversation: they are *Chelius* and *Bommaerts*, the Wild Birds and the Cage Birds. In *The Three Hostages* the clues are to be found in six lines of verse and a country doctor's prescription for what was then known as a 'shocker'.

Buchan's Style

It is often said, with God knows what authority, that Buchan had an attractive literary style. He hadn't. It was entirely commonplace and unadventurous, the sort of language that almost anyone with an orthodox English education could handle. There are very few modern spy writers who could not show him a number of tricks in the evocation of mood and the employment of imagery, even if their syntax might not be so augustanly perfect.

Buchan was utterly insensitive to human feelings and probabilities. Blenkiron, in an apparently inextricable situation in Constantinople, talks about the need for 'a good old-fashioned copper-bottomed miracle to get us out of this fix.' No-one had spoken like that in such a situation since Ballantyne. He goes on to accuse Hannay of being 'mighty indelicate'. It is friendly ribbing at a time when friends don't rib each other. Immediately afterwards Hannay speaks of their hunger. This brings us back to the real world for it was something Buchan could understand. He was fascinated with the physical life, hence the boring chases over moors, the flight over the housetops in *Greenmantle*. Its influence has lain heavy on adventure writing ever since and has damaged the work of otherwise effective writers such as Geoffrey Household. It is only necessary to compare the housetops episode of *Greenmantle* with Casanova's escape from his prison in Venice to see what has been lost. In *Mr Standfast* we have another chase through Scotland and Yorkshire with varying forms of transport thrown in to make it 'exciting'. Buchan aims at boys' adventure excitement and never manages psychological enlightenment. *The Island of Sheep*, which is not a spy novel, is a good example of his story-telling technique, which is to insert a series of lesser stories into the main framework, each told by a different character. Contrary to common belief, Buchan is a very awkward story-teller.

This novel is also an excellent example of his treatment of women. They are obedient, docile, amenable adjuncts to the men. Clanroyden (the ennobled Sandy), Hannay and Lombard are off on a dangerous mission to the Norlands (The Island of Sheep). What about the women?

> LOMBARD: 'Beryl won't object. She's as keen on this job as I am.'
> HANNAY: 'I was certain that Mary would raise no objections.'
> SANDY: 'Barbara would be the first to tell me to go.'

So much for the women. Hannay's Mary in *Mr Standfast* and *The Three Hostages* is a chocolate box girl—plain chocolate, of course, not milk. She is super-human, beautiful and feminine, tough, brave and resourceful—and never does anything that might arouse criticism. Hilda von Einem, the magnificent spy in *Greenmantle*, is equally unreal. Most women in contemporary spy novels are also unreal, but in a different way. They seethe with sex, sometimes genuine, sometimes a trap like a perfume. There is so little sex in *Steps* that the various film treatments have had to inject it.

Hannay admits he knows nothing about women. 'Women had never come much my way, and I knew about as much of their ways as I knew about the Chinese language. All my life I had lived with men only, and rather a rough crowd at that . . .' He rides in a motor-car with Hilda and feels uncomfortable. 'I had never been in a motor-car with a lady before, and I felt like a fish on a dry sandbank. The soft cushions and the subtle scents filled me with acute uneasiness.' This was not a feature of the spy novel that was destined to persist.

In fact, it seems likely that Buchan only managed to look into a woman's eyes for all critical control to leave him. Here is a description of Barbara Dasent from *The Courts of the Morning*:

> . . . her skin had a healthy pallor which intensified the colouring of lips and eyes. These eyes were a miracle—deep and dark, at once brooding and kindling, as full of changes

as a pool in the sunlight, and yet holding, like a pool, some
elemental profundity. The lashes were long and the eyebrows
a slender crescent.

This is bosh. Blathering about the eyes is a sure sign of a writer who
has no idea how to put across his notion of a character. It occurs all
the time in Buchan. Mary, who is supposed to be delectable, had 'an
uncanny power of making her eyes go suddenly grave and deep, like a
glittering river narrowing into a pool.' Even the men are subjected to
this treatment. Sandy had 'brown eyes like a pretty girl's'. Blenkiron
had 'full sleepy eyes'. Peter Pienaar had 'pale blue eyes, a face as
gentle as a girl's, and a soft sleepy voice.' (Incidentally, Buchan loved
the paradoxical appearance—the tough guy with the gentle demean-
our.) And the master spy in *Steps* had hooded eyes like a hawk.

The New Enemy

Hannay's earliest efforts were concerned with the frustration of
German plans, as were Childers's and various characters in
Oppenheim, Le Queux and Valentine Williams. But after the First
War the German menace subsided—at least, for a decade—and a new
enemy was discerned. He is described in *The Courts of the Morning*
which appeared in 1929. The same characters as in the spy novels re-
appear but this is not a spy novel. It is political adventure in the
course of which there is a place for a little espionage. But it is not the
central theme.

The leading character is Sandy Arbuthnot, now Lord Clanroyden,
backed by Sir Archibald Roylance and his wife Janet, with Blenkiron
in a subsidiary role. Buchan's characters are allowed to age from
book to book, which is unusual in a fictional series. Sir Richard
Hannay, who supplies a Prologue, in fact declines to take part in the
action on the grounds that he has settled down into domesticity. As
usual, Sandy is a master of disguise. He appears as a waiter named
Miguel, but from time to time he visits a block of flats and re-emerges
as a clerk with a spruce collar and an attaché case, as an engineer in
rough clothes and large spectacles, and sometimes as a workman
from the furnaces. Later his death is presumed, for fragments of his
clothing are found where an explosion has taken place. But Sandy is
re-incarnated as Black, a police recruit, only to change later into the

cotton trousers and dark-blue shirt of a peon. (The novel is set in
South America.) But Sandy's major role as leader of a rebellion was
that of El Obro. Blenkiron had two disguises: first, his reported
death, and then as the Mexican Rosas, Vice-President of the company.

The new enemy is the megalomania which wishes to control and
perhaps destroy the world, represented here by Castor. He combined
a hatred of democracy with a loathing of America. This latter
prejudice does indicate considerable political insight, for the often
quite irrational hatred of the U.S.A. and all its works is one of the
marks of our time. The destruction of civilization was a theme that
was gaining adherents and may be related, probably quite unconsciously, with the appearance of Dadaism among intellectuals.
Priestley's *The Doomsday Men*, which appeared a decade later,
belongs to the same genre; in all these stories a small group of
dedicated individuals frustrate the master scheme. Sandy puts the
situation like this:

> I need hardly tell you that the world today is stuffed with
> megalomania. Megalomania in politics, megalomania in
> business, megalomania in art—there are a dozen kinds. You
> have the man who wants to be a dictator in his own country,
> you have the man who wants to corner a dozen great
> businesses, you have the man who wants to break down the
> historic rules of art and be a law to himself . . .

This is essentially the background to all the conspiracy novels, even
when they are partly disguised by ideological trimmings. Such men
do not possess a creed, although they have to pretend to one to gain
support. 'He does not want to re-make the world on some new
fantastic pattern, like the Communists. He has none of Mussolini's
arbitrary patriotism. He wants to root out various things but I doubt
if he has a preference for what should take their place.'

This is already an old model in the adventure thriller. Some may
lament its passing—as does the master-spy in Diment's *The Great Spy
Race*. It is in fact possible to discern a distinction emerging between
the spy novel and the conspiracy novel. The former is usually
concerned with ideology because the spies work for national
organizations which profess political ideals, whereas the conspiracy
novel is cruder and more physical because naked power is the only
aim. Buchan began with patriotism and saw megalomania taking its
place. After him would come the international ideologists.

3: THE UNSOPHISTICATED SOPHISTICATES

When Childers's admirable novel appeared there were other spy modes or quasi-spy modes jostling for attention. We have already referred to the North-West Frontier novel, which started well with *Kim* and adequately with Buchan's *The Half-Hearted* but virtually died as the Russian 'menace' appeared to recede. For a while there was an apparently lusty Anarchist novel rivalling the spy, but this also faded as the Anarchist movement became less active. There was still another mode, however, which actually had its roots before *Riddle* and clung on tenaciously well into the new century. This might be referred to as the Diplomatic Spy novel because its main practitioners, Oppenheim and Le Queux, usually used diplomats of one kind or another as protagonists or, if not, made use of diplomatic settings. These novels were the 'shockers' despised by Childers and deplored by Buchan (although he sometimes classed his own work under that title, though they were not in the diplomatic setting). They were sensational, trite, unreal and not worthy of serious attention. We only notice them here because they belong to the genre we are considering and serve as a foil to the better work which superseded them. They are intended to reveal to the innocent reader a world of the utmost sophistication: the settings are liable to be Monte Carlo and the Orient Express; the men are addicted to white tie and tails, monocles, kid gloves and French titles; the women are *soignée* in long gowns and carry immense cigarette-holders; all of them gamble and spend hours in libraries not reading. The sophistication is entirely bogus. They exist in a never-never land of fantasy which no truly sophisticated person would ever tolerate.

But we of the eighties should not be smug. There is just as much unreality among modern spy writers as among their forebears. The difference is that it is, rather oddly, more difficult to detect it in a contemporary than in an earlier generation. This is because we are subject to the same pressures and fantasy-moulders as the writers who are contemporary with us. Exploded ideas and faulty images are easily recognized. Julian Maclaren-Ross, who tried unsuccessfully to write good thrillers, including a spy-thriller, wrote: 'Atom-spies ought to be put on the index with sliding panels and mysterious Chinamen.' If we are to be really severe what hope would there be for John Gardner or Brian Freemantle or even, dare we say it, for some of Len Deighton?

It is amusing to choose an example of the early type of spy writing from *The Crouching Beast* by Valentine Williams. Amusing, because it illustrates the hold this style had on even reasonably good writers when they dropped their guard—for Williams was a much better writer than either Oppenheim or Le Queux, who must be regarded as the pace-setters. Also because *Beast* appeared in 1928. This is well after the prime of the other two, although they were not yet finished. (Le Queux actually died in 1927. Oppenheim lasted longer.) It is also after Buchan's best work had appeared. In a dark room Olivia offers to help an English spy who has just escaped from a German military prison. He gives her instructions:

> 'In the drawing-room of a woman called Floria von Pellegrini, an opera singer, who has an apartment at 305 Hohenzollern-Allee, a sealed envelope is hidden in the gramophone cabinet. It is in the lower part, thrust away behind a lot of old gramophone records, a blue envelope, you can't mistake it. Do you think you could retrieve that envelope without this woman or anyone else knowing, and take it to an address I'll give you?'
> Feeling rather scared, I answered as bravely as I could:
> 'I'll do my best. But how can you be sure it's still there?'
> 'Because the gramophone is never used. Floria hates gramophones . . .'

Also belonging to this corner of the spy-field is what is probably Conan Doyle's one essay in the genre, a short story entitled 'The Adventure of the Bruce-Partington Plans', from *His Last Bow*. The time is November 1895. The B-P is a submarine. Naval warfare would become impossible within its radius of operation. Every effort was made to keep the plans secret, but ten papers were taken from Woolwich and when the story opens three of the most essential were still missing. The patriotic element is stressed. Brother Mycroft urges Sherlock to leave no stone unturned: 'In all your career you have never had a greater chance of serving your country.' The man responsible for selling the plans to a foreign agent was Colonel

Valentine Walter. Holmes is appalled. 'How an English gentleman could behave in such a manner is beyond my comprehension', he exclaims. Some years later writers like Brian Freemantle would have quite a lot to say about the English gentleman and his patriotism.

Sherlock asked Mycroft to send a complete list of all foreign spies or international agents known to be in England, with full addresses! This apparently posed no problem. Holmes decided it would be necessary to break into a private residence without a warrant. Watson didn't like it, but was overruled. 'I knew you would not shrink at the last', he says, and Watson saw in his eye something nearer to tenderness than he had ever seen before. Oberstein, the spy, had put the plans up for auction 'in all the naval centres of Europe.' The Queen rewarded Holmes with a remarkably fine emerald tie-pin. No story could better illustrate the vast gap between the moral codes and patriotic attitudes of their time and ours.

The Anarchist Novel

As a body of work this has disappeared, although it has been partially subsumed by the conspiracy novel. At one time, especially during the first decade of this century, the anarchist novel appeared to be gaining ground over the spy novel as a serious literary form, despite *Riddle*. *The Four Just Men*, by Edgar Wallace, is perhaps the best known of the class, and appeared two years after *Riddle* in 1905. But the purest example of the anarchist novel was Max Pemberton's *The Wheels of Anarchy* (1908) just as Conrad's *Secret Agent*, which came out in the preceding year, was its finest literary flower. It is not always possible to distinguish between the anarchist and conspiracy novels, especially as the conspirators may be anarchists at heart but adopt another ideology to win support. *The Wheels of Anarchy* is based on a conviction that civilization is a sham and that violence and brutality remain constant in human affairs, though there are periods when they are veiled. The frequency of these novels reflects the growth of anarchist activity in the generation before the First World War. Norman Angell also reflected the general concern in his *The Great Illusion* (1910) in which he asserted an advance in man's moral stature signalled by a decline in political torture. We now know that the illusion was Angell's.

The spy novel and the anarchist novel frequently meet in

conspiracy but they come from different directions. One is concerned with the conflict between two concepts, which may be simple patriotic loyalties or quite complex ideologies; the other with the overthrow of all systems. There are also two strains of anarchism: that which is nourished by violence for its own sake, illustrated by *The Wheels of Anarchy*, and a more respectable strain that is suspicious of all government of any kind (represented by the publications of the Freedom Press in this country, but short on fiction). The pure spy novel is concerned with the passing of information and is therefore to be distinguished from conspiracy, which involves political action. Perhaps the best-known modern examples are the novels of Frederick Forsyth, though there are many others: novels by Buchan and Priestley have already been mentioned. Chapman Pincher's *The Four Horses* is another.

The old-fashioned spy novel was still going strong in 1927 (v. Oppenheim's *Miss Brown of X.Y.O.*) No distinction was made between anarchists and communists in the same author's *Gabriel Samara* (1925). An anarchist gained his 'first nourishment from the brutalism of Lenin and Trotsky, suckled on Marx.'

Oppenheim

E. Phillips Oppenheim was the leader of what is often referred to as 'the cloak-and-dagger school'. His novels were severely stereotyped and revolved round the 'black-velveted seductress, the British Secret Service numskull hero, the omnipotent spymaster', to quote Eric Ambler,who is one of the three most intelligent living spy writers. At first it seems astonishing that Ambler should have a good word for Oppenheim, but in his Introduction to his selection of stories entitled *To Catch a Spy* he not only says that Oppenheim is a much better writer than Le Queux (which, even if true, is no great praise) but calls him 'a clever craftsman who manipulated a personal set of stereotypes with ingenuity and, sometimes, humour; and his improbable world of diplomatic salons, cosmopolitan hotels and suave, stiff stuffed-shirted intrigue still has an engaging quality about it.' I think Ambler is being very kind to Oppy, as he was known—and certainly kinder than his biographer, Robert Standish, was in *The Prince of Storytellers*, a title bequeathed by Oppy's publishers, without any signs of modest rebuttal from Oppy himself. There is a big streak of sentimentality in the literary world towards writers who are no longer with us. Intellectuals who would rather have died than be seen enjoying Wodehouse forty years ago now discover immense virtues in him; it appears that Edgar Wallace is a better writer than his contemporaries ever knew; and yarn-spinners like Anthony Hope are given a niche in the literary pantheon. However, it is a pleasant and generous trait and should not be despised so long as it doesn't overturn our judgment. Ambler certainly managed to retrieve one splendidly telling phrase from Oppenheim's *The Great Impersonation* (1920) when he quotes Prince Terniloff saying, 'I detest espionage in every shape and form, even where it is necessary.' On this, at any rate, he was at one with both Childers and Buchan.

Falstaff joked and was the cause of jokes in others. It is very rare to come across a critic who does not combine contempt for the cloak-and-dagger school with an irresistible urge to satirize it. Jacques Barzun wrote a hard-hitting attack on spy writers in general in *The American Scholar* (1964) called 'Meditations on the Literature of Spying'. He quoted with approval (and who would not!) Flaubert's entry for 'spy' in his *Dictionary of Accepted Ideas*: 'always in high society'. That certainly went for Oppy and his friends. Barzun added his own bit of fun:

> But that is the spy of the Age of Reason, polite and cosmopolite, who comes historically between the base fellow and the modern Every Man His Own Secret Agent. E. Phillips Oppenheim gave the ultimate renderings of that delightful intermediate type, a suave habitué of the Orient Express and a willing prey to the svelte seductress whose prerogative it was to transfer the naval plans from his well-marked dispatch box to her bosom, no less well marked. Protocol required these trappings, and this too rested on presumption.

Dollmann of *Riddle* was the base fellow, Bond the E.M.H.O.S.A.

We have already noticed that Oppenheim was producing his spy novels before the turn of the last century. *Mysterious Mr Sabin* appeared in 1898. (William Haggard has a rather mysterious character named Sabin Scott in his *The Arena*. The choice of this unusual name hints at the interbreeding which is so common in the spy novel.) It was a very clumsily constructed book—one of those that appears to end and then starts up again—and a paperback edition in 1963 was greatly abbreviated. Here is Mr Sabin arrayed in Oppy's finest diplomatic style.

> Mr Sabin sat alone in his sanctum waiting for a visitor. The room was quite a small one on the ground floor of the house, but was furnished with taste and evident originality in the Moorish fashion. Mr Sabin himself was ensconced in an easy chair drawn close up to the fire, and a thin cloud of blue smoke was stealing up from a thick Egyptian cigarette which was burning away between his fingers. His head was resting upon the delicate fingers of his left hand, his dark eyes were fixed upon the flaming coals. He was deep in thought.
>
> 'A single mistake now', he murmured softly, 'and farewell to the labour of years. A single false step, and goodbye to all our dreams! Tonight will decide it! In a few minutes I must say Yes or No to Kingenstein. I think—I am almost sure I shall say Yes! Bah!'

A little later he tells the Ambassador: 'When I place in your hands a simple roll of papers and a small parcel, the future of this country is absolutely and entirely at your mercy. That is beyond question or doubt. To whomsoever I give my secret, I give over the destinies of England.' The destinies of England were always being endangered in those days, and in the same plummy language specially chosen for such statements. I pay more detailed attention to the menace in Chapter 5.

This kind of story was full of urgent warnings against complacency on the part of the British public, who believed that one Englishman could account for any ten foreigners. There is a significant conversation between Wolfenden and Felix. Wolfenden says there is no need to worry about intrigue, this isn't Russia or South America. Nine-tenths of your countrymen believe that, says Felix: 'To all appearance you are the smuggest and most respectable nation ever evolved in the world's history', and he goes on to state that Mr Sabin is deeply involved in intrigue against Britain. Ah, but we stand outside all continental alliances, says Wolfenden the simpleton, and then he gets a really nasty one. 'There is no country in the world so hated by all the great powers as England', says Felix. Germany is the enemy and, though Wolfenden might find it difficult to accept, under certain circumstances would win in a contest.

A Good Word for Oppy

Yet he was an extremely compulsive writer. One feels, as one reads, the resistance dissolving. After all, he could tell a story, even if it was a ridiculous one. (In every novel by Oppenheim there is at least one absurdity guaranteed to take the reader's breath away.) For a man who loved to write of spies he had a very low opinion of the breed, as we have already seen. 'I hate spies although I am a spy myself', says Dessiter in *Miss Brown of X.Y.O.* (1927) It is a recurring refrain and, according to Ambler, the probable reason why the spy-hero was so late on the fictional scene. A spy in *Matorni's Vineyard* (1929) belongs to a 'detestable profession'. And when Miss Brown is asked to serve her country in that capacity she is warned there will never be any honours. 'You'll never be made a Dame of the Empire, even if you save the country. No-one will ever have heard of your name or know what your work is.'

In *Miss Brown* a sequence of remarkable circumstances lead to a prudish and very correct little London stenographer being involved in combatting a communist plot to subvert English society. The tale ends with an incredible marriage. Oppenheim's reputation as the Prince of Storytellers was deserved because not even the inevitable dose of incredibility could destroy the effect created by pace, suspense and endless invention. The hyperbole of saving civilization contributes both to the incredibility and the excitement. 'You are a part depository of the greatest secret the world has ever known', Blunn tells Itash in *The Wrath to Come* (1925). In the same novel Grant Slattery has 'the secrets of a world's salvation' in his possession. 'These documents' (documents were the stand-by of the early spy-writers*) 'if they fell into the wrong hands'—as they always do, if only temporarily—'might lead to a terrible and disastrous war.' On the very first page of *Gabriel Samara* (1925) Miss Sadie Loyes is unknowingly 'the unconscious arbitress, not only of the fate of two very interesting people, but also of the fate of a great nation.'

Oppenheim liked to place his SS stories in the near future, when the world would be seen to be recovering from what he considered political madness. In *Gabriel Samara*, for instance, the Bolshevist Government has been overthrown in Russia, which is 'lifting her head

---

* But not without reason. 'Most Government information is in documentary form and the classification process applies in the main to files, papers, diagrams, etc.' (*Security Procedures in the Public Service*, Cmnd 1681. 1978.)

among the nations of the world'. The ordinary people have a 'craving' for Tsardom. By the end of the novel Tsar Nicholas recovers the ancestral throne to universal acclaim. Communists, as always, are indistinguishable from anarchists. It was Oppenheim's abiding belief that the monarchical principle was the only sane one and that it was reviving not only in Russia but also in Germany and even in France. This idea receives expression in nearly all his SS fiction. So unrealistic is he that his work can best be described as sophisticated fairy-tale. 'It is incredible', says the German diplomat, von Hartsen, speaking of a rather nondescript New York stenographer (Oppy's foil to the svelte seductress) 'that you have not discovered the identity of this young lady! I have the honour, then, to present to you the Princess Catherine Hélène Zygoff, Grand Duchess of Urulsk, Countess of Borans and hereditary ruler of the lands of Utoff.' And the little typist is transmogrified into the Tsarina.

In nearly every case, the Germans are the major villains. Either they are cold-bloodedly aiming at world conquest or they are quietly contributing to the downfall of their enemies (the French and the British) by supporting a third party. Their sinister influence lies behind the Italian dictator's attempt to take over the Riviera (*Matorni's Vineyard*). Published in 1929, this novel is set in 1940 and Matorni (Mussolini) is only foiled by the combined energies and intelligence of an English tennis player and an Italian countess. It comes as a surprise to find that Oppenheim held the majority view of the time—that Fascists were worse than Communists, an unexpected view for a resident of Monte Carlo to hold. Matorni was a menace and it was the Red Shirts who were vowed to overthrow him. (But perhaps Garibaldi was in Oppenheim's mind rather than the Red Flag.) All the ingredients of the early spy novel are present; frequent letters give instructions and suggest rendezvous; Mervyn Amory sews the inevitable incriminating documents into his vest; for his country's sake he admits he is prepared to abandon conscience and his sense of honour.

The normal Oppenheim dialogue is astonishing. Except in moments of crisis, or when the agent is faced by a menacing enemy, direct statement is rarely used. Whenever possible, meaning is conveyed via flattery or nuance or circumlocution. Lord Bremner is taken to see Matorni and says it is years since they met. 'Years which have dealt kindly with Lord Bremner', comes the reply, smooth as a well-oiled rifle action. The language is ideal for intercourse between the sexes: 'You sit there like the cold Englishman whose place you are taking, you whose tears have fallen before now upon my hand, whose lips—', complains Princess Stephanie of Eiderstrom in *The Great Impersonation*. 'I am entirely at your service' is the accepted cliché for opening a discussion. Dominey wishes to get rid of Mrs Unthank. 'You must excuse my ringing the bell. I see no object in asking you to remain longer.' And how should a lady accept an invitation to lunch? 'I think I may go so far without indiscretion', says Catherine in *Gabriel Samara*. It is really not surprising that in Oppenheim's 1940 the French and Italian armies still used horse transport!

The Wrath to Come, published 1925, is set in 1950 with Edward VIII on the British throne. (The device of setting spy novels in the near future is still used. Chapman's Pincher's *Dirty Tricks*, for example, appeared in 1980 but was set two Parliaments after Labour had replaced Mrs Thatcher.) The hero is American Grant Slattery, who has officially retired from his country's diplomatic service and now acts on behalf of the British Prime Minister with cover as a representative of Bethlehem Steel. The seizure of documents forestalls a plan by Germany and Japan to dominate the world, though not before the Royal Navy has wreaked considerable havoc. All these British and American agents are noble fellows—the slovenly anti-hero has not yet appeared—yet it was a German who forbade one of his men to trifle with the affections of a lady, for 'to deceive a lady of weak intellect, however beautiful, to make use of your position . . . is not, save in the vital interests of his country, the action of a Prussian nobleman' (*The Great Impersonation*). This novel is the most intriguing (in the psychological sense, not the diplomatic) of all Oppenheim's fiction. The incredibility quotient is even higher here than in the others. An Englishman, believed to be a German, impersonates himself! The mystery is sustained right through to its unfolding, a fine feat of story-telling. The trick wins the documents for the British: war plans and sensitive diplomatic memoirs. And a last word must be said on behalf of Oppenheim's characterization. It is not always the slick puppetry one might expect, although there is plenty of that. In at least three of his SS novels he managed to create attractively real females. In a world apparently dominated by men his women are the most vital forces. They never make the mistake of challenging men on male territory but on their own they are invincible.

Le Queux

William Le Queux was extremely prolific and probably the most influential of the cloak-and-dagger school. His novels were always sensational and his talents were journalistic. He shared one quality with Childers, perhaps only one, but it was very powerful: obsession with the notion that war with Germany was coming and Britain was unprepared. Some people, especially Conservative politicians, took Le Queux seriously, which they never did for Oppenheim. A.J. Balfour said his books were worth several thousand votes for the Conservative party. Political leaders have often been suckers for spy stories, perhaps because they become so wrapped up in the power struggle they lose all sense of reality. President Kennedy put Fleming high on his list of literary favourites.

Before examining his spy novels, or a few of them (he wrote so many!), it is worth while looking at a prophetic novel called *The Unknown Tomorrow* which appeared in 1910. It is not about espionage but it serves as a useful background to his work in general and explains his attraction for politicians of the Right. It contains two major themes: fear of Germany and a detestation of socialism. Le Queux was really far more intelligent than Oppy and gave evidence of actually having read socialist literature. One could not imagine Oppenheim getting down to that! In this novel there is a long quotation from the Fabian tract, *What Socialism Is*. The book is sub-titled: How the Rich Fared at the Hands of the Poor together with a Full Account of the Social Revolution in England. It was dedicated to Sir William Earnshaw Cooper, C.I.E., 'in Friendship and in Admiration of his Splendid Work in Exposing the Fallacies of Socialism.'

'The workers were workless, the poor were starving, and the cup of desolation had been filled until it now overflowed. The night was hot and stifling—the evening of the 28th of July—and the year was 1935.' Seven hundred people had been shot down in a Glasgow riot, leading to smaller riots in Manchester, Leeds and Sheffield. Thus the revolution started. But behind it lay the German enemy, waiting his chance. In 1912 the Germans had actually landed on the East Anglian coast, but had been repulsed, thanks to British superiority in the air.

The Red Terror began on 5 August. It has a ferocity that was not generally believed in at the time—for example, bombs were hurled at a mass meeting in the Albert Hall. The idealist who leads the

revolution in its early stages, Henry Harland*, is displaced by the
rabble-rousing George Sillence, an ex-gas stoker. Harland was really
a mouthpiece for the rich idealist dreamer, Sir Percy Barry, who now
accepted his responsibility. 'All this is my work! I have pulled the
wires and my puppets have danced! Yet I believed in the Socialism as
taught by the old philosophers—I believed it to be possible. I see now
that it can never be—*never*!' For the masses had risen and fallen
fiercely on the classes, and revolution and anarchy were the result.
The Jews, as always, were being massacred. Needless to say, the
revolution destroyed itself.

This was a thesis novel—probably his only one. His more familiar
work, deployed on a much more personal field of activity, was much
more concerned with the German menace. This was illustrated in the
early *Her Majesty's Minister* (1901). Ingram's position as second
secretary at the Paris Embassy was unenviable, even though it was
supposed to be a plum of the diplomatic service. He is aggrieved that
the public care so little about the sterling work and loyalty of the
Queen's servants in foreign parts, though he also admits they know
little. 'With Paris full of spies endeavouring to discover our secrets
and divine our instructions from Downing Street, and the *cabinet noir*
ever at work upon our correspondence, it behoved us to be always on
the alert, and to have resort to all manner of ingenious subterfuges in
order to combat our persistent enemies.'

Number 70, Berlin is subtitled A Story of Britain's Peril and actually
appeared in 1916, during the war. An Admiralty official said: 'There's
no doubt that the Germans, as part of their marvellous preparedness,
made an audacious attempt to weave a network of vile treachery in
our Government Departments and, above all, in the War Office and
Admiralty. As an official I can tell you, in strictest confidence, of
course, that I have, several times of late, had my suspicions seriously
aroused. Information leaks out. How—nobody—not even our
Intelligence Department itself can discover.' The significant phrase in
the foregoing is 'vile treachery'. No-one would use it today. If the
money was good enough, it would be agreed that the treachery would
occur, however vile. In 1916 Englishmen did not behave in that way.

* The choice of this name is astonishing. The editor of the *Yellow Book* had been
named Henry Harland, but he died in 1905. His stories were mild and delicate but he
may well have been a socialist idealist. There is a hint of animosity here—had Le Queux
been rejected as a young man? Many popular writers begin their careers by submitting
work to avant garde and art magazines before discovering their true strength.

Or did they? Jack Sainsbury overheard a conversation between Lewin Rodwell and Sir Boyle Huntley, city men renowned for their patriotism. (This is another quaint characteristic of the time—people could be *renowned* for their patriotism.) The conversation revealed them as traitors! Sainsbury reported it and no-one would believe him. And so the British Intelligence Department became the laughing-stock of our Allies. But the situation was not quite as deplorable as appears. Le Queux's foreign agents were often men who had changed their names by deed-poll—from Ludwig Heitzmann to Lewin Rodwell, for example, from Berenstein to Burton. 'Thousands of Germans have come here, and become naturalized Englishmen.' The later excellent novel, *The Spy Who Sat and Waited* (1975), was based on such a case but in a different war. It became an obsession with Le Queux. 'Germans, with or without assumed English names, controlled our finances, our professions, our hotels, nay, our very lives, wherefore it was hardly surprising that we were unable, in the first few months of war, to rid ourselves of that disease known as "German measles".'

Le Quex, or Le Kooks, or Le Kicks, the 'Mystery Man'

He was born a Frenchman and became an intensely patriotic Englishman. Readers had trouble with his name but we are authoritatively assured that it was pronounced Le Kew. N. St Barbe Sladen, in what is probably the least illuminating biography in literary history, calls him a 'Mystery Man'. He certainly remains completely unknown after Mr Sladen's chatty and anecdotal presentation.

Sladen says he wrote numerous spy novels (which he did) but fails to mention them by name. He says he invented the 'adventurous spy as a literary type' and for many people his spies never became more than 'literary types'. When Le Queux was trying to arouse the nation to the German menace the editor of a well-known newspaper wrote: 'My dear Le Queux, We cannot publish this! Spies exist only in your imagination. We don't want to alarm the public.' Similarly Mr Sladen tells us again and again that Le Queux spent a large part of his life engaged in espionage, yet gives virtually no evidence. All we are told is that 'royalties derived from Le Queux's novels were utilized to meet the cost of fifteen years travel in Europe, Asia Minor and Africa as a spy and counter-spy of Great Britain' and we are given one *fact*—that the Commander-in-Chief of the armed forces, Lord Roberts, formed a new voluntary Secret Service Department and that Le Queux became a member.

But the most serious criticism of this book, which creates rather than presents a Mystery Man, is its claim that Le Queux was on intimate terms with practically everyone of consequence during his lifetime. Mr Sladen names a great many people but they nearly all belong to the second or third rank. Otherwise he prefers to hide behind descriptions such as 'a well-known editor of a powerful paper' or 'one of our leading lawyers'. When one reads accounts or histories of the early decades of this century one never encounters the name of Le Queux as one does constantly of Shaw and Wells or Chesterton and Belloc. Le Queux seems in fact to have been a social butterfly with a pronounced delight in the society of royalty, but always minor royalty or the short-lived potentates of Balkan monarchies. It was discovered that Queen Alexandra, when Princess of Wales, read Le Queux's novels, whereupon he was advertised as 'the Queen's favourite novelist'. But the House of Windsor, as it came to be known, is not very ambitious in its reading tastes. Edward VIII's favourite author was once said to be Gerald Verner, another and much less well-known spy-writer, while his brother, George VI, plumped for Dennis Wheatley. But Sladen tells us little about Le Queux's skill as a writer, apart from his being prolific, and just one point of interest—that one publisher complained that the name of his hero was liable to change in the middle of the book.

4: CLUBFOOT AND BULLDOG

When Buchan was a War Correspondent in France one of his colleagues was Valentine Williams. According to Arthur Turner, in his monograph on Buchan, Williams was advised to try his hand at spy-writing. The result was the Clubfoot series. Williams never caught the public fancy in the way that Buchan, Sapper and Dornford Yates did, but he was superior to at least two of those writers.

In the Preface to *A Clubfoot Omnibus* (1936) he tells us he wrote the first of the series, *The Man with the Clubfoot*, while convalescing from wounds received on the Somme. It provided an outlet of escape from the 'pent-up emotions of the battlefield.' His debt to Buchan is obvious. He uses the *Greenmantle* device whereby the major clue is a few words scribbled on a piece of paper. One spy is actually named Arbuthnot (Sandy Arbuthnot was one of Buchan's spies, although we only hear of his death. (Getting rid of the leading rival?) The manly handshake exchanged by the brothers when they agree to kill Clubfoot is in the accepted Buchan tradition. But Clubfoot, like Professor Moriarty, was too valuable a property to kill, and had to be resuscitated. The first of the series is an all-action story and not very plausible, but it makes compelling reading. Like James Bond, whom the intelligent reader despises yet continues to read about. The early pages are typical of their period—a gloomy atmosphere compounded of fog, dankness, rain and squalor which serves to introduce the criminal aspect, the other side of the sunny Edwardian afterglow. There is an amateurish element in the amazing luck which Okewood always has whenever he needs it. (The comparison is again with Bond, who is even less credible, and yet the impression is always given that he makes his own way out of the messes.) For example, Okewood steals an overcoat and finds an automatic pistol, fully loaded, in the pocket. At the very moment when an extra person is most needed to distract the enemy's attention, Okewood and his friends come across Sapper Maggs, who plays the hero to let the others escape.

The Clubfoot books improve as the series progresses. The characters in *The Gold Comfit Box* (1932) are much more lifelike than in the earlier books. There are still times when credibility is stretched to breaking-point (particularly when Clubfoot appears on the scene from nowhere, like the pantomime demon, whom he in fact resembles) yet in each case the explanations are plausible. I have mentioned Bond in connection with these books. There are hints that *The Gold Comfit Box* in particular might well have had some influence on the young Ian Fleming. The latter's M could easily have been modelled on Williams's Chief, who was a powerful personality, gruff but fair-minded, and often very critical of the people working for him. Bond's relationship with Moneypenny resembles that of Philip Clavering with Garnet, although he does something Bond would never do, he marries her. There were certainly many inferior models for Fleming to work on.

Desmond Okewood is never mentioned these days in the company of Hannay, Drummond, Boysie Oakes and Smiley (or was Boysie a distant relation?) but he belongs to the select company and occasionally expressed himself in a way of which the others would approve. 'The major satisfaction', he says in *The Return of Clubfoot*, (1922) 'of this poorly paid and sometimes dangerous profession of ours is the rare delight of seeing emerge out of some seemingly impossible tale a solid basis of fact.' Fictional agents must take themselves seriously for few others will. And in the same novel he says, 'This job of ours teaches us to live for the present and let the future take care of itself.'

The Accepted Formula

Early spies needed a written message to set them off. The missing box (*The Gold Comfit Box*) contained a few sheets of paper, with names: 'in this bizarre job of ours fellows have lost their lives over a half-sheet of note-paper.' All the early spy-writers, from Oppenheim and Le Queux through Childers to Buchan, based their reputations on random pieces of paper.

The early enemy was usually larger than life, possessed of almost magical powers and enormous physical strength, frightful, menacing, brutal and, rather unexpectedly, fairly chivalrous. Chesterton, Conan Doyle, even the early Priestley, illustrate this aspect. With each book Williams's Clubfoot becomes a little more overwhelming. His simian qualities are constantly stressed:

He was a type to arrest attention in any assembly, less by
reason of his appearance, which was striking enough, than
the extraordinary air of authority, of command he radiated.
There was a vitality, a suggestion of reserve power, about
him that had something of the lion or the tiger or, better still,
one of the greater apes about it. His bulk was enormous, the
span of his shoulders so terrific that it quite dwarfed his
height, with arms so long that, when he stood erect, they
hung down on either side like any orang-outang's.

This simian suggestion was strengthened by his really
disgusting hirsuteness. His eyebrows, protuberances as bony
and projecting as a gorilla's, were overhung with shaggy
tufts; there were pads of hair upon his cheek-bones, bristles
at the nostrils and growing out of the large, pointed ears; a
ridge of hard, iron-grey stubble under the squat, broad nose,
and a thatch of dark down on the backs of the enormous
spade-like hands.

But the most singular thing about the stranger was the
unbridled ferocity of his manner. He was obviously a man of
unusual intellect, with a big head which he carried thrust
forward at an angle, so alert, so suspicious and challenging
that I could think only of some giant ape crashing its way
through the jungle. Moreover, a light smouldered in his eyes,
which were small and glittering and, let me admit at
once, indubitably courageous, that hinted at bursts of
uncontrollable fury. His lips were bulbous, and when
smiling disclosed a row of yellow, fang-like teeth; but for the
most part they were set in a hard, grim line bespeaking an
arrogant and unconcealed contempt for his fellow-men.

Compare this monster with the grey, unremarkable men who oppose
Le Carré's, Deighton's and Freemantle's agents, men with normal
amounts of hair, without fangs, probably beset by wives and worries.
The breed has changed.

Who opposed him? The highborn Englishman, strong in his
ordinariness, opposing a calm confidence to the terror of such as
Clubfoot. Williams emphasizes the type even more strongly than
Buchan. In *The Return of Clubfoot* Okewood encounters a
beachcomber who is also a drunken wastrel and a dope fiend. He was
unemployable, and every consulate in the Central Americas was

closed to him. 'But he was an Englishman; more, by birth an English gentleman.' He was undoubtedly of good family. The contrast with the impeccable Okewood is striking, but nevertheless they have one glorious quality in common. Williams milks the myth of gentility for all it is worth. 'Even amid the ravages which undernourishment, drink and drugs had made in his features, the influence of gentle birth might yet be marked in the straight, firm pencilling of the eyebrows and the well-shaped aquiline nose.' Yet a quick look through portraits and photographs of highborn English gentlemen is sufficient to lay this one by the tail. The beachcomber is grateful to Okewood, who has helped him. 'Race tells, sir! You have helped one of your own breed and upbringing.' Okewood, with no apparent sign of embarrassment, refers to 'that sublime sense of superiority, which we British suck in with our mother's milk.' His advice is, when in difficulties, remember you're British. (After all, believing you're Godzone, this may help!) 'After all, we're British subjects and a little of Britain goes the deuce of a long way in these parts . . .' And another point: 'foreigners can't go about murdering British subjects, you know. They'd have the Foreign Office on them damned quick, send a cruiser and all that sort of thing.'

I get no pleasure in quoting these views because they make Williams appear idiotic, which he is not. Patriotism ran high in those days and it is quite certain that many early readers would have nodded approvingly. But these passages do highlight one extra-ordinary aspect of the British secret agent: the Celticness of his proud Englishness. Williams was presumably of Welsh extraction. Okewood refers to his Celtic background several times and on one occasion calls himself Irish. Then what of Hannay, Drummond and Bond? (Forsyth's hero in *The Devil's Alternative*, Adam Munro, is a Scot.) Buchan constantly used the word 'English' when 'British' would have been more appropriate. Two factors merge here: there is always a temptation, for writers and for all those who are especially concerned with personal identity, to opt for the minority group (they have scarcity value); and upper-class Celts frequently Anglicize very easily.

There is one other ingredient of the Williams formula that deserves attention. There is absolutely no quickfire copulation in his books, as there is in most modern spy stories with notable (and the more admirable) exceptions such as Ambler and Le Carré. Indeed, there is no copulation at all although there are hints and promises. In *The Return of Clubfoot* Marjorie Garth is quite horrified when Dr Custrin ('the beast!') tries to kiss her. But he turns out to be a German and they have no respect for women. Marjorie and Okewood share great dangers and at one point, in the complete darkness of a cave, they actually embrace and kiss. Later she declares herself willing to marry him but he cannot allow this because she is a millionaire's daughter and he is poor. A little later he discovers a fabulous treasure and immediately telegraphs his consent to the marriage. They were made of stern stuff in those days.

Types of Spy

Williams presents three types of spy to his reader. The classic spy is to be found in any popular spy novel of the period. The most perfect specimen is the irresistible female, the Mata Hari—who was, incidentally, a fake but was unconsciously created out of fictional imaginings. In *The Gold Comfit Box* (1932) there is a serious railway accident in Belgium. Clavering encounters a woman who has escaped from the scene, and his suspicions are roused. He informs Vandervliet, the Belgian security boss.

> 'The coup is classic', he cackled placidly, returning to me. 'The beautiful lady and the stiletto—you said she was beautiful, I think?'
> 'I don't think I mentioned it, but as a matter of fact, she is . . .'
> The Belgian rolled up his eyes with a seraphic expression. 'They always are.'

Clavering thinks this over and later reflects on the part played in espionage by women. We can be pretty confident that the author is now presenting his views. The novel is forgotten, realism breaks through.

> Many people are under the impression that the alluring vamp of spy fiction is a recognized figure of secret service work. I hate to disillusion you, but such is really not the case. Women have their uses in espionage, but the general experience has been that their tendency to survey a situation through the glasses of their emotions rather than their reason and, more particularly, to sentimentalize their business relations with the opposite sex, make their value as

regular agents questionable. In my years in the secret service I had dealings with more than one woman agent of the siren order (more or less) and those who were not out-and-out adventuresses, and eminently untrustworthy, usually fiddled around with a little occasional spy work as a side-line to an even older profession.

Of course, women were employed, and, for aught I know, still are. The efficient ones, however, were much more likely to approximate to the type, say, of our Garnet than a Madeleine Stafford. Usually they were selected for the very reason that they were lacking in those qualities which would single out a striking creature like Mrs Stafford from the common herd.

And here is a portrait of Madeleine, whom Williams feels compelled to introduce into his story while admitting that she was unlikely spy material.

This woman had as many moods as she had frocks. She had changed her tailored suit for a close-fitting indoor robe. It was a barbaresque affair, derived from the Boyar fashions which the Imperial Russian Ballet had then but lately introduced into Western Europe, of heavily figured brocade, in which red and gold predominated, fur-edged, with tight sleeves that dropped below the elbow into extravagantly wide panels and came to a point on the back of her tapering hands. Her eyes, darkened with mascara, were languorous behind the upturned lashes and she seemed, in doffing her outdoor clothes for this gorgeous creation, to have taken on the exotic and subtly provocative air that went with it. There was something faintly wanton in her manner that made me think of a high-class cocotte.

Soignée and *svelte* and undulating in her long dress moulded to her exquisite figure and exuding that subtle fragrance of hers that always made my heart beat faster, she entered, a cigarette smoking between her slender fingers . . .

And yet . . . Madeleine is at first sight just another cardboard E. Phillips Oppenheim character. But she is in fact something more. She is individualized and her fate concerns the reader.

Another constant in spy fiction is the amateur spy. He was in his heyday during the early part of this century. His post-1950 successor, even when he is not an official agent, is a much more professional fellow. He understands and uses all the latest technology, he will shrink from no dirty trick and he avoids the impression of naivety or even trust like the plague. Okewood (in *The Man with the Clubfoot*) goes into Germany during the First World War disguised as a German. An old man takes him aside and tells him he is making a lot of mistakes and causing a lot of dangerous attention: 'Hang it all, man, you can't go into Germany wearing a regimental tie!' Okewood's hand flew to his collar and the blood to his head. 'What a cursed amateur I was, after all I had entirely forgotten that I was wearing my regimental colours.' Fortunately the enemy appear to be equally amateurish.

Which brings us to the enemy spy. We have already had a portrait of Clubfoot. He was much more ruthless than his English counterpart; he was declared to be extremely efficient although his failures seem to belie the idea; and, in the end, he wins the grudging admiration of his antagonists. Clubfoot (he is also the Crouching Beast in the novel of that name) is really a counter-espionage agent. Druce, the British agent, describes his role.

> Clubfoot is the Kaiser's man of confidence, the head of the Emperor's personal secret service. When Clubfoot speaks, it is the Emperor speaking: when Clubfoot strikes, the whole German autocracy is behind the blow. You've been long enough in this country to have seen something of the working of German discipline: can you wonder, then, at the man's power? At least the official espionage and counter-espionage services, like the secret police, are controlled by responsible ministers. But Clubfoot is a law unto himself, responsible to none but his master, this wretched mountebank who is the greatest existing menace to the world's peace . . .

Clubfoot is very much a mystery man because of his uncertain status combined with immense power. He works in the dark. Most Germans have never heard of him. His real name, Dr Adolf Grundt, is to be found in (of all places) the Ministry of Education List, as Inspector of secondary schools. When he appears at the palace it is in connection with certain charities in which the Emperor is interested. Everything about him is massive and violent. This is illustrated again and again, which is why I give another example of his style. This is Clubfoot during an interrogation:

> I heard Grundt draw in his breath with a hissing sound, saw
> how his tufted nostrils opened and shut. Behind their thick
> glasses his eyes seemed to distend. The nails of his left hand,
> which rested on the blotting paper, blindly clawed at the
> topmost sheet till it became detached and was crumpled up
> in that huge palm. His whole body shook: I could see how
> the livid cheeks, shadowed by a black stubble, and heavy as a
> mastiff's, trembled.

It is not surprising that he frequently comes near to losing control.
'His eyes, staring and bloodshot, had lost all human semblance: they
were the eyes of an infuriated man-ape . . .' It was the age of enemy-
monsters. Among their offspring were Fleming's paranoiacs,
consumed by desire to control or obliterate the world, not merely to
serve a master. But the parent breed has disappeared.

Bulldog Drummond

One of the great mysteries of popular literature is how Bulldog
Drummond ever became a folk hero. Sapper is indisputably the
worst of all the popular authors, in the literary sense, and also the
most distasteful. Valentine Williams was frequently absurd but there
was always vitality in his writing. Sapper's work is dead, a
compilation of cliché. He probably imagined that he was following in
the footsteps of John Buchan. Buchan was a very correct, orthodox
stylist, in the line of Stevenson. In comparison Sapper was crude and
completely lacking in dignity.

Sapper was not only middle-middle-class (the kind of terminology
Orwell used to enjoy) but he was nastily middle-class. His heroes were
'clean-limbed young Englishmen' which means much more than that
they washed a lot; it signified that they despised everyone who didn't
play golf. (There was a great change with Bond, who loved golf, but
didn't condemn non-combatants.) Sapper's Englishmen, or con-
verted Scots, were always ready for adventure and regarded all
Huns, Wogs and Dagoes—in short, all foreigners—as natural
enemies who must be put in their place. This went for trade unionists
too. Eric Ambler in fact holds Sapper responsible for intensifying
class hatred in fiction. (It persists to this day, as we shall see later,
especially when considering the work of Brian Freemantle.) In his
Introduction to *To Catch a Spy* Ambler wrote:

Sapper did introduce one disagreeable novelty to the British public. In *The Black Gang* (1922) Bulldog Drummond and some of his ex-officer friends get together to form a private strong-arm squad, dressed in black shirts and masked. The villains opposing them are left-wing politicians, militant trade unionists and, of course, foreign Bolshies. Our hero's squad's way is to kidnap them at night, one by one, take them to some lonely spot and flog them within an inch of their lives. This makes the villains change their ways or leave the country. Scotland Yard shakes its head reproachfully over such goings-on, but secretly approves.

McCormick, in his *Who's Who in Spy Fiction*, draws attention to Sapper's rampant anti-semitism and also his view that 'all lovely young Englishwomen are purity personified.' I imagine that most people who know Sapper's works today will find these aspects distasteful. It is a serious criticism of the age in which he lived that it admired him so warmly. He died in 1937 and a friend of his, Gerard Fairlie, continued the Bulldog Drummond series. Few of these works, however, were really spy stories and therefore we are fortunately not much concerned with Sapper.

His main character (though it is stretching the term to call him one) is Hugh 'Bulldog' Drummond. Here is a description taken from *Temple Tower* (1929).

His height was a shade over six feet in his socks: his breadth and depth were in proportion. Which, in boxing parlance, entitles him to be placed among the big men. And big he was in every sense of the word. His face was nothing to write home about, and even his wife admitted that she only used it to amuse the baby. Anyway, looks don't matter in a man. What does matter is his condition, and, reverting once more to boxing parlance, this man looked what he was—trained to the last ounce.

He was very fond of ale which he didn't drink but 'quaffed'. In fact, Sapper had a taste for archaic language which he found amusing. It was another middle-class pose of the day.

Bulldog Drummond was not Sapper's only clean-limbed (and no doubt plus-foured) Englishman. Another was Ronald Standish who figured in a story collection called *Ask For Ronald Standish* (1936).

Most of these stories are idiotic—in fact, the first, 'Partial Salvage', might well be the silliest story ever published and could thus become a collector's item. If Sapper is to be regarded as the Ian Fleming of his day—and his popularity must have been in the same bracket—it is clear that the advance in the degree of literary ability and skill demanded by the mass reading public is immense. Sapper is not only an aggregate of cliché but of the dullest cliché ever dredged from a clubhouse bar. This cannot be said of Fleming. If Fleming offends by his treatment of sex, Sapper offends by the complete absence of sexual feeling from his puppets. Women are introduced as sweet little things; their only function is to accompany Standish or his companion and provide chatter (Sapper probably considered it 'local colour', a favourite phrase in those days) or to represent wealth through the laws of inheritance. In one of the Drummond books the wives actually set off for a holiday in France in the first chapter, allowing the men to get on with the important things in life. But Sapper did not glory in described violence as so many of his successors do. He was not averse to violence—in fact, it was sometimes necessary to teach dagoes lessons—but in these stories there is only one case of mild torture. Murders were frequently 'brutal' but they are only reported, never enjoyed. I cannot, however, attribute this to any delicacy on Sapper's part. The photographed violence of TV had not yet made its impact.

However, Sapper made his name and is included in the pantheon of thriller writers, though few of his novels or stories can be classified as spy. (Only two in the Standish collection, for instance.) It is therefore not surprising that when a much superior writer of a later generation, Len Deighton, describes the dawn sky as 'black and getting lower and blacker' he likens it to 'a Bulldog Drummond ceiling' (*An Expensive Place To Die*). This sounds more like Edgar Allan Poe although in *The Return of Bulldog Drummond* the first intimation of a murder comes when a patch of blood on the ceiling slowly increases in size. As a similar patch is seen in Hardy's *Tess* it seems clear that it is the style and not the story that counts.

And may we assume deliberate symbolism when a German agent shoots a police inspector in Manning Coles's *The Fifth Man* (1946) and the bullet slides off the outside of his skull and ends in a copy of Bulldog Drummond in the bookcase?

5: THE CHANCELLERIES OF EUROPE

Magic words they were: 'the Chancelleries of Europe'! They were always being threatened, if not by bearded men with bombs, then by suave gentlemen in white ties and tails and smoking De Reszke cigarettes. There was hardly a spy novel, written during those early decades of the twentieth century, that did not describe a situation where an apparently powerful and stable government depended on the courage or intelligence or quick wit of an operator whose name would never appear in the morning headlines. It was, of course, fortunate and inevitable that he always succeeded. Life could go on. Bumbling statesmen, barely allowing themselves time to thank their saviour, could stumble into the next crisis, only to be saved again at the eleventh hour.

Behind all this nonsense lay a serious conviction: nothing should be changed. Society was somehow satisfactory and should and would go on timelessly, despite the occasional hiccup.

The scholars did not always agree. Boyle, it is true, wrote in his *Climate of Treason* that 'the stream of first-hand documentary evidence which passed through Maclean to the Kremlin from 1944 onwards undoubtedly affected world events by influencing the shifts in Soviet foreign policy.' And yet the Chancelleries survived. The unmasking of Maclean and Philby may have sent shivers down eminent backs yet it seemed to be part of the traditional process: just in time. Constantine Fitzgibbon is not so sure. Referring to Kim Philby and Oleg Penkovsky he writes, 'It is almost certain that history would have remained entirely unaffected if these two men had remained true to their first allegiances.' (*Secret Intelligence in the Twentieth Century*). And Michael Burn, in *The Debatable Land*, has even fewer doubts: 'It is often claimed for a spy that he or she "changed the course of history"; the only one of whom this is true on a vast scale, Judas Iscariot, did it, so far as we know, for money.'

It seems likely that the importance of the spy and of espionage in general has been greatly overrated. But this imbalance has often affected those who write about spies, with the result that they believe their work deserves more attention than is given to the ordinary run of imaginative fiction. This observation is particularly true of the earlier writers, who frequently found it difficult to conceal their self-admiration. Not all the later ones are free of this fault, either.

The Country is at Stake!

Hitchcock included in his collection, *Sinister Spies*, a story called 'Legacy of Danger' by an American writer, Patricia McGerr. A Security man has been killed. There is no time to lose. There's a great deal at stake. 'Our country's at stake, she thought. Perhaps the world. Against that, what's one man's death?' Put like that, there's little argument.

The idea is never far from Buchan's mind. Bearing in mind his conviction that only a very thin crust controlled the barbarism beneath the surface, he could hardly escape it. In *The Thirty-Nine Steps* there is great diplomatic activity. Royer, the French minister, is coming to London to be briefed on military details. Sir Walter is worried about his safety and confides in Hannay. The enemy are on the prowl, hoping to pick up information wherever they can. They have already murdered the Greek leader, Karolides. 'This murder of Karolides will play the deuce in the chancelleries of Europe.' Hannay is the man for the job. Again and again he is called upon to defend the nation, civilization itself, against a ruthless enemy. He is convinced of his absolute importance. So is Buchan.

When they discovered they had been tricked, Royer kept his head while realising the gravity of the situation. 'Believe me, the need is desperate for both France and Britain.' This sort of thing is contagious. One is reminded of the reaction of press and politicians after the super-spy Blake escaped (if he escaped), their conviction that irredeemable harm had been done to Britain. Was it ever true? How do we measure these things? Is it all a delusion, powered by self-importance?

When Hannay sees the three men going into the suburban house at Bradgate, he wonders if he is making a fool of himself. Then 'I thought of Karolides lying dead and all Europe trembling on the edge of earthquake, and the men I had left behind me in London who were waiting anxiously for the events of the next hours. There was no doubt that hell was afoot somewhere.' This sort of thing is what emerges when you have left the *Boys' Own* paper a few years behind.

There is the same tone in *Greenmantle*. Sir Walter calls up Hannay and tells him something momentous is happening, though he doesn't know what. 'One last question', says Hannay. 'You say it is important. Tell me just how important.' Bullivant replies solemnly, 'It is life and death . . . The stakes are no less than victory and defeat, Hannay.' One can almost hear the jaws cracking as the muscles set.

In *Mr Standfast* it is the supposedly delectable Mary (Buchan could not create a delectable woman, he could only name her such) who supplies the gravitas. 'Tell me one thing', says Hannay, practically repeating his question to Sir Walter. 'Is it a really big thing we're after?' and Mary replies with immense emphasis, 'A—really—big—thing. You and I and some hundred others are hunting the most dangerous man in all the world. Till we succeed everything that Britain does is crippled. If we fail or succeed too late the Allies may never win the victory which is their right.' Later a worried officer quite understandably queries Hannay's credentials. Macgillivray of Scotland Yard rescues him and snaps at the officer, 'It may comfort you to know that your folly may have made just the difference between your country's victory and defeat.' In *The Three Hostages* the new enemy, Medina, is suspected of 'planning the ruin of our civilization'. This theme, which became quite familiar after the First World War and was probably a popular reflection of Dadaism, is to be found in Priestley's *The Doomsday Men*, where it is handled without Buchan's pomposity.

Sapper could not resist the temptation to threaten and then save civilization. (The irony is that any worthwhile civilization could be saved by Sapper, or his representative, Ronald Standish.) In a story called 'The Mystery at Styles Court' an important Treasury official is discovered moving corn stooks in such a way as to convey information to an aeroplane pilot flying overhead. At first it was thought he was passing on financial information but it turns out to be something worse: 'bigger things are involved: international problems of far-reaching importance.' What they were is not stated (neither Forsyth nor Fleming nor Deighton would be so indifferent)—it is most unlikely Sapper knew. But Standish is appalled. He assumed it was need of money that led Sir James to such an act of treason. He shows no pity for the miscreant: 'in his particular code some things were beyond the pale'. He suggests Sir James shoots himself, which he obligingly does. The death is reported by the landlord at the pub in the kind of deadly understatement that impressed Sapper so much. 'Shockingly careless some gentlemen are with guns. Some beer, sir?'

Another Standish story is called 'The Man in the Saloon Car.' It is a conspiracy tale, but Mafia rather than political. Nevertheless, if it had succeeded 'another throne in Europe would have changed its occupant.' This kind of carelessness indicates the contempt which Sapper felt at bottom for his reader. One feels that those who read him from choice deserved contempt. The one matter on which Sapper becomes informative is the general beastliness of foreigners, particularly their agents. 'Crouching on the floor, his teeth bared in a snarl, our prisoner looked like an animal . . . his eyes arrested me. They burned like coals of fire; the eyes of a madman or a fanatic.' Just like Clubfoot, one might say—and yet Williams always managed to endow Clubfoot with a certain dignity. It is possible to grieve with him in his frustrations.

At this point, that is, poised between wars, *Phantom Spy* (1937) by Max Brand is worth notice. Brand was an American (real name Frederick Faust, nicknamed King of the Pulp Writers, author of many Westerns but also Dr Kildare—he was killed in action in the war he foresaw) but this essay in espionage is set in a Europe about to catch fire. In 1937 Brand realized that Germany and Italy were preparing to attack France, although he thought it would be with Russian help. (Nor was this far out, even if it did not come quite as expected.) This novel belongs primarily to the 'Chancelleries of Europe' school. The Head of the Secret Service tells one of his agents that she may have 'set back the progress of the world a hundred years' by killing a Russian. And the French agent, Cailland, is on one occasion told that he has changed the history of the world. Despite the new ruthlessness which Fascism and the Comintern were introducing into European politics, Brand still observes the milder gentilities. For example, Gloster tells Hendriksen he will spare him if he tells him where some plans are hidden. Hendriksen refuses to tell and awaits his death. But Gloster cannot shoot him in cold blood. 'Well, all right', he says. 'You win.' Nor can he harm Raskoi when drunk. Remember Orwell, who was unable to shoot a man with his trousers down.

It is a weird book and one feels the hack-author, who could understand what was happening so much better than politicians who were immersed in the Chancelleries, could be a compound of Akbar del Piombo, James Branch Cabell and T.F. Powys. It is utterly incredible but could be accepted as surreal spy-fi: in other words, it becomes credible in the way that a fantastic dream suddenly seems to make sense. Brand is concerned with language and ideas and never descends to the block-buster style of Sapper. One feels he might have caught the attention of the youthful Ian Fleming, as I am sure Valentine Williams did. He shows an interest in torture and passages like the following remind one of Fleming's sharp, cool visual sense. Hendriksen is expecting to be shot dead.

> The powder would burn the flesh of his temple. The skin would furl back at the edge of the wound, scorched away. He saw, in his mind, how the wound would be. But what he saw more clearly was the dipping and the winding of the school road, near home, frozen white most of the year, and the school stuck on the side of the hill. In that funny little school, he had been brighter than the rest. Now he had found that you can't be bright and win. It makes you different from other people. Somehow, he always knew and could always answer, just as he had now. Nobody could argue with him about it. A man can't sell himself twice.

Hendriksen is a very minor character, who does not appear again, yet the author considers it worth while describing his state of mind.

Fleming himself more than once described plots and conspiracies which were designed to create maximum havoc. In *Thunderball* Bond disturbs the 'exactly-timed machinery of a plot that was about to shake the governments of the Western world.' Government-shaking is a later equivalent of Chancellery-bashing—there was something noble and admirable in the idea of a Chancellery which no longer applies to the seats of power. *Moonraker* and *Dr No* are adaptations of the same theme. These three novels appeared in 1955, 1958 and 1961. In 1959 came Condon's *The Manchurian Candidate* with its unique scheme of government-shaking assassination.

There is a considerable sameness about this type of novel. Underlying them is the assumption that they represent the final horror. Whether it is achieved through an assassin's bullet or a nuclear explosion, civilization itself will be assaulted and possibly destroyed. As representative, let us consider *The November Man* by Brian Freemantle, a recent vintage (1976). There is a fly-leaf quote from Willy Brandt about the Guillaume affair. Freemantle resembles Deighton and Warren Tute in linking his stories to actual political

events and situations. (This is for real!) We are taken into the
Praesidium of the U.S.S.R. and the confidence of the President
of the U.S.A. At the end the outgoing President makes a solemn
announcement in a nation-wide, peak-time television appearance:
'Surveys later showed no other Presidential address in immediate
American history, even including Nixon's resignation speech or
Kennedy's defence of the Cuban confrontation with Krushchev, had
attracted such an audience rating.' Across the world Melkovsky, the
Russian Foreign Minister, is equally satisfied with the outcome of Mr
Freemantle's imaginative flights. A K.G.B. man says they can't bring
the American President down, and Melkovsky agrees but adds, 'But
it puts us in a position virtually to manipulate his re-election. And
stay in complete control of American foreign policy: it's a detonator
we can push any time.'

This delving into the seats of the mighty is becoming commonplace. We encounter it in Forsyth's *The Devil's Alternative*
where once again both Americans and Russians patch things up
together to suit themselves and each other. The Tory-Labour
duopoly which helped create the Social Democratic Party in Britain is
paralleled on the international stage in the minds of many spy
writers. The most we can hope for is avoidance of catastrophe by
super-power manipulation. There is at present no hint of an
international S.D.P. But underneath all this the old theme maintains
itself. 'The Soviet Politbureau was about to begin a meeting that
would change history', writes Forsyth. Radio operators at both ends
(Moscow and Washington) handled as routine 'messages that could
bring down governments'. And finally there is even reference to the
'Chancelleries of Europe and America.' Buchan was not forgotten.

Disillusion and Revaluation

But all was not quite the same, nevertheless. It was no longer accepted
quite so glibly that the Chancelleries represented values worth
preserving. Doubts began to surface after the Hitler War which, after
all, began with the Fascists and Communists embracing each other
before going ahead with the massacre of Poland. No-one expresses
the new bewilderment more forcibly than Le Carré. Perhaps the new
writers are more modest. They found it difficult to believe that
Western Civilization could really depend on the wit and courage of

one obscure man. The new agent, on the whole, cares little or nothing about the wider consequences—he aims to get his man and then ask for leave. There are, of course, exceptions, but with them the same feeling merely takes a different direction. They are disgusted. The politicians have to think of wider circles of effect than the agents they employ (often with considerable distaste) and it is up to them to accept or reject the temptations of pomposity and self-glorification. Bradfield at the Bonn Embassy (in Le Carré's *A Small Town in Germany*) outlines his task thus: 'to maintain at all costs the trust and goodwill of the Federal Government. To stiffen their resolve against mounting criticism from their own electorate.' Not much to ask for. Turner is amused at the idea of the 'two sick men of Europe propping one another up.'

Le Carré is gently nostalgic. William Haggard is much more forthright and declamatory. His man is Colonel Russell, Head of the Security Executive. In *The Hardliners* he has retired but, like most agents of the old school, remains active. Haggard resembles Anthony Price in his careful plotting and measured logic, but writes with more verve—which can at times mean more aggression. There is a rather unpleasant note of self-admiration, engulfing both the author and his favourite characters, running through this novel. In reality it stems from the old Champions of the Chancelleries. (After all, would not you be rather proud if you knew that either you or your creation was the last bulwark against disaster?) Russell has a strong distaste for intellectuals, especially Left-wingers. Among some of his contemporaries this is paralleled by a hatred of politicians, of any colour. Tender consciences and, for the most part, acting from principle, are out. About defectors from the Eastern bloc: we don't want them. They are contaminated. The eggheads wanted them but the Establishment didn't. 'It's not soft in the head yet, the British Establishment.' The eggheads in question are not necessarily Left-wingers. They are non-political, and act out of principle, which is almost a crime to the true patriot.

The politicians, probably activated by academic eggheads, can go soft, whatever Haggard thinks. In *Goldfinger* M tells Bond that the Treasury has decided that the double-O section was redundant. It was out of date. It is like saying the defence of civilization was no longer on the agenda. This ban is also mentioned elsewhere and is always put down to the feebleness of the new race of politicians. Fleming is certainly not alone in this, Freemantle could be quite vicious at times.

When John Gardner continued the Bond series he had to consider the ban but enabled M to get round it by simply re-naming the section.

Le Carré deals with the same situation in a cooler, more measured way. In *Smiley's People* we hear of an inter-ministerial Steering Committee which is part Westminster, part Whitehall, representing the Cabinet as well as the Civil Service. They were called the Wise Men and were placed between Intelligence and the Cabinet 'as a channel, as a filter, as a brake', according to Lacon. Their job was to exercise control and to show vigilance and accountability in the interests of more open government. It was a result of government mistrust of what the Secret Service was up to. The government was Labour, 'our new masters'. (No doubt Haggard's Colonel Russell could hardly contain his rage.) Lacon, representing the traditional politician, is appalled, Smiley non-committal.

> 'Gibes. Suspicion. Mistrust at every turn, even from Ministers who should know better. As if the Circus were some rogue animal outside their comprehension. As if British intelligence were a sort of wholly owned subsidiary of the Conservative Party. Not their ally at all but some autonomous viper in their Socialist nest. The thirties all over again. Do you know, they're even reviving all that talk about a British Freedom of Information Act on the American pattern?'

Domestic surveillance was becoming a thing of the past. Wise Men don't hold with it.

There is a great deal of nostalgia in Le Carré. Here at least is a feeling that the old world had values that were worth preserving. They had been allowed to let slip, partly by people who felt embarrassed by the very idea of patriotism, who found more comfort in ideology than in tribal conventions. And if there was a class of men who deliberately set out to destroy, so there was another class, well-meaning no doubt, that could not be bothered to put up more than a token resistance. Connie (in *Tinker, Tailor, Soldier, Spy*) laments the lost past and even upbraids Smiley, though not very seriously. If he is at fault, so is she. 'All over the world beastly people are making our time into nothing, why do you help them? . . . It was a good time, do you hear? A real time. Englishmen could be proud then. Let them be proud now . . . Poor loves. Trained to Empire, trained to rule the waves. All gone. All taken away. Bye-bye world. You're the last,

George, you and Bill.' There is an obvious link here, though a sad one, with Buchan and his generation. They seem so different and yet they are fundamentally the same, but responding to changed circumstances. Even Bill Haydon, the mole, comes into this category. It is because he laments the lost past he finally turns to the opposition. It is a logically false and twisted act, but it is closer to inverted patriotism than to international conspiracy.

The old-style patriots thought of England (rarely Britain). Their successors are worried about the West. When there is a loss of faith it is in Western values, what the History Departments used to call Western Civilization. When disillusion sets in it is as likely to come from a Frenchman as from an Englishmen. And in fact the best instance of despair in recent spy literature comes through the French agent Ollivier in Anthony Price's *Other Paths to Glory* (1974). When asked why he has lost faith he replies, 'Because our way is wrong.' He is asked if *their* way is right.

> 'Who is *they*?' Ollivier cocked his head on one side. 'When we were young there was *us* and *them* but now we are all the same—all *them* and all wrong . . . When I realized that, I knew I had spent my life trying to repair something not worth repairing. So I have stopped being a repair man: now I am in the business of demolition. I am putting a match to the fire from which the phoenix may rise.'

It is significant that a Frenchman plays this role. (When Chapman Pincher decides that civilization is at risk, in *Dirty Tricks*, he gives this line to a Russian: 'You didn't know it, but for a moment I, a woman alone in your office, could have changed the fate of the world just by lifting the telephone.') It doesn't come easily to an Englishman, who would be less likely to enquire into fundamentals and would be more likely to support his own side simply because it was his own. Audley says Ollivier's Phoenix is more likely to be a vulture. It's another way of pointing out that French clear-sightedness assists the enemy whereas English muddle-headedness gives nothing away.

6: IAN FLEMING

Fleming created Bond, England's most successful spy; among the generality of readers, England's most popular spy; among the cognoscenti, including Fleming's fellow spy-writers, England's most hated and most despised spy. All of this makes him intensely interesting. Fleming is reputedly the biggest earner ever in British fiction as a whole, not just spy-fiction.

Unlike some of his rivals, Fleming served in Intelligence. (This does not mean much—Ambler, a much better writer and much more convincing in his presentation of the espionage world, never did.) When the Second World War broke out the Admiralty had a list of 'gentlemen who had offered their services to the Admiralty in the event of hostilities.' The Director of Naval Intelligence asked the novelist, Charles Morgan, to pick out between forty and fifty of the more promising volunteers. Fleming was one of them.

Peter Quennell knew him fairly well and thinks that Fleming created the man he would have liked to be. Fleming himself completely lacked Bond's self-esteem and unquestioning self-assurance. But Fleming was annoyed if anyone identified him with Bond or addressed him as such teasingly. When writing about Fleming there is always the temptation to use the name Bond, the same kind of identification that exists between Conan Doyle and Sherlock Holmes.

There are two characteristics of this baffling man which compound the mystery. Quennell tells us in *The Wanton Chase* (1980) he was a natural melancholic 'despite his contempt for highbrows and for the elusive sicknesses of the soul that disturb so many modern writers'. Yet in one of his novels he suggests (or Bond does) that the Secret Service needs more intellectuals to understand the brains on the other side. As for the sicknesses, there is no rule about who may suffer from them. Was there ever a less likely candidate than Evelyn Waugh, as confessed in *Gilbert Pinfold*?

And then Fleming was a puritan, 'at heart perhaps an ingrained Calvinist'. As a Lowland Scot (like Buchan) he was brought up to respect the simple virtues. His mother, like Buchan's, preached the gospel of success. His enormous success came after early failures, when he had run away from Sandhurst and made unsuccessful attempts to join the Diplomatic Service. His brother Peter, the travel writer, carried all before him.

In 1958, six years before his death, he informed a well-wisher that he had definitely conquered fame and fortune, but as early as 1955 he had grown tired of Bond. Nevertheless, he left two novels open-ended, perhaps bearing in mind Conan Doyle's experiences when he got rid of Holmes too precipitately.

John Pearson has given us *The Life of Ian Fleming* and he is mentioned in many memoirs and autobiographies, such as the afore-mentioned Quennell book and also in Waugh's correspondence and diaries. It is worth noting that one of our best novelists, Kingsley Amis, confessed himself a great admirer of Bond. But as an indication of the impact Fleming was able to make on the unknown and the anonymous, there is the case of an American named Fletcher Trenchant (probably a pseudonym) who was convinced in 1963 that another Sarajevo was imminent. He went to Washington to make his fears known but was given the 'not-so-classic run-round'. No-one would listen to him and he was told that Soviet-American relations had improved. He told one senior official that 'President Kennedy will meet his end with bullets, bombs or knives.' Finally he wrote to Ian Fleming and received a friendly reply dated 6 November 1963. 'I see absolutely no reason why you shouldn't be right in the broad lines of your reasoning', Fleming wrote. ' "Natural" death as a means of assassination is a much tidier method than assassination. The only problem is access and in two of the cases you mention, which I happen to know something about, I think this would have been extremely difficult to achieve. You make me reflect upon my own coronary thrombosis about $2\frac{1}{2}$ years ago, but in fact I think that was brought about by a mixture of James Bond and smoking too much!'

Trenchant adds tersely that Fleming died of a coronary some months later. It is known that the K.G.B. regarded Fleming's influence as damaging. Trenchant's theory (which he published privately in a book called *The Wobble*) was that in addition to open assassination men of stature and promise almost invariably die of heart, liver and kidney complaints. He believed there was a world-wide poisoning conspiracy, conducted by Marxists.

The Method

Bond is more counter-spy than spy. Therefore his activities often differ widely from those of other fictional agents. The normal duty of the spy is to discover information in the shape of plans, reports, directives and so on. The counter-spy tries to stop this and if possible catch the spy. In a fully developed story emphasis is placed on what the spy is after: weapon design, military placements, political policies, etc. These are the gist and the foundation of the whole affair. But Fleming doesn't concern himself much with this. Bond is always trying to destroy an agent who is working for the enemy; what the enemy does, or why he is important, is not always stated or, if it is, it is played down. The target is always the man. The plan is presumably there, otherwise there would be no man, but it is not divulged. There is also another level, which is subservient to the espionage level but is required by the reader, on which Bond goes for the woman. With Deighton, Le Carré, Freemantle and others we are usually given perfectly clear reasons why it is so necessary to catch or stop the spy. *The Riddle of the Sands* is the classic of this type of spy novel.

Fleming sometimes gets impatient and arranges for what might occupy another agent pages and weeks of hard work to fall into Bond's lap (or his ears) in a few sentences. In *The Man With the Golden Gun* (1965) Bond eavesdrops on Scaramanga and his hoods. 'He had heard his own death sentence pronounced, the involvement of the K.G.B. with Scaramanga and the Caribbean spelled out, and such minor dividends as sabotage of the bauxite industry, massive drug smuggling into the States and gambling politics thrown in. It was a majestic haul in area Intelligence.' With such data there is nothing to stand in the way of freely flowing action.

But Fleming is chiefly remarkable for his detail. It is always extremely precise, though it may be false. The aim is to give the reader the idea that he knows exactly what is happening. Here are examples taken from just one novel, *Dr No* (1958). Major Boothroyd, the Armourer, gives advice on the weapon Bond should carry.

> 'There's only one gun for that, sir. Smith & Wesson Centennial Airweight. Revolver. .38 calibre. Hammerless, so it won't catch in clothing, Overall length of six and a half inches and it only weighs thirteen ounces. To keep down the weight, the cylinder holds only five cartridges. But by the

time they're gone somebody's been killed. Fires the .38 S &
W Special. Very accurate cartridge indeed. With standard
loading it has a muzzle velocity of eight hundred and sixty
feet per second and muzzle energy of two hundred and sixty
foot-pounds. There are various barrel lengths, three and a
half inch, five inch . . .

But for one sentence, this could have been taken straight out of a
catalogue. The only other writer who can challenge this degree of
detail in firearms is J.T. Edson and his accounts are necessarily less
contemporary.

Bond thinks in the same detail—'of the days when he had literally
dressed to kill—when he had dismantled the gun and oiled it and
packed the bullets carefully into the springloaded magazine and tried
the action once or twice, pumping the cartridges out on to the
bedspread in some hotel bedroom somewhere round the world. Then
the last wipe of a dry rag and the gun into the little holster and a pause
in front of the mirror to see that nothing showed.' It's the same with
his drinks. 'Bond ordered a double gin and tonic and one whole green
lime. When the drink came he cut the lime in half, dropped the two
squeezed halves into the long glass, almost filled the glass with ice
cubes and then poured in the tonic.' It is this compulsive detail (some
might call it almost paranoiac) that accounts for the fascination
Fleming exerted on his readers. Along with the incredibility of the
action went the heightened credibility of the detail.

He made effective use of brand names for a readership that was
being immersed in them (especially those with snob appeal) by
independent television and the weekly supplements. Again from *Dr
No:*

There was everything in the bathroom—Floris Lime bath
essence for men and Guerlain bathcubes for women. He
crushed a cube into the water and at once the room smelled
like an orchid house. The soap was Guerlain's Sapoceti,
Fleurs des Alpes. In a medicine cupboard behind the mirror
over the washbasin were toothbrushes and toothpaste,
Steradent toothpicks, Rose mouthwash, dental floss,
Aspirin and Milk of Magnesia. There was also an electric
razor, Lentheric after-shave lotion, and two nylon hair-
brushes and combs. Everything was brand new and un-
touched.

His younger contemporary, John Braine, who also tried his hand (unsuccessfully) at the spy story some years later, used the same device to win the reader's affiliation. At times it seems pointless, as when, for instance, Bond is taken prisoner by Dr No and Fleming cannot avoid noting that the lift was made by Waygood Otis. At other times it may serve to demonstrate Bond's coolness in adversity, as when Dr No asks him what he would like to drink and he says, 'A medium Vodka dry Martini—with a slice of lemon peel. Shaken and not stirred, please. I would prefer Russian or Polish vodka.'

It is important that Bond should never be at a loss. There must be no area of experience where he doesn't know his way around. The opening of *Diamonds are Forever* (1956) is a sort of mini-lecture. In *The Man with the Golden Gun* the emphasis is on Natural History. Bond has struggled through a swamp and sees a large snake approaching Scaramanga. 'He guessed it was a boa of the *Epicrates* family, attracted by the smell of blood. It was perhaps five feet long and quite harmless to man.' Scaramanga kills the snake, cuts off its head and throws it towards a crab hole. He waits to see if a crab will emerge. But Bond knows better. 'The thud of the arrival of the snake's head would have kept any crab underground for many minutes, however enticing the scent of what had made the thud.'

But he can slip up! *Diamonds are Forever* dazzles with his card-sharping expertise. Nothing is too trivial or fragmentary. 'Bond cut the cards and watched with approval as she carried out the difficult single-handed Annulment, one of the hardest gambits in card-sharping.' Yet in the same novel we read that 'his room was extremely comfortable and equipped with expensive and well-designed modern furniture of a silvery wood that might have been birch.' Bond (or Fleming) is confused by the name 'silver birch', but the colour refers to the bark, not the wood. Birch wood is pale brown or cream in colour, with a dull surface, and it is normally used for brush backs, reels and toys, rarely if ever for furniture. Eric Ambler once pointed out that Fleming's knowledge of the area around Istanbul appears to be at fault. Perhaps his geography is rather uncertain for in *On Her Majesty's Secret Service* (1963) a senior official of the Ministry of Agriculture and Fisheries is made to say, 'Fowl pest is running wild in East Anglia and there are signs of it in Suffolk . . .' And it is not only the facts which may be wrong; at times it is the behaviour. Bond is presented as an admirably correct and sophisticated person, completely at home in 'right' society. He is meticulous in describing

IAN FLEMING 77

his aristocratic tastes and matching them in the approved manner. But when he dines with M at Blades (in *Moonraker*, 1955) he orders lamb cutlets and then adds, fatally, 'The same vegetables as you, *as it's May*'! But only a complete bounder would give the reason for his choice of food.

As an adjunct to his love of detail goes his fascination with gadgetry. It is possibly this that caught the public interest, even more than the detail, and it certainly figured prominently in all the Bond films. His cars and his boats were marvels of mechanical ingenuity and refinement, to an extent that we tend to forget that M was no slouch in these matters either. *The Man with the Golden Gun* starts with the brainwashed Bond firing a jet of poison at M, 'but even as the poison hissed down the barrel of the bulb-butted pistol, the great sheet of Armourplate glass hurtled down from the baffled slit in the ceiling and, with a last sigh of hydraulics, braked to the floor.'

Fleming was not really concerned with the real world behind Bond in the way that most modern spy-writers are. For him the background was wonderfully simple: the good West (largely British, American and French) and their enemies the Communists (which in effect meant the Russians and certain independent organizations which supported, or were supported by, them). There was one Russian organization which took Fleming's fancy, probably because of the unpleasant sound of its title: SMERSH. Thanks to Bond there were probably thousands of readers who knew of this body's existence who knew nothing of the Politburo or Praesidium. It was popularized by Fleming as 'the official murder organisation of the Soviet government' with 40,000 employees. Its title was a contraction of *Smyert Shpionam* meaning roughly Death to Spies. Bond's protracted struggle with SMERSH begins in his first book, *Casino Royale* (1953). At that stage there was very little direct contact with SMERSH although they did succeed in branding Bond on the hand. But later there must have been many readers who believed that Bond was our only credible defence against this sinister body.

Here are a few facts that contradict the Bond story. In 1921 the Cheka established units in the Red Army to spy on the military and root out disloyal elements. It was known as the Double-O section (*sic!*) and was attached at every level of the Army. It was expanded during World War II when it became known as SMERSH. By then it was given greater responsibilities, such as the interception of enemy paratroops and the capture of Soviet deserters and enemy spies. It could hand out summary sentences at the front and it could execute spies on the spot. But in 1946 it was dissolved and its personnel became a division of the K.G.B. under the title of 'counter-intelligence'. It still keeps watch over the armed forces.

The post-Bond school of spy-writers had no sympathy with this kind of informational looseness. Len Deighton, in fact, tries to give his books a scholarly respectability by the use of appendices and footnotes. In Appendix Two of *Billion-Dollar Brain*, under the heading 'Soviet Intelligence', he states that a special part of the K.G.B. is devoted to watching the Army. It is called G.U.K.R. and is often translated as Senior Counter-Intelligence. Deighton italicizes the phrase: *watches the Soviet Army*. He adds that before 1946 it was sometimes called SMERSH and was part of the Defence Ministry. The approach to the real political world expressed here is the complete reverse of Fleming's.

The Style

Much odium has been incurred by Fleming for his style. This is mostly undeserved. It is not his style that is objectionable but his view of life. I have noticed that criticisms of his style usually come from academic quarters, whose stylistic preferences are themselves suspect. Compared with writers like Oppenheim and Le Queux, Fleming writes well. Compared with Sapper's, his is a model of English prose. Kingsley Amis, who impresses by his no-nonsense approach to writing, praises him. Eric Ambler, who is superior to all the other pure thriller-writers in his use of English, writes in his introductory note to the Bond story, 'From a View to a Kill', which he included in his collection *To Catch a Spy*: 'Critics rarely remark on how well written the James Bond stories are. I suppose that with a man as civilized and amusing as Mr Fleming, good writing is taken for granted.' Nevertheless, I feel that this statement must be taken with a pinch of salt, just as we rarely take singers' views of the quality of music seriously.

However, there are many things that can be said in favour of Fleming's style. He is clear and incisive. His prose has an easy flow. He is extremely articulate and employs a wide vocabulary. His descriptions have a meticulous particularity. At times, it is true, this becomes too emphatic, 'over-heated'. He has a pleasant, quiet humour. He convinces the reader that he is in full control of both story and detail. He handles suspense effectively. And despite his brand-name snobbery Fleming presents Bond as a modest personality.

This is a list of virtues no-one would be ashamed of. But Fleming's view of life is a different matter and it was this that caused later spy-writers, such as Le Carré and Deighton, to revolt against him. Fleming is careless over psychological credibility. For example, in *Thunderball* (1961) a member of the criminal syndicate does his job and is then ruthlessly slaughtered in front of his colleagues. (In fact, this happens twice.) Is it likely that the colleagues would continue to work for an organization where their lives were obviously at great risk from those they worked with and for?

Fleming liked to start a story or novel or chapter with a set-piece (sometimes about an animal, bird or fish) written in a highly flamboyant style. There was cunning in this, for it set the mood for the physical emphasis, even violence, that was sure to follow. 'From a View to a Kill' which Ambler selected for his collection *To Catch a Spy* seems to me an extraordinary choice. It is not only a ridiculous story but also starts with a passage that shows Fleming at his worst. The writer attacks the reader with a verbal bludgeon.

> The eyes behind the wide black rubber goggles were cold as flint. In the howling speed-turmoil of a BSA M20 doing seventy, they were the only quiet things in the hurtling flesh and metal. Protected by the glass of the goggles, they stared fixedly ahead from just above the centre of the handlebars, and their dark unwavering focus was that of gun muzzles. Below the goggles, the wind had streamed into the face through the mouth and had wrenched the lips back into a square grin that showed big tombstone teeth and strips of whitish gum. On both sides of the grin the cheeks had been blown out by the wind into pouches that fluttered slightly. To right and left of the hurtling face under the crash helmet, the black gauntlets, broken-wristed at the controls, looked like the attacking paws of a big animal.

There is no doubt about the literary skill that is being deployed here. Its purpose, however, is to dehumanize the character and to set a tone which will prepare the reader for the violence that is to follow. This is in direct contrast to the mode adopted by some other writers, according to which violence breaks suddenly and disturbingly into a scene which is relatively peaceful, even idyllic.

Fleming was, of course, a formula writer yet on occasion he tried to avoid or break the formula. He was capable of rejecting the Happy Ending which used to be considered obligatory for the popular writer. When we finish *From Russia with Love* (1957) Bond is poisoned, possibly dead. At the end of *On Her Majesty's Secret Service* his new bride is murdered while they are setting out on their honeymoon. This may be a device to encourage the reader to buy the next book in the series. In each of the above cases the doubt in which one novel ends is cleared up in the succeeding one.

There are indications that Fleming might have been capable of writing a serious and thoughtful novel. *Casino Royale* has passages which encourage such a belief. In the 1961-70 supplement to the *Dictionary of National Biography* Kingsley Amis calls it 'one of the most remarkable first novels to be published in England in the previous thirty years.' If Fleming found the temptations of easy fame and fortune too great to resist, he was not the first to succumb. Literary history is littered with writers who emerged from the *avant garde* of their time to write popular nonsense. In the atypical *The Spy Who Loved Me* (1962) one feels that Fleming is trying to write a non-spy novel—or at least, a straight novel that has an agent for its hero (as Graham Greene has done and, in effect, John Le Carré). Up to page 104, it looks like it. In the first section he (or Vivienne Michel, heroine and supposedly part-author) uses the loose '. . . and . . . and . . . and' style that once suggested literary sophistication. Bruce Merry (*Anatomy of the Spy Thriller*) called it 'atypical', a term I have borrowed for its aptness.

This novel is written from a French Canadian point of view and is not very complimentary about the English. There is, for example, a reference to 'damned English snobs'. Vivienne is very complimentary about Bond, but then he is Scoto-Swiss. In fact, spy novels often illustrate strongly the self-criticism that Ifor Evans considered typical of English writing in his *English Literature: Values and Traditions* and which, in the less thoughtful atmosphere of popular writing, often turns to self-hatred.

Continuations

Fleming died in 1964 but there were some who were not prepared to let Bond die with him. One of these was Kingsley Amis who, four years later, produced a 'Bond' novel under the pseudonym of Robert Markham. In 1981 John Gardner gave the world another 'Bond' novel called *Licence Renewed*, which has been followed by *For Special Services*. These three novels are of immense interest, partly for the simple reason that they were written at all (and one by a novelist of very high reputation) and partly because, as justification, they had to stay as close to the models in spirit, manner and method as was humanly possible. Otherwise they would not have been acceptable to the many Bond fanatics. It is therefore possible to regard these three books as conscious imitations of an admired model, and consequently representative of the model's major characteristics.

Markham's *Colonel Sun* is dedicated 'to the Memory of Ian Fleming.' In an essay entitled 'A New James Bond' Amis expresses his admiration for Bond but also says he wished to annoy the intellectual Left. He is a debunking expert. Now you can't very well debunk Bond so what do you do if you are of a contrary turn of mind? You upbunk him. Fleming's precise touch is reproduced to the point of parody. Bond finds his boss M (who is actually named as Admiral Sir Charles Messervy) drugged and helpless. Then comes the lecture:

> Adrenalin is produced by the adrenal glands, two small bodies situated on the upper surface of the kidneys. Because of the circumstances which cause its release into the circulation, and its effect on the body, it is sometimes known as the drug of fright, fear and flight. Now, at the sight of M, Bond's adrenals fell to their primeval work, pumping their secretion into his bloodstream and thus quickening respiration to fill his blood with oxygen, speeding up the heart's action to improve the blood-supply to the muscles, closing the smaller blood-vessels near the skin to minimise loss in case of wounding, even causing the hair on his scalp to lift minutely, in memory of the age when man's primitive ancestors had been made to look more terrible to their adversaries by the raising and spreading of their furry crests . . .

Amis/Markham obviously showed the best of intentions but as we move into the novel he loses concentration and his writing becomes as slack as Sapper's. And he is guilty of a narrative failure that one might expect in Sapper but never in Fleming. During the torture scene we are told that von Richter and Willi are present, but at some time they seem to leave. When and why? We are not told.

What Amis does well is to emphasize the compassionate streak in Bond which Fleming never disguised. When the Hammonds are killed Bond is deeply upset—'he found himself beset by the irrelevant wish that he had listened more appreciatively to Hammond's anecdotes about pre-war naval life at the Pacific Station, that he had had the time and the kindness to thank and encourage Mrs Hammond for her self-dedication to M during his illness. Bond made a muffled sound between a sob and a snarl.' This aspect of Bond was overshadowed by the violence and the slickness but it was never entirely absent. Amis rescues it. When Bond kills the pilot of a cruiser and throws a bomb down the hatchway, 'not for the first time in his career (he) felt a surge of sickening remorse at the gross, outrageous destruction he had caused, the stabbing of the man in the pilot's seat and the unknown, but probably dreadful, fate of the other.' In fact, this kind of reaction becomes exaggerated. Yanni, a boy of sixteen, knifes a man. Bond feels responsible. 'Bond shuddered. He had to get used to the idea of involving innocent bystanders in the kind of savage, unpredictable violence he traded in, but to have brought about the initiation of an adolescent into the ways of killing was something new to him. He hoped desperately that the relative unsophistication of Greek youth would protect Yanni from the progressive intoxication with lethal weapons that, in an urban British lad of this age, could so easily result from such an episode.'

Fleming showed little admiration for politicians but never portrayed one quite as unsympathetically as Amis does in this book. It is closer to the figures one finds in Freemantle or Melville-Ross. The Minister ultimately responsible for security is surrounded by 'envy, spite, ambition'—and reacts accordingly.

John Gardner also tends to out-Bond Bond without having recourse to some of the subtler shades incorporated by Amis. In his Acknowledgments he thanks the Board of Directors of Glidrose Publications Ltd., owners of the James Bond copyright, for inviting him to renew the Bond series. There is no doubt that Gardner has studied his model very carefully. As a result he not only includes all the Bond characteristics but also hammers them home relentlessly. It was probably the effort of over-conscious imitation that led to the abundance of cliché—a cause frequently followed by that effect in writing. The first paragraph has a sentence beginning: 'A trained observer would have particularly noted . . .' We also get: 'It had about it a distinct air of unreality', referring to a conversation between Bond and the arch-villain Murik.

The Brand-Name touch is done to death. Fleming himself might have been disturbed by this description of a breakfast: 'two large cups of black coffee, from De Bry, without sugar; a single "perfectly boiled" brown egg (Bond still affected to dislike anything but brown eggs, and kept his opinion regarding three and one-third minutes constituting the perfect boiling time); then two slices of wholewheat toast with Jersey butter and Tiptree "Little Scarlet" strawberry jam, Cooper's Vintage Oxford Marmalade or Norwegian heather honey.'

But the particularity is imposed, not lived through, so that any loss of concentration leads to error. The terrorist Franco (apparently based on the real Carlos) spends a long time in a public toilet changing his identity and then leaves without using the flush. This is very careless behaviour for such a man in such a book. In fact, we can be sure that it was the author who slipped up, not his character. Gardner tries to give his story a strong sense of reality by referring to existing terrorist organizations. This is a practice that has intensified during recent years. Some of the earlier spy-writers, such as Manning Coles, still moved in a world of Ruritanias. Bond's terrorist and conspiratorial organizations were closer to reality though still fictional. Gardner, however, brings Bond into what is in some degree a post-Bond world, where Franco has no direct political affiliations but cooperates with groups like Baader-Meinhof, the Red Army Faction, the P.L.O., the I.R.A. and others. As has already been stated, the double-O status has been abolished (the work of 'fools of politicians', a common opinion among the more sensational spy-writers) but M privately lets Bond know he can retain the status merely through a change of designation.

Licence Renewed cannot rank high in the Bond canon, even if it is included. There is a deliberateness in the writing which calls to mind a set exercise—which, in a sense, it is. And as an example of the determination to emulate the Master, not only is Bond captured by his enemies and tortured ('high frequency white noise' beamed into his head!), and then miraculously escapes—but it happens twice!

7: JAMES BOND

Bond is one of those rare fictional characters who is better known than his author. In fact, one sometimes comes across people who speak of James Bond as a thriller writer. Like Sherlock Holmes, he has been imposed on the public consciousness like a tattoo mark.

In *You Only Live Twice* (1964) Commander James Bond, CMG, RNVR, is believed dead. M writes an obituary for *The Times*.

> James Bond was born of a Scottish father, Andrew Bond of Glencoe, and a Swiss mother, Monique Delacroix, from the Canton de Vaux. His father being a foreign representative of the Vickers armament firm, his early education, from which he inherited a first-class command of French and German, was entirely abroad. When he was eleven years of age, both his parents were killed in a climbing accident in the Aiguilles Rouges above Chamonix, and the youth came under the guardianship of an aunt . . .

At twelve he went to Eton but left after only two halves as the result of 'some alleged trouble with one of the boys' maids.' He was sent to Fettes, his father's old school. He fought twice for his school as a lightweight and founded the first serious judo class at a British public school. In 1941 he entered a branch of what was subsequently to become the Ministry of Defence. Owing to the confidential nature of his work he was accorded the rank of lieutenant in the Special Branch of the RNVR and ended the war with the rank of Commander.

M refers to an impetuous strain in his nature, 'with a streak of the foolhardy that brought him in conflict with higher authority. But he possessed what almost amounted to "The Nelson Touch" in moments of the highest emergency, and he somehow contrived to escape more or less unscathed from the many adventurous paths down which his duties led him.' He became, against his will, something of a public figure, with the inevitable result that a series of popular books came to be written about him by a personal friend and former colleague.

> If the quality of these books, or their veracity, had been any higher, the author would certainly have been prosecuted under the Official Secrets Act. It is a measure of the disdain in which these fictions are held at the Ministry, that action has not yet—I emphasize the qualification—been taken against the author and publisher of these high-flown and romanticised caricatures of episodes in the career of an outstanding public servant.

In this passage Fleming pre-empted his critics. This must be the least entertaining of the Bond books. The action is constantly held up by disquisition on (of all things) Japanese culture and customs. Twelve pages are spent putting the villain, Dr Shatterhand, into context. It provides another instance of Fleming's odd desire to be taken seriously, and the contrast with the opinion of his work expressed in the obituary is rather touching.

Bond's Way

I have already noted the prevalence of Celts among fictional Secret Service personnel. M actually preferred Scots, and said so. This is no quirk of Fleming's—or Buchan's or Valentine Williams's. John Le Carré in *Smiley's People* asked: 'Why are Scots so attracted to the secret world?' It puzzled Smiley: 'Ships' engineers, Colonial administrators, spies . . . Their heretical Scottish history drew them to distant churches, he decided.'

One of the first things we notice about Bond is his constant attention to detail. 'He was a secret agent, and still alive thanks to his exact attention to the detail of his profession. Routine precautions were to him no more unreasonable than they would be to a deep-sea diver or a test pilot, or to any man earning danger-money' (*Casino Royale*, 1953). He apologizes to Vesper for being so particular about his food. It was partly due to his being a bachelor, but mostly from his habit of taking a lot of trouble over details. On the other side of the same coin was the absence of emotion in his make-up. This is always stressed in any description of his relationship with women. When he slept and the warmth and humour of his eyes were extinguished 'his features relapsed into a taciturn mask, ironical, brutal and cold.' As a symbol of his hardness we are twice told of Bond's detestation of tea, with its hint of softness and domesticity in contrast with the exoticness of coffee. 'Bond loathed and despised tea, that flat, soft, time-wasting opium of the masses . . .' (*Thunderball*, 1961). He once told Moneypenny it was partly responsible for the decline of the Empire. M, who was no softy, not only drank tea but drank it from a vast cup, 'as big as a baby's chamber pot', but black, without sugar or milk (*On Her Majesty's Secret Service*). Bond called for whisky which M called 'rot-gut'.

In *Moonraker* we are given a typical day in the life of James Bond. An assignment requiring his special abilities came along only two or three times a year. Otherwise he led the life of an easy-going senior civil servant with elastic office hours from around ten to six, lunch usually in the canteen, and 'evenings spent playing cards in the company of a few close friends, or at Crockford's; or making love, with rather cold passion, to one of three similarly disposed married women; week-ends playing golf for high stakes at one of the clubs near London.'

> He took no holidays, but was generally given a fortnight's leave at the end of each assignment—in addition to any sick leave that might be necessary. He earned £1500 a year, the salary of a Principal Officer in the Civil Service, and he had a thousand a year free of tax of his own. When he was on a job he could spend as much as he liked, so for the other months of the year he could live very well on his £2000 a year net.
>
> He had a small but comfortable flat off the King's Road, an elderly Scottish housekeeper—a treasure called May—and a 1930 $4\frac{1}{2}$ litre Bentley coupé, supercharged, which he kept expertly tuned so that he could do a hundred when he wanted to.
>
> On these things he spent all his money and it was his ambition to have as little as possible in his banking account when he was killed, as, when he was depressed he knew he would be, before the statutory age of forty-five.

He would have eight years to go before he was taken off the 00 list (there were two others with a licence to kill) and given a staff job at HQ. As we have already seen, the politicians took away this licence at a later date, but M managed to restore it by jiggery-pokery. This meant he could look forward to at least eight assignments, probably sixteen and possibly twenty-four before he retired, if he ever reached that point. The jurisdiction of his Service ran only outside the United Kingdom. The Prime Minister had to give permission for him to operate on the Moonraker job.

Bond loved women and always managed to work a slim-lined beauty into the folds of his assignment. McCormick claims that only twice in thirteen books did Bond fail to seduce the girl he fancied (*Who's Who in Spy Fiction*). It may surprise many readers that he failed even once. Sex, or easy-sex, plays such an important part in spy fiction I am leaving a fuller consideration of it to a later chapter. Let us go back to Bond's official vocation.

Like all spies, he needed cover. In *The Man with the Golden Gun* (1965) he has a forged British passport under the name of Frank Westmacott, company director, on his first appearance. But then we find that he has been brainwashed by the Russians and is therefore acting as a counter-agent. By the time he reaches Jamaica in search of Scaramanga he is Mark Hazard (surely a dangerously suggestive name?) of the Transworld Consortium. In earlier days it had been Universal Export but this was now discarded. Companies, like agents, can be 'blown'. In fact, in *Dr No* (1958) it is made abundantly clear that his description as an Import and Export Merchant is quite useless for espionage purposes, for everyone knows who he is. Bond didn't go in for false beards and moustaches, wigs and plastic noses. That belonged to an earlier generation. Neither the KGB nor SPECTRE were likely to be fooled by that sort of thing.

The agent's security depended not on trying to change his personality and appearance so much as on integrating himself with the society in which he intended to operate. In *Live and Let Die* (1954) Bond makes his first visit to America since the war. He goes in with all his senses at full stretch. He examines his environment keenly, 'picking up the American idiom . . . all the small fleeting impressions that were as important to his trade as are broken bark and bent twigs to the trapper in the jungle.' These included the advertisements, the new car models, prices of second-hand ones in the used-car lots, 'the exotic pungency of the road signs', the standard of driving, the number of women at the wheel with their menfolk docilely beside them. Obviously a society dominated by the automobile, so the automobile must be known as thoroughly as a peasant knows his cabbage patch.

He must be able to make a lightning assessment of people and situations. There may be no second chance. We see Bond on his toes when a driver calls to take him to the airport in *Diamonds Are Forever* (1956). The driver tells Bond not to talk. 'Bond smiled and said nothing. He did as he was told. Forty, he thought. Twelve stone. Five feet ten. Expert driver. Very familiar with London traffic. No smell of tobacco. Expensive shoes. Neat dresser. No five o'clock shadow. Query shaves twice a day with electric razor.' And the necessary precautions. When men meet they retire to the urinal where their secrets will be flushed away by the sound of running water. This has become more than a cliché, it is a joke. Every worthwhile urinal in a modern capital must be equipped with hydrophonically stabilized microphones. And then there are the women. Where can they go? Bond took Mary Goodnight into the bathroom and turned on the shower. At that stage in the adventure they were still clothed.

Professional Killer–with the Soft Centre

Moonraker (1955) opens with Bond in the underground shooting gallery with his instructor. His scores are entered on his Confidential Record. He was the best shot in the Service but only M was allowed to know that. Bond had been shooting against a machine and had lost. He was satisfied with his score but not proud of it. He wished the light might be better but M insisted that all shooting should be done in 'averagely bad conditions'. A dim light and a target that shot back at you was as close as he could get to copying the real thing. 'Shooting hell out of a piece of cardboard doesn't prove anything' was M's single-line introduction to the *Small Arms Defence Manual*.

Bond's favourite weapon was the Beretta. M and the Instructor were contemptuous of it. Colonel Butler in *Colonel Butler's Wolf*, by Anthony Price, even referred to it as 'a whore's gun'. It is little facts like these that help explain the fascination that Bond held for so many readers. Thinking of him *in vacuo* one might be tempted to imagine a superman who never failed. But this was not true. Bond could and did fail, although he always succeeded in the end. Bond could surprise the reader (as Bulldog Drummond never could) and reveal his humanity. The gap between me and him, thinks the poor nine-to-five clerk, may not be so enormous after all. Think of Bond's Russian adventure. He didn't come out of that very well. M was sarcastic. 'Your gun got stuck, if I recall', he says, and orders him to have another model. The

Armourer is called in and sniffs at Bond's Beretta, a 'ladies' gun'.
Bond thinks, 'He's got it in for me over the last job. Feels I let him
down. Won't trust me with anything tough.' And so we come to the
heretical moment, in the first few pages of *Dr No*, when Bond looks
into M's eyes and 'for the first time in his life he hated the man. He
knew perfectly well why M was being tough and mean. It was deferred
punishment for having nearly got killed on his last job.'

This was not the only occasion when Bond seemed to slacken in a
way that would be considered unBondlike if we accepted the
stereotype. In *The Man with the Golden Gun* he is sent out to eliminate
Scaramanga. He sits in a car behind his prey and wonders whether to
shoot him now, in the back of the head, in the old Gestapo-K.G.B.
style.

> A mixture of reasons prevented him—the itch of curiosity,
> an inbuilt dislike of cold murder, the feeling that this was not
> the predestined moment, the likelihood that he would have
> to murder the chauffeur also—these, combined with the
> softness of the night and the fact that the 'Sound System' was
> now playing a good recording of one of his favourites, 'After
> You've Gone', and that cicadas were singing from the *lignum
> vitae* tree, said 'No'.

He knew that he was disobeying orders and being a bloody fool. In
fact, if we didn't know that Fleming was ultimately in control, we
would consider Bond's sentimentality as a very dangerous weakness.
And in the end an unexpected languor nearly allowed Scaramanga to
escape and certainly led to Bond's hospitalization. The older reader
might well be reminded of those early film serials in which the villain,
seeking to kill the hero, constantly had him at his mercy yet never
delivered the *coup de grâce*. The Bond stories are in this tradition,
though Fleming has the skill to make them more credible.

Goldfinger (1959) starts with Bond in what appears to be an
uncharacteristic mood. He has killed a Mexican and he feels guilty.
Now he is reading a SMERSH publication called *Defence* and is
depressed by the nauseating toughness of the blunt prose used by the
Russians. 'What was wrong with him?' he wonders. 'Couldn't he take
it any more? Was he going soft, or was he going stale?' It is certainly
these human doubts and misgivings which attracted Robert
Markham, alias Kingsley Amis.

It should be remembered that Bond's training was not entirely in firearms and combat. It was necessary for him to be a skilled card-sharper. An American named Steffi Esposito had taught him the tricks of the trade.

> Made me work ten hours a day for a week learning a thing called the Riffle Stack and how to deal Seconds and Bottoms and Middles . . . He knew every trick in the game. How to wax the aces so that the pack will break at them; Edge Work and Line Work with a razor on the backs of high cards; Trimming; Arm Pressure Holdouts—mechanical gadgets up your sleeve that feed you cards. Belly Strippers—trimming a whole pack less than a millimetre down both sides, but leaving a slight belly on the cards you're interested in—the aces, for instance . . .

Here we have a player who really knows how to cheat at cards. Formerly there had been several cheats, and they often won (depending which side they were on), but it was never divulged how they won. We know exactly how Bond wins at cards—and at golf!

Bond's Reputation

Bond is the dean of British spies. No-one is referred to more frequently than he—in fact, his name is invoked wherever espionage matters are concerned more than all other fictional spies put together. (His real-life rival is Philby.) The references are often made by fellow spy novelists in their fiction and also by journalists and commentators on the actual world of espionage. It would be pointless to enumerate all the occasions when Bond has been held up as a standard by which to measure others but a few examples in the nature of evidence may be presented.

First of all, it is always assumed that, once a fictional spy has taken the public's fancy, that there must have been an historical model. When Dusko Popov, one of the most successful spies of the Second World War, died, Martin Walker of the *Guardian* pointed out that in the days of satellites and *Sigint* listening posts there seems to be less and less scope for 'the James Bond figure, the spy who uses bribes, blarney and the bedroom to unravel the enemy's intentions' ('A Wartime Double Dealer who Gambled on Two Fronts', *The Guardian*, 24th August 1981). But Popov was one of the last, if not the last, and we are told that Fleming used him as a model for James Bond. Walker continues:

> Popov was short, dapper and Jugoslav, whereas Bond was tall, casually elegant and Scot-Swiss. But Fleming's first novel *Casino Royale* was based upon an evening at the casino at Estoril, in neutral Portugal, where Popov gambled away $50,000 while bankrupting a German spy-master. Commander Ian Fleming was watching, and holding the spare cash in case Popov needed more.

It had to be Bond. A generation earlier it would have been Bulldog Drummond, a generation before that Richard Hannay. These fictional favourites accrete legends as easily as whores, drunks and millionaires.

It is no wonder, then, that Bond holds the position he does within the circumscribed trade of espionage. Seth's *Encyclopaedia of Espionage* is strictly about real-life spies but not even he can resist a mention of James Bond—the only fictional reference in the whole book. The meetings of Captain Nikolai Khokhlov, the SMERSH agent who defected to the West in 1954, with the Americans 'read like something out of a James Bond novel.' Seth makes a few references to novelists who were themselves agents, such as Compton Mackenzie, Somerset Maugham, A.E.W. Mason and Ian Fleming himself, including an unjustified one to Len Deighton (the book is woefully inaccurate) but to no other fictional character.

After the Bond cult came the anti-Bond cult. The case of John Gardner is a strange one. According to McCormick, he detested Bond. Boysie Oakes was 'a positive antidote to Bond.' And yet Gardner wrote two of the Bond continuation novels. If the spy novel was to develop it had to develop against an accepted model and this could only be James Bond. Anti-Bond statements are to be found in novels by Robert Merle, Ted Allbeury and Warren Tute, and include the following in Desmond Bagley's *The Freedom Trap* (1971):

> The cult of James Bond has given rise to a lot of nonsense. There are no double-o numbers and there is no 'Licence to kill'. As far as I knew I didn't have a number at all, except perhaps a file number like any other employee; certainly no-one ever referred to me as number 56, or whatever it was—or even 0056.

But the point is that, traditional or modern, friendly or antipathetic, they find it difficult to get him out of their systems. There is a shadowy figure in Anthony Price's *Tomorrow's Ghost* named Trevor Bond whom we never actually meet—although he is not the ghost of the title—and he is interrogated about K.G.B. contacts. He was classified as of 'low mentality', 'a near-idiot'. In the same author's *Soldier No More* three young women tease Captain Roche, pretending he is a spy—which in fact he is. They say he isn't much like the popular idea of a spy and they mention James Bond among others. Lexy, who is represented as the dumb one of the trio, asks who he is. Meriel says, 'we told you—we gave you *From Russia with Love* to read.' There are suggestions here of Price's, and his generation's, attitude to James Bond.

Most of the later references are unfriendly. In Forsyth's *The Devil's Alternative* the Cabinet secretary, Sir Julian Flannery, fears the worst. Terrorists are holding a huge oil tanker and its crew as hostages. The PM enquires about the Special Boat Service, the sea-based counterpart of the better known S.A.S. (Special Air Service), which had helped the Germans at Mogadishu and had acted in the Balcombe Street siege. 'Harold Wilson had always wanted to hear all the details of the lethal games these roughnecks played with their opponents. Now they were going to start another James Bond-style fantasy.' But then Mogadishu was sheer James Bond, so how is he to be rejected as mere sensationalism? Some writers just get angry—for example, Antony Melville-Ross in *Tightrope*. Rafferty interrogates enemy agents. Someone refers to him scornfully as belonging to a 'crummy Secret Service government outfit' and asks him if he's 'James bloody Bond's bloody father'.

The works I have quoted from (and I could quote many more) all appeared after 1970, six years after Fleming's death. They all gnash their literary teeth at Bond's sensationalism, implying that he should be put in the same class as Sapper or Creasy or Horler. This prompts the query: If he is so unrealistic, why is he still universally remembered? The answer is surely given by Kingsley Amis in his entry for Ian Fleming in the 1961-70 supplement to the *Dictionary of National Biography*. 'There is hardly a page in the 3000 and more of the saga that does not testify to Fleming's ability to realize a unique personal world with its own rules and its own unmistakable atmosphere. His style is plain and flexible, serving equally well for fast action, lucid technical exposition, and serious evocation of place

and climate; if it falls here and there into cliché or the language of the
novelette, it never descends to pretentiousness. The strength of his
work lies in its command of pace and its profound latent
romanticism.'

Among spy writers only Childers, Le Carré and Deighton possess a
style more honed to its purpose.

Epilogue

Bond and his author may be fiercely decried these days but there is no
doubt about their impact. The very reaction against them is evidence
of this. Amis analysed Bond's adventures and character in *The James
Bond Dossier* and said it was inaccurate to describe him as a spy. A
more accurate description would be counter-spy, and agent would be
even more comprehensive. If I were to stick strictly to the function of
espionage as a criterion for inclusion in this book, I would have to
omit Bond. It would then become a rather pointless exercise.

Fleming is said to have read Peter Cheyney very carefully. His
attitude was ambivalent. Early in his career he said he wanted to 'get a
bit closer to Eric Ambler and exorcise the blabbering ghost of
Cheyney'. Bond was an upper-middle class variation of Lemmy
Caution. The intellectuals despised both writers but there was
probably a large element of envy in their attitude. Both writers were
immensely popular and popularity is only something you pretend to
despise when you don't have it.

But if Bond wasn't always appreciated at home, the Russians took
him seriously. They regarded him as a powerful propaganda
weapon. The K.G.B. persuaded the Bulgarian, Andrei Gulyashki, to
take up the challenge. His Avakum Zakhov set out to destroy James
Bond, the 'supreme example of imperialistic espionage'. *Zakhov
Mission* (1966) was a great success and was serialised in the Soviet
youth paper, *Komsomolskaya Pravda*, under the title *Avakum Zakhov
versus 07*. (McCormick says the Bulgarians were unable to get
copyright permission to use Bond's name or 007, but it doesn't seem
likely that the copyright law would have worried them much where
security was concerned.)

Le Carré wrote that 'the really interesting thing about Bond is that
he would be what I call the ideal defector. Because if the money was
better, the booze freer and women easier over there in Moscow, he'd

be off like a shot. Bond, you see, is the ultimate prostitute' (quoted from McCormick). This is a hypothesis which was never tested. But it was possible to test his facts and his famous detail and these were often found wanting. He was out of date about SMERSH, as has been already noted. He called the French *Deuxième Bureau* a counter-intelligence agency when in fact it is a military agency which coordinates the Intelligence Services concerned with national defence. But the only result of drawing the critic's attention to these matters is to illustrate, once again, how idle it is to judge literary matters by factual accuracy and how necessary to gauge flair, style and the reader's potential.

8: THE ACCEPTANCE OF TORTURE

One of the major differences between the contemporary spy novel and its forerunner lies in their treatment of torture. Torture was rare in the early group, and when it occurred it appeared to be half-hearted by later standards. Bond was constantly tortured in a way that Hannay and Oppenheim heroes never were. And Bond set the tone. After Bond torture becomes a necessary ingredient of all but a few spy novels. It is often described in gruesome detail. (One Russian had a blow-torch used on him and then had his fingers chopped off one by one before he finally succumbed—not to death but to surrender!) The agents are fantastically tough, superhumanly tough. Bond suffered but never gave in and always recovered.

This aspect of the spy novel gives a truthful reflection of the real world to the extent that torture has become a recognized practice in nearly every state, whatever its political complexion, in the contemporary world. Security apparently justifies any inhumanity. What is not a truthful reflection, in all probability (it is impossible to know unconditionally), is the victim's ability to withstand and recover from torture. This comes closer to the cartoon mouse, embedded in a brick wall without damage to flesh or bone, than to real life.

Fleming produced a formula which others have followed. Bond takes on enormous odds. He is captured, beaten and tortured, but manages to turn the tables. Sometimes, as in *Live and Let Die*, this happens twice. He then manages to consign the enemy to a death as horrible as the one planned for him; perhaps the same one, which adds a sense of poetic justice. When facing death Bond is usually accompanied by a girl with whom there has been no sexual intimacy, but this will be his final reward. Meanwhile, as the enemy moves in the reader can experience that well-tried frisson cooked up by the mingling of the sexual and sadistic impulses.

Fleming's merit is that although he is not a realistic writer he makes sufficient concessions to the reader's workaday world to convince him that he is. Bond recovers miraculously from his savage treatment, but concern is expressed for his health. On one occasion the Medical Officer actually drew M's attention to the hazards of Bond's life and its possible consequences. On another (in *Thunderball* 1961) he made out a medical report which was read by M. But it appeared from this that Bond was more likely to suffer serious damage from his domestic habits than from what characters like Dr No and Drax and organizations like SPECTRE and SMERSH might do to him.

> This officer remains basically physically sound. Unfortunately his mode of life is not such as is likely to allow him to remain in this happy state. Despite many previous warnings, he admits to smoking sixty cigarettes a day. These are of a Balkan mixture with a higher nicotine content than the cheaper varieties. When not engaged upon strenuous duty, the officer's average daily consumption of alcohol is in the region of half a bottle of spirits of between sixty and seventy proof. On examination, there continues to be little definite sign of deterioration. The tongue is furred. The blood pressure is a little raised at 160/90. The liver is not palpable. On the other hand, when pressed, the officer admits to frequent occipital headaches and there is spasm in the trapezius muscles and so-called 'fibrositis' nodules can be felt . . .

Bond was getting off easily.

The Punishment of Bond

Casino Royale is the first and best of the Bond novels. The style is cool and controlled and is geared to the passing on of information. The main action appears to be finished two-thirds of the way through and for a while one has the impression that the novel is broken-backed—but the thought persists that no publisher would accept anything that moved quite so sluggishly. And one is right, for the final chapter reveals a situation shocking in its abruptness. This is very skilfully handled.

But it is obvious that we have here a man who enjoyed describing torture. Bond sits naked on a cane chair whose seat has been removed and he is lashed on his genitals with a carpet-beater. Chapter XVII, 'My Dear Boy', luxuriates in the description. But the most impressively 'realistic' piece of writing ('realistic' is the cant term—perhaps 'positive' would be more apt) is the description of Le Chiffre's death at the hands of SMERSH agents. It is cold and clinical and reduces death to the level of a sabotaged machine.

> There was a sharp 'phut', no louder than a bubble of air escaping from a tube of toothpaste. No other noise at all, and suddenly Le Chiffre had grown another eye, a third eye on a level with the other two, right where the thick nose started to jut out below the forehead. It was a small black eye, without eyelashes or eyebrows.
> For a second the three eyes looked out across the room and then the whole face seemed to slip and go down on one knee. The two outer eyes turned trembling up towards the ceiling. Then the heavy head fell sideways and the right shoulder and finally the whole upper part of the body lurched over the arm of the chair as if Le Chiffre were going to be sick. But there was only a short rattle of his heels on the ground and then no other movement.

This is not exactly a description of torture but there is an obsessive concern with physiological distortion. (Compare the passage already quoted from the story 'From a View to a Kill'.)

In the next novel, *Live and Let Die*, Fleming appeared to luxuriate in the cruelty. As usual, there were no ill effects for Bond. Others may have parts of the body torn away (as happens to Leiter) but pain is mentioned only conventionally and in passing. At most, Bond goes into a temporary faint. The sadistic element is revolting. Leiter is picked up and his face is hurled against the wall. 'It nearly smashed his nose'—it is astonishing that it didn't succeed. A few moments later Leiter is smiling at Bond through blood-stained teeth. Bond is captured by Mr Big. One of his henchmen bends the little finger on Bond's left hand back. 'Suddenly it gave. There was a sharp crack.' This doesn't seem to inconvenience Bond. He escapes, gets back to his hotel and holds a long and quite rational telephone conversation with Leiter. Leiter begins by asking what the damage was. 'Broken finger', says Bond. 'How about you?'—'Blackjack. Knocked out. Nothing serious', replies Leiter. Obviously this is the sort of stuff Fleming must get out of the way as quickly as possible so that he can get on with his story. To hell with credibility.

Come to think of it, Leiter was right to be undemonstrative about his injuries, considering what was to follow. Thrown to the sharks, he loses one arm and half a leg. (In a later novel, this is matter for joking repartee.) However, he seems to be pulling through. It was gratifying to know that Mr Big was actually eaten (live) by the sharks, with barracuda helping. When it is all over Bond gets into the bath and Strangways, the chief Secret Service agent for the Caribbean, soaps him down and bathes his body in merthiolate. Bond has been attacked by a barracuda and his naked body has been tossed about by heavy seas on a reef. 'He was raw and bleeding in a hundred places and his left arm was numb from the barracuda bite. He had lost a mouthful of muscle at the shoulder.' The sting of the merthiolate made him grind his teeth.

It is just as well Bond was capable of quick recovery else he would not have been ready for *Moonraker* and Drax. He swims in the sea with Gala and is sitting with her on the beach, relaxing beneath a cliff. A bomb is exploded above them and a large section of cliff is torn away and falls on them. He throws himself, gallant-like, on Gala and is inevitably covered with dust and rubble. 'Blood dripped from his cut back and arms and mingled with the chalk dust . . .' He was so angry he felt no pain.

Krebs and Drax, chased by Bond in his Bentley, release huge rolls of newsprint in his path. He is thrown twenty feet out of his car, which is wrecked. When they find his body his face is covered with blood but he is still breathing. Bond is now completely at Drax's mercy—this is part of the formula. He is tied to a chair and Drax, mad with rage, beats him furiously. 'His head felt as if it had been used as a football, but there was nothing broken.' Later Bond is crawling through a shaft. (This provides good training for *Dr No*.) 'Slither, scrape, rip. His shoulders carefully expanding and contracting; blistered, bloodstained feet scrabbling for the sharp knobs of iron, Bond, his lacerated body tearing its way down the forty feet of shaft . . .' Then there is a ten-foot drop out of the shaft and he runs, 'leaving a trail of red footprints and a spray of blood-drops from his raw shoulders.' When his work is done and he is back in the office with M, 'under his clothes Bond was latticed with surgical tape. Pain burned up his legs whenever he moved his feet. There was a vivid red streak across his left cheek and the bridge of his nose, and the tannic ointment dressing glinted in the light from the window. He held a cigarette clumsily in one gloved hand.' In the shaft he had been drenched with boiling steam.

In *Diamonds Are Forever* Bond gets his meed of punishment mainly from kicking. This time there is no description but we see the administrators sitting down to take off their shoes and put on their boots. Instead we are given the aftermath. 'It ought to be all right but he just didn't want to move. His will-power had gone. He just wanted to sleep. Or even to die. Anything to lessen the pain that was in him and all over him, stabbing, hammering, grinding him—and to kill the memory of the four boots thudding into him, and the grunts coming from the two hooded figures.' Bond of course makes a remarkably quick recovery. We are also told in this novel what a life-time of working for the cause has done to poor Felix Leiter. He naturally limped. 'The right arm had gone, and the left leg, and there were imperceptible scars below the hairline above the right eye that suggested a good deal of grafting . . .' Here Fleming's usual care deserts him for we are not told how Bond perceived the imperceptible scars.

Bond suffered grievously in *From Russia with Love* and needed a rest. The doctor said he could be near his limit of endurance and recovery. He is sent to Jamaica where he meets his old friend and accomplice, Quarrel, who looks at him keenly and says, 'Dere some pain lines in you face since de las' time.' The real pain in the succeeding novel, *Dr No*, starts with Bond's attempt to escape from the doctor's prison. Trying to tear out a grille, he gets an electric shock: 'The next thing he knew was a searing pain up his arm and the crack of his head hitting the stone floor.' The current is turned off and he manages to get through the grille. The next task is to worm his way up a shaft, inches at a time. His feet begin to sweat and slip, and whenever he loses ground his shoulders are scalded with the friction. The next test, after getting into a horizontal shaft, is heat. 'How could his bruised flesh stand up to that? How could he protect his skin from the metal?' He has to go on, and he does, screaming. 'He went on screaming, regularly, with each contact of hand or knee or toes. Now he was finished. Now it was the end. Now he would fall flat and slowly fry to death. No! He must drive on, screaming, until his flesh was burned to the bone.'

The final test comes when he hurtles down another shaft and hits the sea at forty miles an hour. Although he lost consciousness, the impact failed to smash him. He manages to hook himself on a wire fence. 'Now there was nothing much left of Bond, not many reserves. The last dive down the tube, the crash of impact and the half-death from drowning had squeezed him like a sponge.' He is attacked by the giant squid, he screams as its suckers bite into his flesh. 'God, his stomach was being torn out!' He manages to cut off a sucker and the squid ejects its ink. 'The stinking, bleeding black scarecrow moved its arms and legs quite automatically. The thinking, feeling apparatus of Bond was no longer part of his body. It moved alongside his body, or floated above it, keeping enough contact to pull the strings that made the puppet work. Bond was like a cut worm, the two halves of which continue to jerk forward although life has gone and has been replaced by the mock life of nervous impulse.' All that could be said for Bond, unlike the worm, was that he was not dead.

Thunderball is relatively mild. In fact, the only deliberate torture occurs when Bond is racked beyond the safety limit at a Health Farm. He has a gruelling fight under water before he wins through but this was a pretty routine affair for Bond.

When *You Only Live Twice* (1964) starts, Bond appears to be nearly finished. M is even considering pensioning him off. Although he had suffered so much physical damage, he took good health for granted. (His suffering was merely, for him, 'the extension of a child falling down and cutting its knee.') He had been to GP's, specialists, quacks, even a hypnotist and told them, 'I feel like hell. I sleep badly. I eat practically nothing. I drink too much and my work has gone to blazes. I'm shot to pieces.'

He is now sent to Japan on an 'impossible' assignment. As usual, he finds himself at the mercy of his enemies—in this case, Ernst Blofeld (masquerading as Dr Shatterhand), and his hideous camp-warder wife, Irma Bunt. Bond had already fallen down an oubliette and cracked his skull, and now a thug named Kono deals him a fearful whack directly on the bruise on the side of his head. There were ten blows altogether. Bond sees his tormentors 'through a mist of blood'. He is next threatened with a periodic geyser, which is about to erupt up his naked backside, but he manages to avoid that one. Later he fights Blofeld, who is armed with a samurai sword, and Bond is wounded in the rib area. He escapes and a doctor tends him. 'He will live', said the medico, 'but it may be months, even years before he regains his memory. It is particularly the temporal lobe of his brain, where the memory is stored, that has been damaged.'

When Bond reappears in London (*The Man with the Golden Gun*) he says he had had a bang on the head in Japan. Then he was picked up by the Russian police who roughed him up and he got another bang on the head. On the final train journey in this novel, where the hoods are eliminated, he gets a bullet in the shoulder and a fever starts. In the final reckoning with Scaramanga he gets a poisoned bullet through his stomach from close quarters, and loses consciousness for a week. Massive anti-snake bite injections saved him and, no doubt, British security. Felix Leiter, his American friend, who had also suffered horribly on behalf of his country, is on crutches at the end of this story.

Robert Markham (or Kingsley Amis) added the expected quota in *Colonel Sun* although, not surprisingly, he shows more interest in the theory of torture than Fleming ever did. Chapter 19 is called 'The Theory and Practice of Torture'. Thus Amis goes to the heart of the Bond cult: he is a man who soaks up immense amounts of torture but never succumbs to it. Colonel Sun is an expert in the administration of pain. From Sade he had gained the idea that to inflict torture would raise him to the status of a god. (Later he acknowledged that he had been mistaken and he felt 'sick, guilty and ashamed'.) Here Amis goes far beyond anything Fleming ever had in mind.

Sun begins with mental saturation. He tells Bond in detail what awaits him.

> At the proper moment I shall cause your death by a method that has never, as far as I know, been tried before. It consists, firstly, of breaking all twelve of the main bones of your limbs, and, secondly, of injecting you with a drug that will send you into convulsions. Perhaps you can form some sort of mental image of the agony that will be yours when your muscles pass out of control and your shattered arms and legs begin to heave and twist and thrash about of their own accord.

Bond usually evaded the final torture through his own ingenuity but here he suffers immensely until he escapes through the outraged sympathy of one of the enemy camp. It will be seen that although Amis seizes on an essential part of the Bond cult he departs in his treatment from his model. Dr No and Blofeld showed no signs of possessing feelings as delicate as Colonel Sun's, nor did they have anyone in their employ who were capable of experiencing sympathy with suffering.

Sick World, Sick Job

This aspect of Fleming's work is absurd. Other spy writers have been quick to follow suit. One has the feeling that in some cases the description of torture is the major attraction. The more responsible writers, such as Deighton, acknowledge the ubiquity of torture in our world but restrain the lure of fantasy. Fleming gives us in the fullest detail an account of how Felix Leiter is bruised and broken. Deighton merely tells us, without a narrative, that Loiseau, of the Sûreté Nationale, has a face pitted with tiny scars and that part of his left ear is missing (*An Expensive Place to Die*). In the same novel we are told how information may be obtained—in other words, how Davis was made to talk. No heroics can save him when he is taken prisoner in Datt's establishment and is injected with LSD and Amytal.

> 'You will answer any question we ask', said Datt to me.
> I knew he was right: a well-used barbiturate could nullify all my years of training and experience and make me as cooperatively garrulous as a tiny child . . .

As a result, Davis has a sense of failure.

> I had told them everything. I had betrayed my employers, my country, my department. They had opened me like a cheap watch, prodded the main spring and laughed at its simple construction. I had failed and failure closed over me like a darkroom blind coming down.

Bond, of course, is strong enough to withstand a drug. So is Ken Follett's Roper (see *The Bear Raid*). There is in fact no torture in this case. It is not necessary—the threat is sufficient, for it inevitably lay behind the barbiturate. But Fleming prefers immediate torture because it provides the violence his readers appear to look for. Not that Fleming always ignores subtler methods—at the beginning of *The Man with the Golden Gun* Bond has been so successfully brainwashed by the K.G.B. that on his return to London he tries to kill M. It takes several months at The Park to undo the process.

Deighton gives a good example of the successful threat in *Twinkle, Twinkle, Little Spy*. The Russian Bekuv has defected but is not as cooperative as the Americans wish. Mann tells him what happened to one of their men who had been captured by the Russians. 'When we got him back, his arse was raw with untreated cigarette

burns, and his bloodstream was full of pentathol. We flew him back
to the best surgeon in the States but he never got the full use of his
right hand again . . .'

The Thayer Street outfit (in Antony Melville-Ross's *Tightrope*) use
the abattoir for getting information from captured enemy agents.
Fiona Langley, a beautiful sadist (though it is said at one point that
she loathes cruelty!) is guaranteed to break anyone down. Rafferty,
the new director, says it's sick. Jane replies: 'It is, isn't it? So is an
atomic explosion in a heavily populated area'—this is being
planned—'so is Al's putting his life on the line to no purpose because
we failed to anticipate the possibility of other danger points. So is the
world and the job we do in it.' In the Buchan-Oppenheim world the
agents were protecting civilization from barbarism. Now it often
seems that barbarians are protecting the world from barbarians. So
what is being protected. Civilization? or Barbarism A against
Barbarism B? As the football managers say: It's not the clubs, it's
society!

9: THE ORGANIZATION OF FICTIONAL ESPIONAGE

Which is the crazier or more sensational or more absurd: real-life espionage or its fictional reflection?

A woman contact gave a spy instructions on how to communicate with the Russians. On a certain Saturday in January he was to make his way to a street corner on New York's lower East Side carrying a tennis ball in his left hand. There he would see a man carrying a book with green binding and wearing gloves and carrying an additional pair of gloves. This man would introduce himself as Raymond. Question: is this from Le Carré, Oppenheim or Warren Tute? Answer: the spy was Fuchs and Raymond was Harry Gold. The year was 1944.

The two espionage worlds merge and overlap but on the whole (and only on the whole) the fictional specimen exceeds credibility in its frequent superhumanity. Fiction can provide supermen, real life cannot. Bond's capacity for punishment and the machine-like efficiency of Deighton's agents are cases in point. Real spies often make pathetic errors such as actually calling at an Embassy to enquire for his contact, as did Nunn May. The only fictional spies who might be expected to be so gauche will be found in novels where the emphasis is on the person rather than the plot: writers of the calibre of Le Carré, Greene and R. Wright Campbell.

There are areas where it is impossible to know (without actual personal involvement) whether an activity is historical or imagined. The Official Secrets Act is an impassable barrier. There is a minor character in Le Carré's *Tinker, Tailor, Soldier, Spy* named Roy Bland. He was one of Alleline's main supports. His value to the organization came from his proletarian background, his father's membership of the Communist Party, his knowledge and understanding of Marxist doctrine and his teaching post in Economics at the University of Poznan. We are told that he wrote 'leftish papers for tiny magazines that would have died long ago had the Circus not subsidised them.' Was this and is this a method of surveillance of a suspect group? We cannot answer for the real world. But for the fictional world we can. All is clear.

The Excellence of the British Secret Service

It used to be considered the best in the world. At least, the British thought that and all the early spy writers refer to it in the most favourable terms. But foreign agents were also convinced—it seems they had been brainwashed. Buchan's Blenkiron, an American, could not hide his admiration. But a later generation of writers has strong doubts. The new situation is expressed neatly by Geoffrey Household in *A Time to Kill* (1952). Dr Losch, still living partly in the past, holds the conventional view. Pink says he will have nightmares when he learns the truth. 'God, he ought to see Roland calling a conference to decide whether it's safe to pass a traffic light!'

The British Secret Service has lost efficiency and its agents no longer command the fullest trust, but it is still the repository of immense cunning. In A.J. Quinnell's *The Mahdi* (1981) the British and Americans work together on the master plan but it is entirely funded by the Americans, who also supply the technological expertise. The British are treated quite openly as poor relations. Later, when the Russians also come in on the scheme (this novel disturbs the normal tensions of the post-war spy story), the British just tag along as side-kicks. But the point of the novel is that the British come out on top through superior cunning. There is a similar dénouement in Chapman Pincher's *Dirty Tricks* where, after a series of crosses and double-crosses, it is the British who display the most successful deviousness.

In *The Mahdi* there is an early reference to 'the much-vaunted British intelligence' coming 'apart at the seams'. Hawke, the American Director of Operations (C.I.A.) had a deep suspicion of the British. 'They were more riddled with "moles", he had pointed out, than Windsor Great Park.' He ticked them off on his fingers—the usual litany of Philby, Burgess, Maclean, Vassall and Blunt (the list gets longer as the years pass by)—and only God and the K.G.B. knew how many more there might be. It is interesting that Blake was not mentioned. Spy writers have reservations about Blake which may illustrate British deviousness more clearly than any fiction.

The Americans have never recovered their faith—Blenkiron's faith—in British efficiency. Len Deighton's Americans are rarely complimentary. Schlegel, in *Yesterday's Spy*, stresses that something happened long before his time 'to emphasize that this was a British cock-up, less likely to happen now that we had him with us on

secondment from Washington'. Schlegel liked 'what he described as
cutting through British red tape and deviousness'. Deviousness is
always the key word in this connexion.

Of course, the espionage world is in itself devious. The success of
British deviousness might well compensate for failure in other
departments. But it is possible that sometimes what appears to be
devious may be merely accidental. Anthony Price does not take the
old line that the British Intelligence Service is beyond reproach. In
fact, in *Soldier No More* Captain Roche, who is working for the
Russians, starts by thinking they are immensely efficient. He changes
his mind when he discovers they don't know about Steffy's death,
where murder was passed off as an accident. Now he realized that 'the
Comrades were as criminally incompetent as the British'. Which is
comforting for the domestic reader—until it is revealed that Steffy's
death *was* accidental after all.

Price reminds us that accidents do happen. This is almost heresy in
the world of fictional espionage.

A Superfluity of Outfits

God and the K.G.B. know how many organizations in Britain are
concerned with the gathering of intelligence. Each of the armed
services has its department and so have the Treasury and the Bank of
England. What the man in the street understands by the term Secret
Service is otherwise sponsored. In fact the term has no official
justification and can be found in no list of organizations. The correct
name for non-departmental intelligence activities is Special Intelligence Services. The initials S.I.S. naturally lent themselves to
Secret Intelligence Service. Fiction abounds in these off-beat
organizations. Each writer spawns his own. For example, Le Carré is
usually associated with a group called the Circus. But in *The Looking-
Glass War* we are introduced to a rather amateurish group under
Leclerc who are openly envious of the Circus. (There is little interdepartmental love in these latitudes.) Referring to the Circus:
'They're a curious crowd. Some good, of course. Smiley was good.
But they're cheats. That's an odd word, I know, to use about a sister
service, John. Lying's second nature to them. Half of them don't
know any longer when they're telling the truth.'

It would be possible, but pointless, to list these semi-autonomous groups. Most of them are not, outwardly at any rate, very impressive. George Mado worked in 'a dreary little Soho building, where his branch of the outfit' was situated (*The Resident*, by Warren Tute). These outfits are barely on speaking terms with the Embassies when they operate overseas. The Embassy loathes them for ill-mannered upstarts, with no concern for diplomatic decorum, and they regard the Embassy as an effete hangover from the Horace Walpole era. Mado and Padstow create some embarrassing situations which the Embassy has to clear up. The Ambassador is furious, they regard him with contempt, and there are frequent clashes. Just once the Ambassador relaxes and says, 'You must find us a pain in the neck, Mr Padstow' and Padstow thinks, 'A pain in the arse is what you should have said, you pompous oaf.'

Fleming's M sometimes worries about the independence of his unit. In the story, 'From a View to a Kill' (*For Your Eyes Only*) Bond sees the chance to 'wipe the eye' of the whole security machine of no less an organization than SHAPE. This would win a feather in the cap of the British Secret Service vis-a-vis the SHAPE High Command. 'Private armies, private wars. How much energy they siphoned off from the common cause, how much fire they directed away from the common enemy!' One can imagine a modern Duke of Wellington saying, 'I don't know whether they frighten the Russians but by God, they frighten me!'

This seems the place to outline briefly the organization of British Intelligence on the understanding that it is merely a background to the extremely active fictional departments. MI5, concerned with counter-espionage, operates at home. MI6, the espionage proper organization, operates abroad. It is hard to maintain a neat division between the two areas, and this has led to confusion, rivalry and ill-feeling between the two branches, for each feels it has to spy on the other to prevent enemy infiltration. This situation certainly provides a pattern for the fictional antagonisms. Cooperation is easier between MI5 and the Special Branch (originally the Irish Special Branch because it was formed to deal with Irish troubles) but there is still no hard and fast line of division. When the three service departments were subordinated to the Ministry of Defence MI5 became, strictly speaking, DI5. The Head of Security has for years been referred to as C. There have therefore been a series of C's. Spy-writers have followed suit by using other initials for their department bosses. Fleming's M is the best known of these.

By the time of the Second World War the original distinction between 'traditional' espionage (stealing or photographing of documents and the reporting of conversations by straightforward listening or bugging) and cipher-breaking became blurred. Secret intelligence must always be checked against open intelligence (monitoring of the press and radio and the censorship of letters) and by battlefield intelligence, aerial reconnaissance, prisoner interrogation and plain visual observation. Open intelligence can also be provided to the enemy to mislead him. All these activities are illustrated by the more accurate spy-writers. Others, however, prefer to concentrate on the sensational and omit what seems to them to be boring routine work. If properly compiled, the latter can be fascinating, as shown by Conan Doyle in another field. During the War the Special Operations Executive (S.O.E.) was concerned with military activity, political activity in German-occupied countries (including assistance to resistance movements) and sabotage or commando-type operations usually against intelligence targets. Cipher-breaking was done at Bletchley Park. A Joint Intelligence Committee, with immediate access to the cabinet and the supreme command, co-ordinated material.

Change in Character of Espionage

It will be clear from the foregoing that espionage is no longer what it was. Spies are not likely to dodge helicopters on the Yorkshire Moors, nor are they expecting to find naval plans in a woman's cleavage on the Blue Train. For the writer who values accuracy and wishes his work to be contemporary, this poses a problem.

Whatever the methods employed, the three essential aspects of intelligence work have always been and remain the collection, collation and evaluation of material. But the development of short-wave radio has revolutionized the means of passing intelligence. There are two significant differences between the old and the new: the transmission of information has been speeded up, and the agent has been placed in almost instant contact with his control. Therefore the most valuable information can be rendered utterly useless if delayed in transmission, and the gathering of information has become much more intensive. Exact details of what is required, much more fully expressed than formerly, can be sent to the agent. It is also easier to curb personal inclinations. The radio-operator, practically unknown fifty years ago, is now indispensable in espionage. In practical terms (though not in fictional) this can mean that Bond is less important and more readily expendable than Sparks. Efficiency has been further increased by the putting of communication satellites into orbit. Signals can be sent to a satellite as it passes overhead and stored until it passes over home territory, when it is released to special receivers which record it. Moreover, whereas the early equipment was cumbersome and needed expert operators, today the average agent can operate it.

As an illustration of this point, let us consider the German Enigma and Japanese Purple machines, highly sophisticated pieces of machinery which could be easily operated and originally defied all attempts at decoding. The principle was that of a typewriter which enciphered a message which could be deciphered by another machine at the other end. A mechanism at both ends could change the cipher used either at regular intervals or whenever desired, providing the recipient was informed. American experts eventually collated a mass of Japanese messages and proceeded to work backwards and build their own Purple Machine in Washington. There are different stories about the acquisition of an Enigma. One claimed that it was taken from a sunken U-boat, another that the Poles got possession of one in September 1939 and smuggled it to the West. Another story was that the Germans employed Polish labour in the factory making them, and one man memorized the parts and passed the information to the Polish Government or the French. This is all fascinating stuff, and provides an excellent story in itself, but it is not a conventional spy story. The human element is being squeezed out for there is a limit to the number of times the Purple or Enigma Machine could be broken down, copied or stolen. It is significant that coded messages play a far smaller part in fictional espionage today than they did fifty years ago.

Andrew Boyle, in *The Climate of Treason*, says it did not take Philby long to grasp the fact that spies in the classic tradition of John Buchan's virtuous hero Richard Hannay were outmoded. Slowly and reluctantly, the more serious type of spy fiction must adapt to reality. But the options are not attractive. Philby is a fascinating figure (repulsive to some) but the fascination lies in the degree of treachery he managed to conceal so successfully for so long, not in his routine espionage activity. A novel about a man who merely passes on classified information through virtually foolproof channels, with full-scale electronic back-up when needed, would be immensely boring. Philby knew where the information was and how it was passed on. To take one recent historical example: Col. Felix Cowgill, Head of Section Five of the British Security Service, manoeuvred his agents in Spain, Portugal and Africa, but it was not they who supplied the crucial information that helped destroy the German war effort. This came from the intercepts supplied by Bletchley Park. It was a change equivalent to the industrial switch from the individual craftsman to mass production. It is remarkable how often the contemporary spy novel introduces domestic discord into its story. Broken marriages, for instance, such as Smiley's and Tute's Mado's. Roper in Ken Follett's *The Bear Raid* is getting over a broken love affair. The situation is treated with great nostalgia. This is a human compensation for the dramatic loss imposed by the new situation. At a pinch Smiley can be confronted by his Russian opposite number, but it takes a good deal of working up; on the other hand, his errant wife is always at hand to provide heart-burn and nerve-wrack.

Ronald Seth in his *Encyclopaedia of Espionage* makes the same point. The American N.S.A. (National Security Agency officially but some call it Never Say Anything) engages in top secret cryptography and electronic espionage. Seth says their work has little interest for novelists because it is too technical and backroom to have mass appeal. The N.S.A. lacks the glamour of some other agencies, such as the C.I.A., which at least conducts its politics with reference to human beings and individuals, if only on the best way to get rid of them.

10: FICTIONAL ESPIONAGE IN THE FIELD

'The ideal spy is not one who is introduced—an extraordinarily difficult task—but one who is, as it were, already *in situ*, who has already obtained the security clearance of those for whom ostensibly he works. These may be "sleepers", to be activated only in a period of crisis; if they have in appearance loyally served their ostensible masters for several years they will have become increasingly valuable as they obtain access to increasingly secret information. The ideal location of such an agent is at a high level of the enemy's own intelligence service.' (Constantine Fitzgibbon, *Secret Intelligence in the Twentieth Century*.)

The Russians have proved particularly skilful at this kind of long-term infiltration; they have been helped by their international ideology and various Agitprop organizations and fronts. Although espionage has become increasingly the work of machines, particularly satellites, radio intercepts and cipher-breaking computers, there is still a place for the individual, human (sometimes all-too-human) agent.

The early writers leaned heavily on personal disguise: facial hair, clothing and physical defects. Among the moderns, John Gardner has been known to make use of such tricks but on the whole disguise has been replaced by what is known as 'cover', which is both less personal and more dependent on extraneous matters. The lead in Len Deighton's *Funeral in Berlin* is contacted by radio while driving through London. 'Message for you oboe ten from Northern Car Hire'. Deighton cannot resist a footnote and supplies one here. (This adds to the air of authenticity.) 'Our radio procedure is designed to make an eavesdropper think we are a taxi service. For this same reason our car pool uses radio-equipped taxi-cabs with the flags always set at "hired".' Thus it is not the agent but the car which is disguised. This seems reasonable in the light of modern espionage developments. It does not mean, of course, that Deighton's outfit confined their movements to false taxis. Later Jean 'wangled a Jaguar from the car pool.'

Much of the excitement in reading about spies lies in waiting for the first mistake. It is likely that real-life spies are more prone to mistakes than fictional ones. If our hero triumphs through a mistake of the opposition the author may be accused of cheating. Hannay and Bond and Muffin must win through, against enormous odds, by superior intelligence, courage and skill. It should not be forgotten that the partial elimination of the human element does not mean that mistakes will occur less frequently. All that happens is that a semantic change takes place. Machines do not make mistakes; they break down.

In Simpson's *Moscow Requiem* Modin is angered by his contact's carelessness.'The usual recognition signals had been arranged by the K.G.B. resident, but for some reason—nervousness, perhaps—the man launched straight into conversation.' But there are no serious consequences.

It is known that little mistakes can have considerable consequences. No self-respecting author could allow his agents, of whatever colour, to be as inefficient as some historical ones have been: for example, the German who was landed on the East coast during the last war, stole a bicycle and rode away—on the wrong side of the road; or the other German who landed in Scotland and asked for a ticket to Aberdeen at the local railway station. The clerk said 'Two and ten' and the German gave him two pounds and ten shillings.

Contact

First of all, the agent must pretend to be someone else. Very often he is supposed to be the representative of a commercial company—we have already noted one of Oppenheim's heroes posing as a representative of Bethlehem Steel, while Bond was apparently concerned with the export trade. In *Moonraker* the 'Secret Service' was stationed in a nine-storey building. In the entrance hall the tenants were named as Radio Tests Ltd., Universal Export Co., Delaney Bros. (1940) Ltd., The Omnium Corporation and Enquiries (Miss E. Twining, O.B.E.)

The agent would then have to establish contact with his control or someone who was supplying information—perhaps a 'mole' or a defector. There were a large number of possibilities. In the story 'Risico' (*For Your Eyes Only*) Bond was told to look out for a man with a heavy moustache sitting by himself drinking an Alexandra. 'Bond had been amused by this secret recognition signal. The creamy, feminine drink was so much cleverer than the folded newspaper, the flower in the buttonhole, the yellow gloves that were the hoary slipshod call-signs between agents.' Another old favourite was the torn banknote—you matched your half with the other fellow's. Graham Greene uses another banknote device in *The Human Factor*. You give someone a marked note and wait to see where it will turn up. Deighton calls this 'seeded material'. Greene, whose emphasis is always on the character rather than the plot, actually shows his plan going wrong. The suspect is told a bogus story about researches at Porton. Unfortunately for him he innocently mentions it to the real spy, with the result that when the note turns up in the other camp it incriminates him and not the guilty man.

The telephone is naturally very important in this connexion. Le Carré's Guillam is the expert in this area. He knows all the ropes, including the G.D.R. ones. He explains how it works in *Call for the Dead*: 'You dial the number from a call box and ask to speak to George Brown. You're told George Brown doesn't live there so you apologize and ring off. The time and the rendezvous are pre-arranged—the emergency signal is contained in the name you ask for. Someone will be there.' In *Tinker, Tailor, Soldier, Spy* Guillam rings Mendel. He phones from a box on Waterloo Station. When Mendel answers he asks for Jenny and Mendel replies tersely that no Jenny lives there. Guillam apologizes and rings off. He gives Mendel time to get to a callbox at the end of his avenue, then rings it. 'This is Will', says Guillam. 'And this is Arthur', says Mendel. Guillam says he wants to give him 'the headlines'. They used a scholastic cover: exams, students, stolen papers. Mendel ends by saying he's got 'those happy snaps from the chemist'. They had come out well, no misses. Then he rings off.

Guillam got some of his knowledge of G.D.R. techniques from the Americans who had intercepted a courier. 'Never waiting at a rendezvous, never meeting at the stated time but twenty minutes before; recognition signals—all the usual conjuring tricks that give a gloss to low grade information. They muck about with names too. A courier may have to contact three or four agents—a controller may run to as many as fifteen. They never invent cover names for themselves. They get the agent to do it for them. The agent chooses a name, any name he likes, and the controller adopts it.'

This is all run-of-the-mill stuff. The interposition of a machine between man and man might be expected to depersonalize the proceedings, but this is not so. Fleming, who rivalled Deighton in his fascination with technology, could not resist summarising a NATO paper called 'Radio Signatures' which Bond reads in *Moonraker*.

> The almost inevitable manner in which individuality is revealed by minute patterns of behaviour is demonstrated by the indelible characteristics of the 'fist' of each radio operator. This 'fist', or manner of tapping out messages, is distinctive and recognizable by those who are practised in receiving messages. It can also be measured by very sensitive mechanisms. To illustrate, in 1943 the United States Radio Intelligence Bureau made use of this fact in tracing an enemy station in Chile operated by 'Pedro', a young German. When the Chilean police closed in on the station, 'Pedro' escaped. A year later, expert listeners spotted a new illegal transmitter and were able to recognize 'Pedro' as the operator. In order to disguise his 'fist' he was transmitting left-handed, but the disguise was not effective and he was captured.

Le Carré makes use of a similar mannerism in *A Murder of Quality* when two type-written messages are traced to the same operator, although purporting to come from different sources. Again, the operator is betrayed by his 'fist' just as surely as a thief can be betrayed by his finger-print.

There is another kind of contact between operators which occurs regularly in spy-fiction. It is 'tailing', which is the reverse of recognition. This practice is often described at some length and with considerable exactitude. There is a good example in Le Carré's *The Honourable Schoolboy*. Jerry sets out to visit Frost at the bank. He knows that he is likely to be watched, or 'tailed'; he knows the different methods that can be used, and he must be prepared to frustrate them.

Time is important. There are twenty minutes to go. He only needs seven. As a result, he saunters, but never idly. According to Sarratt, the training centre, you should give yourself plenty of time. You could post a letter (to yourself), walking half way down the street and then stopping dead at the postbox, checking whether feet faltered or faces turned away. You would look for the 'classic formations', a two this side, a three across the road, a front tail floating ahead of you.

Tailing could be a delicate instrument. It could be put to a variety of uses. Chapman Pincher in *Dirty Tricks* mentions the deterrent tail, consisting of 'watchers who deliberately let their quarry know they are being followed to scare them out of achieving their purpose.'

Any reader of spy thrillers knows that tailing is often done by car. This is an even more skilled job than the pedestrian method. A following car very quickly becomes noticeable. It should be obvious that the car employed should not be unusual or noteworthy in any way. Nevertheless, official car-tailing in fiction is frequently done by huge and heavy high-powered black limousines. There may be good reason for this. The action may be deterrent. Frances in Anthony Price's *Tomorrow's Ghost* uses a department car but her job is to be as invisible as possible. Therefore it is a small family saloon. But a tail-car is useless if it cannot keep up with a much bigger and faster car; therefore her saloon had a souped-up engine and an enlarged petrol tank. It could be a very useful machine and yet it had its own built-in drawbacks. A mechanic at a petrol station very soon discovered that it was not an ordinary car and this would set him wondering.

Codes

If communication could not be personal codes were necessary. They might also be used as recognition signals. 'I gave the operator the week's code', says the lead in Deighton's *Funeral in Berlin*: '"I want the latest cricket scores". The operator said, "Are you a subscriber to the service?" and I said, "I have country membership of two years' standing—Mr Dawlish, please."' Incidentally, this agent is strangely inconsistent over security. While radioing a message from his car he deliberately upsets the operator by playing the fool; but now he decides to report the operator because he is careless with the key and the lead hears what he says to Dawlish. But this is observation of commonplace human weakness, ignored by most writers, is a mark of the writer who still relates to the real world.

However, some of Deighton's agents, especially the Americans, are practically encased in technology. Schlegel in *Yesterday's Spy* had a remarkable machine that fitted in a case like a typewriter. It was the newest model of acoustic coupler. He typed a message and dialled a Paris number, then scrambled the message by putting the phone handpiece into the cradle switch inside the case. He pressed the 'transmit' button and the coupler put a coded version of what he'd typed through the phone cables at thirty or forty characters a second. There was a short delay, then the reply came back from the same sort of machine. This time Schlegel's coupler decoded it and printed it on to tape in 'plain English'. Schlegel read it, pushed the 'memory erase' button and rang off. This machine was in a metal case that was intended to make it look like a cheap typewriter. He could plug it into any computer with terminals. He had used the C.I.S. TELCOM from a callbox.

This represents the peak of sophistication in coding devices. The old book codes have been superseded. The best known example of these is to be found in Greene's *Our Man in Havana* where the Lambs' *Tales from Shakespeare* was the source book. In Antony Melville-Ross's *Tightrope* it is Bulwer Lytton's *The Last Days of Pompeii*. Ken Follett used *Rebecca* in the same way. The advantage of the book code is that it cannot be broken without a copy of the book. But compared with Schlegel's machine it is extremely slow and cumbersome.

Fifty years ago things were much simpler. Sapper's Ronald Standish is faced by a code; he goes to his bookcase, takes out his 'Bentley' and immediately breaks the code. Ernest Lungley Bentley was a sort of Coding King, with dozens of publications on the subject to his credit. He produced ready-made codes which in one way was convenient but in another (as illustrated by Sapper's story) was absolutely useless in a situation where the codes were common property. Among Bentley's titles are these: *Bentley's Complete Phrase Code* with two separately published supplements, *Bentley's Geographical Code* and *Bentley's Oil Code; Bentley's Check Indicator for Letter Codes; Bentley's Second Phrase Code; Overseas Two-Phrase Code; E.L. Bentley's Sectional Cyphers;* and *Bentley's 30,000 Numbered Codewords.* Here is the title-page of his *'U' Supplement,* published in 1922.

'U' Supplement
for use with
Bentley's Complete Phrase Code
(Or Separately)
2,477
Five Letter Artificial Words
(With no Meanings attached)
All ending with 'U' and having a 2-Letter difference between
each and those in 'Bentley's Complete Phrase Code'.

> Any one of these Half Cyphers can be joined to any other or
> on to any one of those in the Complete Phrase Code,
> none of which end with 'U'.

This supplement had 76 pages, with 5-letter codes (beginning with
abbtu and ending with *zyzyu*) in a column down the left-hand side of
the page, leaving the rest of the page blank. The 'U' cyphers were
given in terminational order (from *rabbu* to *lyzzu*) at the end of the
book, with these final instructions:

> If a mutilated Cypher should arrive reading *dackunabnu*
> divide the word into *dacku* and *nabnu* and by turning to this
> Terminational Order and working backwards through
> *dacku* you find that the Code contains *backu* and similarly
> through *nabnu* you find *gabnu*. These would give the correct
> Cypher, viz., *backugabnu*.

These cyphers and codebooks were used in the real world. They
were not the invention of a frenzied spy-writer. Contemporaries were
no doubt impressed as we feel impressed by Schlegel's technology. In
fifty years' time it may seem as weird and wonderful as the Bentley
codes. This is something worth remembering and to which I will
return in my final chapter: fictional espionage appears to be a crazy
business but in fact it is no crazier than the world it reflects. The spy
novel is probably closer to the 'truth' than the detective novel. It only
seems more remote because few of us are tempted to spy whereas all
of us are tempted to kill at some time or other.

Jargon

Each profession has its jargon and writers who aim at verisimilitude
feel obliged to employ it. Spy writers relish jargon and even add their
own usages to those made use of by the C.I.A., the K.G.B. and MI5
and 6.

Blackmail is a valuable weapon in the spy-game. For blackmail
you need information. This is how they went about getting it in
Smiley's People. Their intended victim is Grigoriev, who has a false
Swiss passport and an account at a Swiss bank. Two girl hikers do a
double act. One of them dumps a rucksack carelessly at Grigoriev's
feet, recording whatever he says to the cashier—hidden cameras snap

away from toggle bags, ruck-sacks, brief-cases, bedrolls, or whatever. ('It's the same as the firing-squad', says Toby Esterhase. 'Everybody hears the click except the quarry.') When Grigoriev gets into his car a woman starts an altercation because he is partly parked on the pavement. She has a handbag under her arm and Grigoriev has been snapped in his car with the bank in the background. And now everything is set up for the *burning* of Grigoriev.

Any reader of spy fiction soon becomes familiar with this language, with the *sleepers* who simply wait until they receive instructions, the *safe houses* to which they retire when the enemy is closing in, the *moles* (who need no longer be defined, even to those who never open a spy novel), the *branch lines*, or contacts thrown up in the course of surveillance but not necessarily run to earth, and so on. Le Carré probably derives a creative thrill from inventing terms used by no other writer, such as *lamp-lighters* who provide support for mainline operators, and *pavement artist* for a surveillance agent (or team) watching premises. Trevanian is another writer who likes to indulge himself in this way. But Trevanian is consciously satirical. One feels that Kingsley Amis, in *The Anti-Death League*, finds it difficult to remain entirely serious and there is a strong tongue-in-cheek element in his writing. His agent, Brian Leonard, is very earnest and constantly refers to his instruction manual. We understand that he is engaged in *phylactology*, or spy-catching. He thinks Dr Best is a *non-transvasive defector*—in other words, he has defected without physically joining the enemy. Best is mad and imagines his mission is to save civilization from the holocaust. He is strong on jargon and is happy to *shake a tail* or *lose a tag* when he gives a follower the slip.

Once again, it is very easy to relate this semantic free-for-all to the actual world of espionage. When Gouzenko defected in Canada the police made a valuable haul of cover-names of Russian agents and also a considerable vocabulary of code-names used by the K.G.B. Canada was referred to as *Lesovia*; the Soviet Embassy was *Metro*; the N.K.V.D. was *The Neighbour*; Communist Parties (except for that of the U.S.S.R.) were called *Corporations*, with members as *corporants* or *corporators*; passports were *shoes*, a hiding place was a *dubok* and a legal front for activities was a *roof*; the military espionage organization was referred to as *Gisel*.

11: THE REAL AND THE FICTIONAL

Few of us, I have said, are tempted to spy professionally. And yet some say espionage is the oldest profession, even older than the other one. In fact, spying can occur over a very wide range of activity, from seeing what the neighbour's doing up the garden to stealing the plans of the new nuclear reactor in Sao Paolo. Fiction concentrates on the latter. But as armies and navies are massive organizations and nuclear industries are still few in number, it is virtually impossible to fictionalize them. If you are concerned with murder, your victim can be any Mr Smith or Lord Longbottom. But if your concern is espionage you will lose all credibility if you invent a country. Ruritania is always a mistake in spy fiction, as Compton Mackenzie recognized when he explained in the Preface to *The Three Couriers* that he was avoiding a 'Ruritanian air' by setting the action in an identifiable Greek location.

Manning Coles did not avoid this mistake in his *Death of an Ambassador*. Instead of relating his agents and diplomats to real countries and situations, Coles chose Esmeralda. Immediately the novel takes on the air of a fairy tale, not to be taken seriously. Coles tries to compensate for this by setting his action in London and Paris, but the damage has been done. He also makes an allusion to the familiar world, an absolutely unexpected one, by bringing Archdeacon Grantly and his wife from the diocese of Barchester to attend an ecclesiastical conference! As Grantly is more real to some readers than the present Archbishop of Canterbury, this must be viewed as an attempt to establish a known context.

The contemporary spy novel has become increasingly related to the actual political world. Oppenheim and Le Queux referred frequently to the policies of the great powers, but they were shadowy and without definition. The modern spy writer refers constantly, not only to the sovereign states by name, but to their actual policies, their leaders, their espionage organizations, their successes and their failures. Sometimes historical personages appear as characters in the novels—spies like Philby particularly, but also Prime Ministers and Presidents. Every effort is made to create an impression of actuality.

No-one does this more vigorously and successfully than Frederick Forsyth. His books are so closely linked with current events they read like history. *The Devil's Alternative* (1979) moves from the Kremlin to the White House to Whitehall. Names of political leaders bear a family resemblance to contemporary ones: PM Thatcher becomes Carpenter, President Carter becomes Matthews, Chancellor Brandt becomes Busch, and so on. There is a very early reference to the Big Three Traitors, and British Intelligence is once again in the hands of professionals. 'This is a service, not a trapeze act', the new director of the S.I.S. told novices. 'We're not here for the applause.'

For a popular writer, Forsyth makes considerable demands on the reader's powers of concentration. There is always a thorough background of historical and political information. Some of it is hypothetical and predictive, for the action is set one year in advance of publication date. This device is virtually necessary for any writer who deals with contemporary political situations; his world must be recognizable but he deals in situations which are new to the reader. (Oppenheim was as much aware of this as Forsyth.) *The Devil's Alternative* (1979) proceeds by a series of short and often impersonal chunks of reportage, the same method as the author followed in *The Day of the Jackal* (1971), though it is not so compelling, probably because there is no single character who dominates the whole story as in the earlier book. As happens so often with Deighton, technology at times overwhelms the human interest. This is an analogue of a situation that has already been referred to, that the human agent is giving way to the electronic device. Both Forsyth and Deighton wish to capture the reader's interest by their emphasis on contemporary processes, but it is at the expense of human interest. As human interest declines, so it seems to increase in falsity. But fundamentally creative writing is about people. The spy writer faces the same dilemma as the science fiction writer.

True or False?

The probable truth or falsity of the information he is getting from his spy novel (for it is likely to contain more straight facts and pseudo-facts than any other kind of novel) is an important matter to the reader. Are these accounts of the K.G.B. and the C.I.A. accurate? Is this what really goes on behind the newspaper headlines? There is a class of reader, unsophisticated no doubt, who takes the spy novel very seriously. It is an extension to the politics he acquires from the *Mirror*, the *Sun* and the *Express*.

In an interview with Richard Helms, the ex-C.I.A. chief, Kenneth Harris of the *Observer* said that 'the Russians have the reputation of being better at Intelligence work than anybody else.' He asked Helms if this was true. Helms's answer does not concern us here, but the question does receive consideration in various ways in a number of spy novels. Let us take Warren Tute, author of *The Resident*, as our example. He explains that 'Resident' is the Soviet term for the top official under diplomatic cover in an embassy. (In Secret Service parlance, he is 'legal' as opposed to the 'illegal' non-diplomatic agent.) The network he directs is called the 'residentura'. Ideally he lives in and operates from a country bordering on that in which the network operates. If the network is compromised the Resident is safe from arrest, since espionage against another power is not usually an indictable offence.

Tute is a novelist and he is telling a story, but in this kind of story he has to ensure that the reader understands all the implications. To do this, he must impart information, even mini-lectures. He explains that the Resident is the senior K.G.B. officer in any given territory. He is never the Ambassador and usually not even a senior Embassy official. Inside the Embassy everyone knows who he is. He may nominally hold down some minor post on the commercial or cultural side. This will enable him to move about the country on legitimate Embassy business and to receive each and every kind of visitor without attracting undue attention from the security services of the country concerned. His power is immense because he is the one man in the area whom Moscow trusts. No-one on the spot has direct control of the Resident unless and until things go wrong. Then an inquisitor with plenary powers is sent out. (This is exactly what happened in the non-fictional Gouzenko case.) It is therefore a major aim of Western Intelligence services to win the defection of a Resident. This can be done by blackmail or through the agency of fear when he has failed in some assignment. Tute's novel has a parallel theme to Le Carré's (or Smiley's) plot to win Karla for the West—and a previous novel had defection of a British agent, Tarnham, just as Le Carré had recounted the treasonable activities of Haydon.

The British spy novel works against a background of extremely serious, high level defection, and this is rarely lost sight of. It doesn't matter how splendid the fictional spies are, their real-life colleagues have a deplorable record. The Burgess-Maclean escape to Moscow came on top of the Fuchs and Nunn May defections. The first could have been avoided if the Americans had passed on to the British the details of Basil's (the Fifth Man) confession in 1948. American opinion began to harden after Nunn May: could Britain be relied upon? A once great nation now dabbling in socialism—the Americans began to feel uneasy and F.B.I. agents were encouraged to discount British agents as security risks. The atmosphere is reflected in fiction, again and again. In Fleming's *Live and Let Die* Captain Dexter of the F.B.I. is irritated when Bond says there must be a huge leak somewhere in Washington for the enemy to know why he had arrived in New York. 'Why should it be Washington?' he asked testily. Deighton makes much more of the situation in *XPD*. Stuart meets his C.I.A. opposite number. Referring to a colleague, Stuart says he will never give a definite opinion. The American laughed: 'Especially when that opinion might explode in his face and dribble all down his Eton tie.'—'Harrow', says Stuart. 'Leslie went to Harrow, and his tie is Guards Armoured Division.' Although the two sides sometimes shared information, it was sometimes withheld. At a weekly intelligence meeting the chief of G.C.H.Q. always left early. He did this because his best hardware was financed by Americans who had National Security Agency employees in the most sensitive posts. The chief left when the agenda included as a last item 'non-electronic systems.' 'It was a polite way of asking him to leave the room. It was better that he did not know what was discussed, rather than have to feign ignorance to his American colleagues.'

In the *Observer* interview Helms said that terrorism was the subject to which the Intelligence services should be applying themselves most vigorously. The spy novel, which overlaps the conspiracy novel to an extent that they can no longer be separated, is increasingly concerned with this menace to civilized society. It has moved on from an almost parochial concern with naval plans to the complete overturn (and possibly destruction) of something more than a régime: a social complex. The stimulus may be ideological but it can also be mere greed, that is, the desire of a gang to control the world's wealth. Some novelists have been quick to incorporate this situation into their fiction. Antony Melville-Ross's *Tightrope* (the title is extremely evocative) makes frequent references to actual conspiracy organizations such as the Baader-Meinhof, the Red Brigades, the

I.R.A. and the P.L.O. The Melody file is mentioned. Chapman Pincher is also keen on this approach. In *The Four Horses* the reader believes he is actually in the presence of the famous terrorist, Carlos. It is a false alarm. It is noteworthy, however, that in this type of novel the characterization is usually paper-thin. Alan Williams not only mentions Philby but puts him at the centre of his story. Philby even emerges as a person.

William Haggard stresses a point that it is impossible to check. According to him, there is a superfluity of intelligence organizations in all the major countries. Certainly, if all the outfits written about by a few dozen spy writers actually existed, there would be a considerable accommodation problem. But we cannot actually know how many there are because the Official Secrets Act will not allow a public count. Haggard writes in *The Hardliners* (1970):

> British security, like American and more so Russian, was a jungle of overlapping empires, or if that sounded too like official jargon you could simply call it a shocking mess. It wasn't so bad as the French perhaps, a world of parallel police—enchanting phrase—of riot squads and internal scandal. But it was a mess just the same and one had to walk warily.

It was bad enough for the authorities. Who should Sir Albert Bull, Junior Minister at the Foreign Office, call in to do a special job? If he was doubtful there was small hope for the reader.

The Philby Obsession

All modern spy writers work under two shadows: those of Bond and Philby. And Philby really stands for a nest of traitors, particularly the public school crew of Burgess, Maclean and Blunt.

No-one despises the Old Boy network more vehemently than Charlie Muffin and, presumably, his creator, Brian Freemantle. Another Freemantle agent, Adrian Dodds in *Goodbye to an Old Friend* (1973), is amused by the courtesy extended to one of the Russian defectors he is debriefing. The question arises whether he should have consular access. Common sense says no; the Permanent Secretary says he must be given every opportunity. It seemed to Adrian that nothing had changed.

Play up, play up and play the game, he mused. Those who cheated were called rotters and those who did what was expected, according to the public school dictum, were jolly good chaps. Adrian thought that the confessions of Kim Philby, whose background the security services had not probed because one gentleman does not question another from the same social stratum, had eradicated such attitudes.

The Philby obsession reached its climax with the publication in 1974 of Alan Williams's *Gentleman Traitor*. Philby is actually a character in this novel—he is fed up with Russia and wants to return, but is sent (by MI6) to Rhodesia to wrap up UDI! At the time everyone was still wondering who the Fourth Man was. It appears to be Roger Laval Pugh Jameson-Clarke (the name would have delighted Charlie Muffin) who had been recruited into the Soviet Intelligence Service in 1931 while reading Greats at New College, Oxford. 'He had never been a member of the British Communist Party but had remained, throughout his career in the British Diplomatic Service, an unflinching supporter of the new social and ideological order which had found its roots in Soviet Russia.'

> The man was a true Imperialist: he admired strength and order; he hated the flabby, insipid affluence of the West, the anaemic Britain over which he had so long presided, with its permissive liberalism and tatters of colonial glory.

This was the worst defection yet. Philby had been slightly bohemian and a heavy drinker; Blake had been half Jew, half foreigner; Burgess and Maclean had both been alcoholics and homosexuals. But Sir Roger was a frequent visitor to the Palace, a pillar of the Establishment and a member of the Royal Yacht Squadron Club! He seemed to come from a milieu similar to Blunt's.

Williams's theory (and it was held by many others) was that Philby had been allowed to escape because he could compromise too many prominent people. He is about to read out the names of five men who all held high positions in contemporary Britain and had been for more than thirty years in the employment of the Soviet State Security Organization, when he has a heart attack and dies on the spot! It is a strange novel in many ways. The leading character, a newspaperman named Cayle, is killed during the course of the novel. (No fictional genre has left the idea of the neat, happy ending so far behind as the spy novel.) Williams is fiercely anti-Russian in his judgments, to such an extent that at times it is difficult to take him seriously. (Most spy writers are anti-Russian but the best ones in a measured and rational way.) He also seems to have little time for the police—at least, Cayle is one of those newspapermen who simply have to make things as difficult as possible for the police, and consequently for themselves. He is also unusual in cutting out the sex content. Certainly there is no easy sex in the Bond-Mado (Warren Tute) fashion. He is also deadly serious and quite humourless.

The conventional wisdom in Whitehall these days is that the day of the politically committed spy (especially commitment to Communism) is over. As an ideology it has lost most of its attraction, largely due to the activities of the Soviet régime and its satellites. Character defects, providing a target for blackmailers, are important but it is believed increasingly that money (the 'quick buck') is the main stimulus for passing on classified material. Goronwy Rees, interviewed just before he died by Andrew Boyle, described the classic agent as a 'controlled schizophrenic' who has so thoroughly mastered the art of lying that nothing will shake him or break him down (*Observer*, 13 January 1980). But whatever the motives for becoming a spy, few spy writers have any sympathy with the defectors. In many cases, especially the actual historical cases, they express pity. When the mystery is cleared up in Anthony Price's *Soldier No More* we are told that the Russians and their agents will have to get back to 'their Moscow *dachas*'. This included Philippe Roux. 'Philippe out of range of Paris didn't bear thinking about—that was greater punishment than Burgess and Maclean had had to bear, in swopping London for Moscow.'

The most intense examination of the lives of British defectors ending their days in a dreary and oppressive capital is to be found not in a novel but in a play, *The Old Country* by Alan Bennett. The novels are concerned with spying but this play treats the aftermath. Two English defectors, now settled in Russia with their wives, provide a striking contrast of the two types most prone to defect. One is a pretentious left-wing, public school product, the other a bewildered technician. A British Embassy official tries to arrange a swop of a Russian spy for the former. The Old Boy network stands firm, there is nothing for the technician who is in fact eager to return home and face the music. There had previously been a homosexual relationship between the two spies but the older man blots it from his memory. The atmosphere is one of hopelessness, waste and spiritual emptiness. One senses considerable bitterness and disgust on the author's part.

There are frequent references to writers who were influential during an impressionable youth. For example, E.M. Forster and his famous pronouncement about the betrayal of friend and country. The diplomat's wife has no doubts about the relative importance of friend and country: 'The old boy must have had nice friends. I'd plump for the old Union Jack any day.' Hilary is in fact doing this when he rejects the claims of Eric, his one-time lover. But he never faces any issue squarely. He either ignores it or conceals it beneath verbiage.

The suggestion in this play is that the Establishment, *au fond*, is eager to forgive the transgressor, perhaps because there, but for the Grace of God . . . Duff, of the Moscow Embassy, makes an appeal to the defecting diplomat which is nauseating in its moral flabbiness. Come back, he says in effect, you've been out for fourteen years which is surely long enough! Not everyone can forget but, by and large, after a very short and probably comfortable period in some kind of institution ('more hydro than house of correction') you'll be able to settle down somewhere. What about Gloucestershire? Quite near to Bristol with the Old Vic, good restaurants . . . Financially, an excellent pitch. Television, newspapers, publishers, all clamouring. Some may turn their backs, but who cares?

Forgiveness is an admirable quality. The language in which the offer is made is fairly repulsive. But what makes the whole transaction abominable is the injustice that lies behind it. For no comparable offer is made to Eric. The English class system extends its curse beyond the ideological boundaries. There is little doubt that many among the novelists, including Le Carré, Deighton, Gardner, Tute and Freemantle, would share Bennett's distaste. But it is not their territory. They may follow the spy into exile but from then onwards he ceases to concern them, at least as far as their fiction is concerned.

Homage to Spy Writers

It is clear that, despite the apparent vastness of the field their agents operate in—it is world-wide and is always prepared to jump into space—the spy writers occupy a confined associational space. They write about the rivalries of governments. Their models, heroes and villains are to be found in the world around us, yet in certain segments in a few capital cities, and historically they probe backwards for about a generation and no more. But there is one other field of activity which hems them in and conditions their thinking. This is each other. Every spy writer is as aware of Bond as he is of Philby. They form a very self-conscious fraternity.

A very few examples will suffice, but many could be given. Flying out to Istanbul Bond reads Ambler's *Mask of Dimitrios*. He is still reading it on the Orient Express, returning to England (*From Russia, with Love*). When he is trapped by Grant (of SMERSH) on the train, Grant warns him against trying any tricks: 'No Bulldog Drummond stuff'll get you out of this one.' The name Bond assumes on this assignment is Somerset, which could be a tribute to Maugham. In other words, three separate references to spy fiction. The Ambler-Maugham references are interesting as they are regarded as the two writers who were most influential in leading the spy novel out of the Buchan-Oppenheim dead end. Sapper was not admired. In *On Her Majesty's Secret Service* Bond meets the hideous Fräulein Irma Bunt whom he silently dubs Irma La not so Douce, after Sapper's *femme fatale*. (For some of the many references to Bond himself made by other spy writers, see Chapter 7. They outnumber all references to other fictional spies put together.)

Warren Tute makes a neutral reference to Bulldog Drummond in *The Golden Greek*. It is, in a sense, a historical note and conveys no judgment, but is interesting for that reason. 'We had both been brought up on Bulldog Drummond and the novels of Dornford Yates. No doubt most boys at one time or another see themselves as crusaders or master spies. I have not checked up lately but Bulldog Drummond remains in my mind as a large, clean cut Englishman with a jaw, steely eyes and a meaty punch.' And the Buchan influence is still invoked by John Gardner in his *A Killer for a Song*, as late as 1975. On the run in France, Boysie Oakes signs a hotel register as Sir Richard Hannay. There is much irony here, for Oakes would never have made those exhausting journeys over heath and moor. He would have employed a local gillie.

Who Are the Spy Writers?

'To define spy fiction is not as easy as to define detective literature', Donald McCormick writes in *Who's Who in Spy Literature*. He points out that the main characters in many 'spy' novels are not spies at all. He may be a counter-espionage agent like Bond or an Intelligence chief sitting at his desk, controlling spies but not spying himself. 'In fact, when we speak of the spy story we are talking of spy-catchers as well as spies, of double and treble agents as well as agents, or hired killers, planters of misinformation, or sometimes even of that unassuming little man at the corner shop who operates a kind of letter box for agents.' McCormick himself casts his net very wide and is extremely generous in his acceptance of many very marginal cases. Nevertheless, his is an extremely valuable book for the addict and it contains much intelligent comment.

The accuracy of spy novelists is often debated, along with another old favourite: does experience in Intelligence help? The answer must surely be equivocal. On the one hand we have Ambler, greatly admired and setting new standards of credibility, yet quite inexperienced in the practice of espionage. But a superb novel such as *The Levanter* is much more than the work of a man who has had or not had 'experience'. It is a work of a very high literary order. Graham Greene has been particularly successful in his novels dealing with espionage (whether in his *novel* vein or his *entertainment* vein). I doubt if any reader would be much concerned whether Greene had had 'experience' or not. In fact, during the war he belonged to the same subsection as Philby (it was called the Iberian) but he operated in Sierra Leone. Philby wanted Greene to stay in the service and even offered promotion, but Greene turned it down.

So generalizations about the background of the good spy writer are not much use. Bernard Newman, who has written a few indifferent spy novels himself, is extremely contemptuous of most of his colleagues. He never names them but condemns them as a class. But his attitude, as expressed in his book *The World of Espionage*, is far from convincing. When F.B.I. agents were trying to get evidence on Harry Gold (Fuchs's contact), they found a map of Santa Fe which had slipped behind a bookcase in his room. Gold had told them he had never been West of the Mississippi. Newman writes: 'But then a trifle came to light—so trivial that a fiction writer would dismiss it as absurd.' But it is Newman's comment which is absurd. This is just the kind of detail that spy writers delight in. Its use is not the sign of a good writer but merely of one who possesses the necessary degree of invention. Elsewhere Newman says that the suggestion that nuclear bombs could be transported in sections through the diplomatic bag 'sounds like an episode from a spy thriller' but adds that it could be done. So where does the spy thriller diverge from life? Newman also claims that most spy memoirs are fictions. He dismisses the Mata Hari story as pure legend. Somehow he seems to imply that such statements invalidate spy fiction.

McCormick quotes Aaron Latham, who made a study of American secret intelligence and wrote: 'There is more truth in some spy fiction than there is in books supposedly non-fiction.' We get into logical hot water if we claim that spy fiction is unreal because it is not so apparently fictional as real-life espionage. What we can say is that experience of espionage cannot make a good writer but it can supply useful guide-lines to the dimensions of a spy novel. In fact, a large proportion of spy-fiction writers have served in Intelligence. Far more spy writers have served in Intelligence than sci-fi writers have been in space. The general attitude towards spy writers resembles that towards sci-fi writers: it begins with contempt but leads to grudging respect as their forecasts are realized and actualized.

There are some very intelligent men working in this field. (It has not attracted the women yet. The so-called Queen of Spy Novelists, Helen MacInnes, is an exception. Although born in this country she must be classified as an American writer, and therefore does not qualify for this study.) By this I mean that they cannot be dismissed as mere pulp-writers. I dare say there are many bright teenagers who could write an adequate Western or Oppenheim-type thriller. One invents a world as one goes along. The world described by Deighton, Forsyth and Le Carré goes way beyond a pass in O-Levels. Oddly enough, it is Bond, who has never been credited with high intellectual or educational attainment, who puts the case most clearly. In *From Russia, with Love* he argues with Paymaster Captain Troop, R.N. (ret.), Head of Administration. Bond said they must concern themselves seriously with the atom age 'intellectual spy', and must employ intellectuals to counter them.

> Retired officers of the Indian Army can't possibly under-
> stand the thought processes of a Burgess or a Maclean.
> They won't even know such people exist—let alone be in a

position to frequent their cliques and get to know their friends and their secrets. Once Burgess and Maclean went to Russia, the only way to make contact with them again and, perhaps, when they got tired of Russia, turn them into double agents against the Russians, would have been to send their closest friends to Moscow and Prague and Budapest with orders to wait until one of these chaps crept out of the masonry and made contact. And one of them, probably Burgess, would have been driven to make contact by his loneliness and by his ache to tell his story to someone.

Fleming appends a cryptic footnote: 'Written in March 1956'. Shortly after that Burgess made it clear that he had had enough of Moscow and asked to be allowed back. He found no takers.

12: THE GREAT GAME

What made Philby tick? Ideological conviction? Money? Love of adventure? Alan Williams, in his *Gentleman Traitor*, tried to answer the question. Hennison, a publisher, says of Philby:

> He was a thief. He'd steal anything—reputations, jobs, State secrets, wives, people's affection, trust, loyalty. About the only thing he didn't steal was money. Which is perhaps what's meant by that sanctimonious guff about his having a "higher loyalty", as Mr Greene chooses to call it. Kim Philby had about as much higher loyalty as a black mamba . . .

Then what attracted him to communism?

> Power, and mischief. Look, if you're going to get anywhere trying to understand Philby's real motives, you've got to realize that he wasn't fired by any passion for the working class, which he's never had anything to do with, or a love of Mother Russia, which he'd never visited until he fled there, or even a belief in Marxism, which I doubt he really bothered to study. With Philby it was all a game.

It was a game that, like other games, could be enjoyed by spectators as well as participants. When Cayle meets Philby in Moscow he tells him that he had a following among those who like to see 'the Establishment get egg all over their faces.' This is perfectly in order so long as such people do not imagine they are giving their support to historical determinism or dialectical materialism by so doing. What was Philby's relationship with Pol, the French financier? 'Cayle decided that they were very much opposite sides of the same coin: vain, devious, extravagant adventurers with childish ideals that were half-honest, half a sham to cover their playful machinations against authority.' And Philby held a whip over many prominent people who had played the same game though not so boldly. 'Before fleeing from Beirut he had left implicit instructions that if he—Harold Adrian Russell Philby, only son of the great St John Philby—should ever be arrested or meet with a violent death, his final testimony, lodged in a vault in Berne, should be offered to every newspaper in the Western hemisphere, together with the Director of Public Prosecutions in London.' Presumably Philby did not believe in life after death but he was prepared to let the game continue for the benefit of survivors.

Espionage has always been referred to as the Game (or even the Great Game) by members of the European ruling classes including, naturally, the diplomats. It was necessarily secretive and was confined to a small number of players. It has surprised some people that the post-war British spies have nearly all been ex-public schoolboys yet there could be few better training grounds for espionage than the hothouse games-playing atmosphere of the public school. Constantine FitzGibbon says that 'the events of 1914 and after have made its flippancy repulsive' but the equation is not easily abandoned. In the last War the operations of Colonel H.J. Giskes, chief of Abwehr counter-espionage in Holland, were known as *Englandspiel*. They were immensely injurious to the Allies, whose own espionage in Holland was negatived for an incredible period of twenty months. At one time the Dutch believed that the British were playing what Ronald Seth calls an even 'deeper game', as every plan ended in disaster and the agents were liquidated. Deaths of agents and also innocent people do not deter the gamesman. Attempts have been made to calculate how many deaths Kilby was responsible for. One of the most famous of all modern spies was Leopold Trepper, conductor of the Red Orchestra, the Soviet spy network which operated in Western Europe from 1940 to 1943. He called his published memoirs *The Great Game*. They give a clue to the attraction many men feel for espionage: it is a love of pitting one's wits against the enemy, short of war. Valentine Williams said that spying became of secondary importance once war broke out.

The Metaphor

The spy writers adopted the game metaphor, on the whole without questioning its validity. 'It's a great game as Blunn plays it', wrote Oppenheim in *The Wrath to Come*. But Oppenheim was not given to thinking carefully about the words he used.

There is a huge contradiction at the heart of the Great Game. It is obviously a most cynical description of activities which were regarded as despicable by many people and yet the players often insisted on a high code of morality. This is well illustrated in Valentine Williams's *The Man with the Clubfoot*. Okewood finally meets his brother Francis, who is on intelligence work in Germany. (He seems to spend all his time avoiding capture, none of it in acquiring information!) Francis explains why he has never confided in his brother. 'You know there are issues in this game of ours, old man, that stand even higher than the confidence that there has always been between us two. That is why I wrote to you so seldom out in France—I could tell you nothing about my work: that is one of the rules of our game.' But Clubfoot is beyond the pale. He has slaughtered British agents in cold blood. Francis comments: 'There is a code of honour in our game, old man, and there are lots of men in the German secret service who live up to it. We give and take plenty of hard knocks in the rough-and-tumble of the chase, but ambush and assassination are barred.'

But the rules have changed since 1918.

Let us look forward to 1941: Eric Ambler's *Uncommon Danger*. Zaleshoff, the Russian agent, is assisted by his sister Tamara. Kenton is greatly attracted by her. During a lull in proceedings he asks her how she got mixed up in such dangerous work. She refers to it as 'an imbecile game of snakes and ladders'. He says he doesn't care for such metaphorical expressions. She agrees but adds, 'It saves thinking.' This is interesting on two counts. First, Kenton is no longer prepared to accept a comfortable metaphor to disguise the true nature of what he is doing, and second, even if Tamara still uses the metaphor she calls it 'imbecile'.

When we come to the later writers it is no surprise to find Bond (or Fleming) referring uncritically to 'The Game', as in the story 'Risico' (*For Your Eyes Only*). One of the major switches in feeling which occurred after Bond in the spy novel, especially in writers like Le Carré, was a disgust felt for treating as a game an activity which so often led to suffering, treachery and bereavement. There were still operators who were immersed in the sporting aspect, however. One feels surprise at realizing that Anthony Price's highly intelligent and cultured David Audley was one of them. He and Ollivier, we are told, were born intelligence men: 'big, clever children entranced with their game because short of war it was the most exciting game of all.' (*Other Paths to Glory*). But in fact there is no contradiction here. Audley is a scholar who is engrossed in his scholarship. Nothing, including espionage, would deflect him from its priority. Audley was certainly created for the Sabbath.

Trevanian, in *The Loo Sanction*, employs irony to expose the game. The agents still play the game. The author neither shares the excitement nor rejects the cynicism. He laughs at the convention. The Vicar, who is in charge of Loo, corresponds regularly with the C.I.I. boss (read C.I.A.) He also has arrangements with his Russian and French counterparts. 'After all, every game must be played by certain rules', says he.

Rules of the Game

Different writers have different ideas of the kind of game they are playing. In Fleming's *From Russia, with Love* both Bond and Kerim (part Turk, part English, and Our Man in Istanbul) refer to 'the Game'. Kerim compares it with chess, at which the Russians excel. But later he changes the metaphor to billiards, which is quite straightforward, everything occurring on a smooth and level table, with smooth and perfect spheres. But outside a jet pilot has fainted and his plane is plunging straight at the table. This is not as comforting as the game's metaphor requires. In fact, the real world is making an unwelcome intrusion. Later Kerim has yet another idea: espionage is really a business, but Bond is a gambler. Therefore Bond treats it as a game which he can win or lose.

It was John Le Carré who attacked the game metaphor most effectively. When an Englishman of the upper classes thinks of games at all he tends to speak of cricket—or he used to. This, like many other pastime, is changing. But if ever there was an activity that was *not cricket* in the accepted meaning of that term, it was espionage. The only thing that matters in that field is success. This was not supposed to be true on the traditional cricket field, although Lillee and Thomson may have changed all that. In espionage, game or not, the *not cricket* gibe comes readily to the tongue. In the book which made Le Carré's name, *The Spy Who Came in from the Cold*, Leamas tells Peters that Fiedler is 'a savage little bastard' and Peters replies sourly, 'Espionage is not a cricket game'. If we want a date for the effective end of the metaphor as a useful counter, this is it: 1963. A little later Fiedler reminds Leamas that their work is rooted in the theory that the whole is more important than the individual. 'That is why a

Communist sees his secret service as the natural extension of his arm, and that is why in your own country intelligence is shrouded in a kind of *pudeur anglaise*.' Nothing could explain the idea of the game more gracefully. He goes on to add that they are not there 'to observe the ethical laws of English country life.'

Two years later, in *The Looking-Glass War*, we are given a shrewd portrait of the gamesman in Leclerc. He is almost totally devoid of human imagination. For him the metaphor serves as a crutch. Espionage is simply a job with rules like a game. He doesn't trouble to call it chess or cricket, it is a game in its own right. It is a very serious game, of course. Danger is to him merely a matter of success or failure and has nothing to do with the nerves or the emotions. Le Carré alternates the story chronologically between Leiser on his journey across the frontier and the rest of the outfit back at the farm. It is superbly handled and, when the final accounts are totted up, it may be regarded as Le Carré's finest achievement. We see poor Leiser getting deeper and deeper into hot water from which we know he will never escape. Meanwhile, back at the farm . . .

> 'You both deserve great credit', Leclerc said, nodding gratefully at Haldane and Avery. 'You too, Johnson. From now on there's nothing any of us can do: it's up to Mayfly.' A special smile for Avery: 'How about you, John; you've been keeping very quiet? Do you think you've profited from the experience?' He added with a laugh, appealing to the other two, 'I do hope we shan't have a divorce on our hands; we must get you home to your wife.'

It had been a good work-out. Hopes for the Spies World Cup ran high.

In *A Small Town in Germany* Le Carré went a step further. He showed that the Game had been replaced by something else, neither enjoyable nor admirable. Spying was not really work for an honourable man—this had been said many times before. Hannay had only stooped to it for patriotic reasons and in any case was mainly concerned with counter-espionage, which is not so tainted. The metaphor hid the unpleasant reality. Some of the younger generation of spy writers still treated espionage as a game and they were aided in this by the growth of a new concept which regarded the whole of life as a form of play (*The Games People Play* was the title of a popular book and it was not concerned with either cricket or chess). The new approach was extended to war itself, and war was studied as a Game. But the more thoughtful writer, such as Le Carré or Graham Greene, was impressed by the baneful effect on the actor, the courses he was compelled to follow if he was to succeed. The old axiom: He who touches pitch will be defiled, was recalled. In *A Small Town in Germany* De Lisle, one of the more pleasant Embassy characters, says that Siebkron's job is 'muddy pools' and adds, 'Your world in a way'. Being a nice guy, he is embarrassed and apologizes, but both he and Turner know it is true. Bradfield turns the screw a little more when he refers to Turner's 'unsavoury profession' and couples it with 'your ignorance of diplomatic practice and your uncommon rudeness.'

In *Spy Story* Deighton is quick to relate espionage with the increasingly popular war games indulged in by the military, although he makes no explicit connection. The background to this novel is a War Game played at the War Studies Centre. Each chapter has a headquote from the Rules and Routine and Glossary of the Games. It would be hard for Deighton to resist that. His love of academic quotation is compounded by one on the flyleaf from William Cowper of all people! (Not to be outdone, Fleming gave his reader lines from a 17th Century Japanese poet in *You Only Live Twice*.) Ferdy Foxwell no doubt felt guilty about the use of the word 'game' to describe these activities and made strenuous efforts to replace it by 'studies', but it was no use—the other 'players' insisted on 'game.' But a year later, in *Yesterday's Spy*, Deighton resorts to the traditional games terminology. Charlie tells Champion that romantics can never beat realists in a battle of wits. Champion stared at him. 'That's not cricket, old pal', he said. Charlie said, 'I thought we were all-in wrestling', which is an interesting comment, because as a game all-in ranks very low in the gentleman's estimation, owing to its almost complete *lack* of rules. Champion has a ready answer. 'You have to learn cricket *and* all-in wrestling if you are the only boy at Sandhurst who plays cricket in second-hand togs.'

But the introduction of all-in wrestling is really an admission that the game metaphor is no longer adequate. There are no longer rules or, if there are, they are broken with impunity. Admiration is for the man who commits the professional foul and gets away with it. For sentimentalists and traditionalists the Game is certain to be cricket. Marcel d'Agneau, in his excellent *Eeny, Meeny, Miny, Mole* (the only successful satire on spy writing, apart from Connolly's brilliant little story) sticks to cricket. Men working in the field are called

Outfielders. Willy, who has retired from the position, sees the whole intelligence operation in terms of cricket. There are several oblique references to the Honourable Schoolboy (the whole book is a friendly joke at Le Carré's expense), whose love of cricket was frequently mentioned. Real cricket, that is, although he was also an admirable performer in the metaphorical game. D'Agneau also has two sets of defectors who are referred to as the First and Second Elevens.

The Sixth Sense

All spy writers claim that all operators possess a sixth sense. They know they are being followed even if they are blindfolded and have their ears stopped. In fact, they are rarely in that situation, especially when proceeding down the street, but they always know what is happening behind them. It must make tailing extremely difficult and frustrating and one wonders why the services persist with it.

This sixth sense has ostensibly nothing to do with games except that it is really intuition and no games player is worth a bean unless his intuitive powers are exceptionally strong. To walk through a strange city in the knowledge that you are being silently tailed and to throw off the tail is a supreme game in itself. What explains Bond? What explains Philby? It is the joy they experience in pitting their wits against an enemy and winning. The apparent purpose is merely cover, something to justify the expenditure of public money. Again and again the writer will mention this faculty and sometimes he will explain that it is a necessary part of the agent's armoury. It applies to more than sensing a tail. In *A Small Town in Germany* Turner is pulling suits out of a wardrobe in Harting's empty house, hurriedly looking through the pockets. 'Then an extra sense warned him: go slowly.'

Oppenheim was aware of it. 'The instinctive apprehension of being followed, common to most criminals and SS men, is one which speedily becomes developed . . .' he writes in *Matorni's Vineyard*. Fleming lived by it. 'Bond had walked for only a few minutes when it suddenly occurred to him that he was being followed. There was no evidence for it except a slight tingling of the scalp and an extra awareness of the people near him, but he had faith in his sixth sense . . .' Bond is always right; he knows when he is being watched or followed, he knows who not to trust, and he can always pick out the person in a landscape whose behaviour is false. In this particular case

(*Diamonds Are Forever*) the follower was doing a front tail, and therefore wasn't technically a follower at all, but this was something Bond didn't know until he discovered it. One of Bond's Russian enemies, Kronsteen, a chess champion and a master spy, judged people by what he considered their basic and immutable instincts (*From Russia, with Love*). To him all people were chess pieces. You could always tell their reactions. Self-preservation, sex and the herd instinct were the basic impulses, in that order. He held the old medieval theory that temperaments were sanguine, phlegmatic, choleric or melancholic, and each individual temperament would depend on their balance. Such ideas may or may not be related to intuition and what the writers call the sixth sense, but they indubitably support the view that an agent depends on his feelings rather than logical thought processes.

The post-Fleming era is even more insistent, if possible, on the importance of intuition. Zayat (a code name for the hero in Deighton's *Horse Under Water*) has a mild disagreement with Jean who says he is paranoiac 'but she hadn't been in the business long enough to develop that sixth sense that I was always telling myself I had.' But in *Yesterday's Spy* there are misgivings. Champion and Charlie have reached denouement. Champion says Charlie didn't discover his plan, he only sensed it. 'No plan is proof against a hunch. You told me there was no place for hunches any more'. And then he says perhaps they are both Yesterday's Spies, implying that modern technology has eliminated the Bond-type spy with his intuition. Could a computer sense a tail?

Leonard, Kingsley Amis's rather prim agent in *The Anti-Death League*, may not be naturally intuitive but he knows it's his job to become so. His 'training had stressed the importance of attending to hunch and instinct, especially in what he had learnt to call under-facted situations . . .' Charlie Muffin always trusts his instinct. 'It had been nothing more than instinct, eight years before, that had initially made him suspect that he was being set up as a disposable sacrifice by the American and British Intelligence Services . . .' (Freemantle's *Charlie Muffin's Uncle Sam*). Coincidence always aroused his curiosity. Like instinct, it was worth consideration at all times. But Charlie is temperamentally and sociologically opposed to any form of pretence. He is determined to see things as they are and he admits, unusually for an intelligence agent, that his instinct might play him false. But it was right 'just a very high proportion of the time.'

It is inevitable that Marcel d'Agneau, in his splendid send-up, *Eeny Meeny, Miny, Mole* (even the title reflects the modern spy story's concern with the nursery, which is implicitly acknowledged by Graham Greene in *The Human Factor*), should turn his attention to Wonder Spy receiving Vibrations at the Right Moment: Welland 'stopped twenty feet from the house, sensitive to his fears, a sixth sense that kept a good agent alive.' And surviving to continue the Great Game.

13: THE SPY AND HIS ETHICS

There is a strong schoolboy-honour tone running all through Buchan's work: a man's word is his bond linked with a powerful sentiment of the 'side' (not yet the 'gang'), shared values, complete trust and confidence in each other, all in the service of undoubted patriotic ends. It is nowhere more evident than in the concluding pages of *Greenmantle*. The story becomes wilder and less credible, as when Hannay with a broken arm seizes the weighty Blenkiron and jumps over a parapet with him, yet it is sustained by a sense of utter rightness. It is virtue that overcomes all obstacles. In the last chapter the friends congratulate each other. 'It's the job that matters, not the men that do it. And our job's done. We have won, old chap—won hands down—and there is no going back on that.' Blenkiron (an American—but who can resist the High British Ethic?) is exultant. 'I'm about the luckiest man on God's earth, Major. I've always wanted to get into a big show, but I didn't see how it could come the way of a homely citizen like me . . . I used to envy my old dad that fought at Chattanooga . . . but I guess Chattanooga was like a scrap in a Bowery Bar compared to this. When I meet the old man in Glory he'll have to listen some to me.' Sandy, the English aristocrat, weighs in. 'We're lucky fellows, we've all had our whack. When I remember the good times I've had I could sing a hymn of praise. We've lived long enough to know ourselves and to shape ourselves into some kind of decency . . .' and he continues moralizing about the boys who had given their lives before they knew what life meant, the fellows with wives and children and homes. 'For fellows like us to shirk would be black cowardice. It's small credit for us to stick it out.' And meanwhile the shells whistle all around them, and they prepare for their end. But they are relieved and Sandy shouts, 'Oh, well done our side!'

Such exultation, in the awareness of virtue! But what a falling-off has there been! Can the modern agent still luxuriate in his victory? Certainly not. At the most he can tell himself that the greater evil is beaten off by the lesser. Virtue lies bleeding and has no role to play. In one of the great spy novels of our time, Le Carré's *The Spy Who Came in from the Cold*, Control says 'We do disagreeable things, but we are *defensive*. That, I think, is still fair. We do disagreeable things so that ordinary people here and elsewhere can sleep safely in their beds at night . . . and in weighing up the moralities, we rather go in for dishonest comparisons; after all, you can't compare the ideals of one side with the methods of the other, can you now?' Leamas told Liz there was only one law in the game. 'What do you think spies are: priests, saints and martyrs? They're a squalid procession of vain fools, traitors too, yes; pansies, sadists and drunkards, people who play cowboys and Indians to brighten their rotten lives. Do you think they sit like monks in London balancing the rights and wrongs?' The last sentence in the book provides a shocking image: 'As he fell, Leamas saw a small car smashed between great lorries, and the children waving cheerfully through the window.' There is absolutely no trust and no fidelity in the spy world.

Ends and Means

It is agreed that espionage has entered a new phase. This is due to the employment of advanced technological processes but, as always, the outer world has its effect on the inner one. Since the last World War the major powers have been building up huge espionage establishments (they were large before but nothing compared with what exists now) and these were bound to collide eventually in spectacular fashion. It was the U2 incident, when an American spy plane was brought down by an SA-2 missile over Sverdlovsk on May Day 1960, which heralded the new age of espionage. Its confirmation became the topic for an important new fictional genre.

After the U-2 was shot down President Eisenhower said: 'No-one wants another Pearl Harbour. Intelligence-gathering activities . . . have a special and secret character. They are, so to speak, "below the surface" activities. They are secret . . . They are divorced from the regular visible agencies of government . . . These activities have their own rules and methods of concealment which seek to mislead and obscure . . . It is a distasteful but vital necessity.'

The contemporary ethical situation in espionage seems to be approached by two avenues. First of all there is the conviction that anything can be justified on the grounds of a 'higher morality', although the measurement of 'height' may be extremely dubious, and secondly, it is admitted that machines have no morality and therefore there can be no ethical rules where technology is king. The net result is a reversion to the morality of a fantasy childhood world. It is sometimes remarked that children usually behave decently with each other but that is normally at a stage where adult training has had its effect. The usual child reaction to a situation where it wants something is to grab it and, if frustrated, to bawl. (In politics we call this 'Fascist aggression'.) In an essay on the modern spy entitled 'Meditations on the Literature of Spying' in *The American Scholar* for Spring 1965 Jacques Barzun wrote: 'What is reprehensible is for the modern world to have made official the dreams and actions of little boys'. The spy enjoys 'permissive depravity' (permission granted by, among others, President Eisenhower), for 'in exchange for a few dirty tricks there is also power and luxury, cash and free sex . . . the advantage of being a spy as of being a soldier is that there is always a larger reason—the reason of state—for making any little scruple or nastiness shrink into insignificance.' He adds, 'The soul of the spy is somehow the model of us all'.

The moral rights of the spy have been argued about for centuries. In 1585 Alberico Gentili, an Italian Protestant exile who became Regius Professor of Civil Law at Oxford (thanks to Walsingham's influence) declared in *De Legationibus* that an ambassador was not bound to obedience if a prince's wishes contravened the moral law. At the time the role of spy was often part of the ambassador's duties—the sharp cleavage between the two was a later development. 'Soul was superior to State', Burn wrote in *The Debatable Land*. Gentili admits that even then his view was not widely followed. 'I paint ambassadors not as they are but as they ought to be.' There has been quite a lot of evidence that some embassies have reverted to the earlier role in recent years.

One of the most successful spies of Elizabeth I's reign, Nicholas Berden, wrote: 'Though I am a spye (which is a profession odious though necessary) I prosecute the same not for gayne but for the safety of my native country.' The spy always flies to the security aspect to gain respectability. Burn's comment on Berden is that his gains were not always negligible. Perhaps the twilight situation of the spy has been best expressed by Geoffrey Household in *Doom's Caravan*, when he called the perfect A.D.S.O. (Assistant Defence Security Officer) 'a first-class crook with an immaculate sense of honour.' Bernard Newman has said the same thing in different words:

'A spy *must* be a man of integrity and yet he must be prepared to be a criminal. A man with scruples is useless in our business.'

The novelists illustrate the point through their characters. Snelling, in his light-hearted review of Bond called *Double O Seven*, notes that they 'really fight their battles with the gloves off in the Secret Service. There are no gentlemanly agreements about not hitting a man when he is down, and all that sort of rot.' One of the accepted procedures in modern security has earned the name of Dirty Tricks, and Chapman Pincher uses it for a novel. 'Falconer had no residual conscience feelings about political assassination, which he regarded as no more than the necessary removal of a threat to his country's security, or of an obstacle to its progress. In his job he was permanently at war, and to win wars enemies had to be killed. Like pain and rain, any guilt was forgotten within a few hours of freedom from it.' Taylor 'did not feel badly about being deceived because it was routine practice in the Intelligence game'. 'In the Intelligence game a successful end justified every terrible means.' It is odd that this willingness to do anything for the country's security comes at a time when patriotism is regarded as a rather shameful emotion. The explanation is that the patriotic sentiment has been transferred from country to ideology: men now kill for Communism, Fascism or Democracy. Guilt is roused when it is done in the name of the latter which alone honours the life of the individual above that of the community or the gang. But not all agents are concerned with the ideology. In many cases they may have started their careers with such concern but had it eroded by the years. When Gemmel is asked in Quinnell's *The Mahdi* if he is worried by moral issues, he replies, 'They don't bother me at all. I'm an intelligence agent. I gave up being concerned with moral issues a long time ago.'

One of the few who remains worried and tries to retain an element of moral compunction in his work is Smiley. In the early *A Murder of Quality* we are told that 'it was a peculiarity of Smiley's character that throughout the whole of his clandestine work he had never managed to reconcile the means to the end.' He tries to conduct his relations with his Russian opposite number in gentlemanly fashion, thus refuting Snelling's claim that 'all that sort of rot' is now out of court. There are even suggestions that Charlie Muffin holds generous feelings towards his official enemies but in his case this may be no more than a by-product of the contempt he feels for his colleagues. If put to the test, he would probably prefer to torture them first!

Ruthlessness brings in its train a new vocabulary. Orwell pointed out how the Russians never killed their enemies but liquidated them, how the Imperialists never bombed natives but pacified them. According to Deighton, if you bump off those who are inconvenient to your plans, it is a case of 'expedient demise'. Thus he calls one novel *XPD*, the accepted abbreviation. No sentimentality or sense of justice must be allowed to get in the way of this expediency. It is 'for defectors. For traitors. For people with heads filled with secrets like the whereabouts of field agents. Then only after the department is certain that they are on the point of giving everything to Moscow. They never XPD field people pursuing an operational task to the best of (their) ability.' Such concessions presumably bring some consolation. John Braine's *Pious Agent* is based on the idea that every year a number of people disappear silently and mysteriously in this way.

Jacques Barzun, whom I have already quoted, finds it impossible to accept these apologies. He jeers at *The Spy Who Came in from the Cold* as a 'really real realistic tale of modern spying.' Leamas 'wants to quit but is compelled to go on by professional routine. This is enough, I imagine, to make him congenial to all of us. He does not believe in what he is doing; he is anything but a hero; he is a good deal of a masochist.' This happens to be true and one does not usually criticize an author for telling the truth. But Barzun is sickened (with good reason) by the whole business, only he allows this to warp his critical sense (without good reason). He realizes that we see our own situation in that of the spy—how else can one explain the fascination of James Bond? It is the modern equivalent of one's earlier recognition in the role of pioneer, warrior, saint or poet. 'We are the spy—an agent, mind you, not a man . . .' This suggests that Smiley is an agent but not a man, whereas Sherlock Holmes (presumably) was a man as well as a detective. One can play a lot of games like this. Bond is not a man, we can all agree. What about Price's Audley, Haggard's Colonel Russell, Freemantle's Charlie Muffin, Deighton's unnamed lead? There is a danger in regarding James Bond as the only agent.

One can nevertheless sympathize with much of Barzun's complaint. There is always a larger reason for allowing any little scruple or nastiness to sink into insignificance. 'As always in trashy literature, it is the satisfactions that produce the illusion of reality: man despising and betrayed, listless in his loves, dying pointlessly every second, scared, scared, scared . . .' This is true exactly for what

Barzun says—trashy literature—and no more. A whole genre cannot be dismissed except by smothering it with a blanket. Barzun makes the point that the novel has always been prying; this is a very good point too, for it is usually spying on the other half, high life, a fraudulent society, it is always revealing discreditable information. It might be true to say that's why we read it. But one wonders if Barzun really approves of any novel. He praises the *Iliad* for being about war and the gods, human character and the brevity of life, as well as about money and sex. But the mainline novel is about 'malice domestic' which ends by stunting our souls. Is this academic snobbery, dressed up in rather unusual garb? Barzun had just re-read *Clarissa Harlowe* and was shocked. But he returns to the spy novel.

> To know in advance that everything and everybody is a fraud gives the derivative types what they call a wry satisfaction. Their borrowed system creates the ironies that twist their smiles into wryness. They look wry and drink rye and make a virtue of taking the blows of fate wryly. It is monotonous: I am fed up with the life of wryly.

This is witty but not very selective. Surely there is a difference between the borrowed wryness of Follett and the felt wryness of Le Carré?

The great illusion (Barzun continues) is to believe that these borrowed impulses and enjoyments betoken maturity, worldliness, being 'realistic'. We can accept this—I made a similar charge against Oppenheim and Le Queux when I called them 'unsophisticated sophisticates'—and we can also agree that it characterizes ninety per cent of the spy-fi output. In fact, the 'spy's ingenuity . . ., his shifting partisanship without a cause, like his double bluffs, his vagrant attachments, and his love of torturing and of being tortured are the mores of the pre-adolescent gang.' But there is another ten per cent and the major difference between the two groups (apart from stylistic qualities) is that the larger group expects us to admire the shoddiness and the smaller group expects us to deplore it.

A World of Contempt

Because of its nature, secret intelligence arouses the enmity of the uninitiated. This, at least, was the traditional view. With the virtual collapse of the old morality among large sections of the population this is no longer true. People can take betrayal, torture and the rest with a shrug: shall we say wryly? But it used to be claimed that spying was contrary to the British character—we're not so sure of the foreigners, who didn't go to public schools. Ambler believes that this belief actually hindered the development of the English spy story. Murder was often forgivable but espionage never. Thus the first British spies in fiction were often counter-spies. It is not difficult to find this distaste expressed in the literature of the past. A good example may be found in Sir George Otto Trevelyan's account of the Siege of Cawnpore in his book *Cawnpore* (1865). He describes how a spy made his way into the British entrenchment. 'Our spies were less lucky; or, it may be that the sturdy and straightforward British nature cannot promptly adapt itself to those frauds which are proverbially fair in war.' We've gone a long way since then and yet the prejudice lingers on. In Freemantle's *The November Man* Dennison, an American diplomat, discusses Altmann's request for political asylum with the Director of the C.I.A. They are not entirely in agreement about what to do. 'After all', says Dennison, 'he's not important, is he? He's only a bloody spy.' The Director agrees. They must have been brought up in the English school.

One of the most interesting debates on the morality of spying is to be found in the least expected quarter: a novel by Baroness Orczy called *A Spy of Napoleon*, published in 1934. This spy is a dancer, Juanita Lorendana, who acquires an aristocratic name through a trick marriage to a young nobleman who had been blackmailed. The period is the Second Empire of Louis Napoleon. Gabriel Prévost, the Deputy Chief of the *Cabinet Secret*, explains to her why spying is so necessary. There is constant intrigue against the security of France, particularly by Prussia and Austria, and it is necessary to acquire the correspondence relating to the intrigues. 'What we want is someone who can move within the inner circle of diplomatic society, someone who has the *entrée* to the *salons* of those *grandes dames* who lend their houses and the prestige of their position for the brewing of political hot-pots—someone who can see and hear what is going on, without arousing suspicion.'

The conventional female is needed—one who is beautiful, fashionable and sophisticated, who can move with ease in the highest society and have a fatal attraction for the male sex. Juanita manages this, and her presentation is both credible and impressive. Talk was going round the clubs: 'I am told that in Germany and Austria the government employs beautiful, fascinating women to put the police on the track of any conspiracy that may be hatched by young men in society, or in the army. A woman can ferret out a secret far more easily than the most astute police officer.' The job is a patriotic one. It is for the glory of France. This is the official view. But Gerard, the young man who has been tricked into marrying her, sees it differently. She says she serves her country. 'By taking blood money', he retorts, 'by carrying on the dirtiest, filthiest trade that ever disgraced man or woman.' And throughout the novel, after he has discovered her trade, he is tortured by the shame. But now and again he has doubts. Perhaps it is necessary. But he wouldn't do it for money. 'But without the money, was the trade any less filthy? To track a human being down, as a hound tracks the fox: to be the direct cause of bringing a fellow-man to a violent death . . . was that filthy in itself—without the money?' (And it is exactly this that he did eventually.) 'Had he performed a laudable service to his country such as is demanded of every patriotic citizen? Or had he, on impulse, soiled his hands and stained his honour with the filthy trade of a spy?'

It is a problem he never really resolves. Juanita, whom he loves, despite everything, was guarding the safety of France. Was that wrong? Was it despicable? Was it 'filthy'—the word he first used? 'And Gerard, brought face to face with the problem in all its crudity, could only wonder what the right answer to it could be.' The situation is complicated by a circumstance that Maugham also exploited. (*Ashenden* appeared six years earlier.) When the major spy is caught and summarily executed, another spy, his wife, commits suicide. But her only motive had been love—not of money, but of her husband.

The dilemma can bring out the best in a writer and it does in the case of the little known and rarely mentioned *The Spy Who Sat and Waited* by R. Wright Campbell. This is not merely a spy story that happens to be well written but a novel that happens to centre round an espionage situation. There are very few novels of high quality in this group; besides this one there is Greene's *The Human Factor*, Le Carré's *The Spy Who Came in from the Cold* and *The Looking Glass War*, Ambler's *The Levanter* and Conrad's *The Secret Agent*. Campbell's novel is not so much about the incidents of espionage as the private agony of Wilhelm Oerter who, through normal human carelessness, allows himself to be used by others. Under orders after the first World War, he changed his name to Hartz, adopted a Swiss passport and went to live in the Orkneys where he became a successful publican, married and had a son, became a British citizen and was admired and liked by his neighbours. But he was playing a double game.

At first there seemed nothing particularly reprehensible. Goldman, the German spy, put it to him like this:

> No special skills are required. In this last war most spies were whores, thieves or confidence men. Why was this so? First, the existence of such a thing as a spy was anathema to the aristocratic military of all nations. Second, they had access to information and understood the devious ways of intrigue. From this moment, we shall find that, while still clandestine, intelligence organizations will gain a certain respect. There will be as much need for clerks as for assassins, for men who have the patience to wait, perhaps fruitlessly, as for active saboteurs.

It sounded harmless. Goldman made no mention of the clash of loyalties that were bound to develop. When Wilhelm heard Chamberlain declare war on Germany he felt a shudder of self-revulsion. 'He felt himself somehow obscene. A parasite thrilling at the grand emotions of the host it was sworn to destroy.'

He passed information about Scapa Flow to the Germans, the Ark Royal was sunk by submarine and he was taken to Germany where he was a stranger. (At home he was believed drowned, heroically trying to save British sailors!) And now he comes under suspicion in Germany for it is clear he has many sympathies for his British family and friends. He is approached by the Canaris conspirators but refuses to join them. It can only lead to more killing. For what? The Fatherland? 'He felt hollow and useless, like a puppet dangling from its strings waiting to be manipulated. It was a feeling he had lived with for many years and it was surpassingly unpleasant and terrifying to be so disposed once again.' When he refuses to join the conspirators he makes a statement which his lack of imagination had prevented him from making before: 'I will not be a small piece in a large game, moved from square to square as though I were filled with sawdust. I won't be used for high and mighty intrigues any more.'

There are obviously two ways of looking at the spy. Either he is beneath contempt or he is a little man who has allowed himself to be used for contemptible purposes, in which case he deserves sympathy.

When Rebecca West's *The Meaning of Treason* was re-issued in 1982 she wrote a new introduction which ended with this passage: 'I am glad to have this opportunity to state that as a result of having watched the form of our traitors for a number of years, I cannot think that espionage can be recommended as a technique for building an impressive civilization. It is a lout's game.' As no-one, not even Oppenheim, had ever recommended espionage as a model for civilization, this hardly ranks as a serious statement, but it evoked a furious response from Ted Allbeury when it was printed in *The Guardian*. He attacks Ms West's 'smugness' and 'ignorance' and recalls his experience as an intelligence officer during the war when he had interrogated the 'so-called SS Freikorps England'. Their offences were 'pathetic and humdrum'. They joined the 'silly circus out of boredom and desperation'. They were working-class youths who had been prisoners for years and saw no end to the war. Allbeury says they were gutless and foolish 'but traitors in any real sense they were not.' As for the non-working-class traitors, such as Anthony Blunt, it was more important to offer them immunity in return for a full confession than to put them away for thirty years (like the members of the Freikorps) and get nothing in return. Spying is an ugly trade but vindictiveness is no cosmetic.

'On Your Own'

A curious result of the sordidness of espionage is that the authorities will not recognize their own involvement. If a spy is caught he can expect no help from his employers. They will not acknowledge him. He is on his own. The reader will find instances of this in the earliest spy novels. In Valentine Williams's *The Crouching Beast* (1928) for instance, Olivia and Druce find themselves in a very hot spot. She says she will go to the Embassy. He laughs.

'I don't want to scare you, but you've got to get this right. I'm a properly accredited secret agent, as much a salaried servant of the Crown as our Ambassador over there in the Wilhelm-Strasse. But he wouldn't lift a finger to help me. He's not allowed to. It's one of the rules of the game. When we're on the job, my dear, we're the untouchables, pariahs, with every man's hand against us . . .'

Deighton makes the same point more than once. In *Close-Up* (not a spy novel) he writes: 'Espionage and show business have in common that tradition that everyone abandons you when you are in trouble.' The agent may not only be deserted, he may even be betrayed by his own side. (After all, betrayal is the mark of the beast.) At one point, in Deighton's *Billion-Dollar Brain*, when the lead is in a thoroughly desperate situation, the thought crosses his mind that he may have been betrayed by London. 'It had been done before, it would be done again.' Not even the highest in the land are exempt. There is a hint of this in Antony Melville-Ross's *Tightrope*. After Rafferty and Trelawney have saved London from a nuclear explosion, the Minister recommends the resignation of Trelawney (Rafferty is dead) on the grounds that 'a government agency which acts on its own initiative over a situation from which the most appalling consequences might well have ensued with no reference to those in authority over it is in need of new leadership.' The fictional agencies frequently act in this way. Government is represented as slow, bumbling and lacking in initiative. (Freemantle's otherwise admirable work is often spoiled by this kind of exaggeration, according to which all politicians are fools and everything would be put right if academics/scientists/business men were put in charge. Recent history has demonstrated the falsity of this idea.) Trelawney points out that there are times when even Ministers come under suspicion. No-one will accept failure. Despite the agency's independence of action, Sir Charles Barry and his wife, two members of the agency, are disciplined for acting on *their* own initiative. There is a chain of irresponsibility.

This situation increases the degree of ruthlessness exercised by the Secret Service. The political editor in John Gardner's *To Run a Little Faster* says they have a reputation for 'a certain ruthlessness. Ham-fisted at times.' They are ready to put their own man away if he has become an inconvenience. It was in fact the Service that wrecked Darrell's flat and threatened him and his girl-friend on the tube. They are trying to frighten him off because he's in the way, but giving the impression that the dirty work is being done by the 'other side'. Clarke, the Intelligence agent, says to Darrell: 'There are some things that people don't understand. The secret war that goes on all the time. It's impossible for us to unlock the door and let you in just like that.'

Nor will recognition normally come through rewards. At the end of *Moonraker* Gala Brand was awarded the George Cross. M told Bond, 'The Prime Minister had something in mind for you. Forgotten that we don't go in for those sort of things here. So he asked me to thank you for him. Said some nice things about the Service. Very kind of him.' So Bond couldn't even collect a diamond tie-pin from the Palace, as Sherlock Holmes once did.

More than one writer has commented on the unexpected fact that the Russians apparently do look after their own. This may come as a surprise, for the Russians are not known for their concern for the individual. But there is probably another consideration at work here. A captured spy may give away valuable information; it may be worth while attempting to rescue him, or promising him earthly delights on his eventual return. It is decided in Deighton's *XPD* that Parker, the Russian illegal resident, must be brought out of danger, for 'that was the code of Moscow Centre. None of the professional Russian-born agents were ever abandoned to their fate.' The same point was made by Freemantle's Charlie Muffin. The actual rescue of Blake is a good example of this policy, although it is suggested by Alan Williams in *Gentleman Traitor* that he was helped from inside the British Secret Service.

The Double Agent

The double agent is a natural character in this murky drama. If he did not exist something would have gone wrong with natural invention. It is not necessary to spend time on considering his position. Just as there is a corpse in every crime novel, so there is a double agent in every spy novel. Spreading misinformation is as important as gathering true information and most spies will be involved to a greater or lesser extent.

One of the major questions that is always being posited and answered, successfully or otherwise, is: can you trust your own men? Next, can you trust the defectors? Are they double agents? You know that some of your own men are double (you hope their first loyalty is to you) and it is quite certain that some who come over are playing the same role. McCormick says Conrad was the first serious writer to deal effectively with the double agent in *Under Western Eyes*.

The double agent has a special appeal for the serious writer because he illustrates a crisis of conscience. In most spy novels he does not air his conscience (of course, he may not have one, or it may not be active) but for some writers it is the conscience and not the plot that

counts. This point is clarified in J.B. Priestley's *The Shapes of Sleep*.
He calls it A Topical Tale and it borders on spy drama. Ben
Sterndale, a freelance newspaperman, is down on his luck. He
becomes involved in an international intrigue concerning the
possession of some coloured shapes which a German psychologist
has discovered have a hypnotic effect on the viewer. The effect was
slight, but sufficient to weaken the will in the unguarded human
mind—just the thing for a modern government to use in its
propaganda. Sterndale is not really a spy and for most of the time he
doesn't know what he is doing, except that he has been paid to recover
a piece of green paper. In his enquiries he encounters German
communists, British Intelligence, a group who have dedicated
themselves to saving the human race from psychological exploi-
tation, and a double agent.

Priestley uses the thriller formula to attack the vices of modern
society and political management. He can express sympathy for the
double agent who is in effect saying, 'A plague on both your houses!'
This is not a sentiment we often come across in this kind of literature.
Nearly all spy writers take sides (their agents usually work for their
government, and as I am writing about British spy fiction they usually
work for the British government). A few of them express reservations
(Le Carré is the obvious example) whereas others are fiercely
patriotic in the old, uncritical sense. But Priestley's double agent lives
in a no-man's-land between the warring factions. 'He lies to people
who've been lying to the wide world for years. He's treacherous to
men who are nothing but traitors to the whole damned human race.'

Probably the clearest expression of the agent's situation is to be
found in Deighton's *Funeral in Berlin*. Stok, the Russian, says, 'I make
my plans upon the basis of everyone being untrustworthy' to which
the lead replies, 'The moment that you think that you know who your
friends are is the moment to get another job.'

14: MOTIVES

'The spy is a uniquely characteristic and significant figure of our time', says Leonard in Amis's *The Anti-Death League*, quoting (as he does endlessly) from the introduction to one of his manuals and trying to make it sound casual. Lucy replies, 'I thought it was moulders of the communal mind by means of manipulation of the mass media who were meant to be that. So somebody was saying in the newspaper on Sunday anyway.' Leonard decides it is possible to have two characteristic and significant figures of our time at once. This ironical, tongue-in-the-cheek novel is really more concerned with spy-mania than with spying. It also makes fun of the posh weekly-popular donnish tone of much temporary discussion.

So the spy is one of the characteristic and significant figures of our time. Then why does he do it? Spy writers sometimes pause to ask this question and usually give an answer. Warren Tute asks it in *The Tarnham Connection* (1971) but does not attempt a positive reply. John Padstow of the Intelligence Service tells his uncle he has no personal ambition, otherwise he wouldn't be in such a job. This sets him thinking.

> Why was he doing the job at all? Why did anyone bother these days? Not for the Queen of England, as he had been brought up to think when a boy, even though his uncle did happen to be 'her man in Malta', even though the English way of doing things still struck him as civilised, intelligent and—allowing for the lower reaches of Whitehall—as uncluttered as the conditions of any modern bureaucratic state would allow.

Patriotic Duty

This was the only motive for the good spy in the early days. Bad spies (that is, working for the enemy) could be tempted in other ways, although some of them might also be slaves of their own brand of unenlightened, reverse patriotism. Carruthers and Davies, Hannay, Okewood, Drummond and the many agents of Oppenheim and Le Queux, never had any doubts. And they retained their enthusiasm. Some modern spies remain patriotic but they try to keep it quiet, being partly ashamed of the emotion. Goldman, the control in *The Spy Who Sat and Waited*, is a good example of the reluctant patriot. He is a German, but this is a serious novel and this situation is treated as sympathetically as if he were on 'our' side. Remember also that these events took place during the second World War (although the book did not appear until 1975) and that Goldman's feelings are rather in advance of their time, anticipating those of Le Carré's major characters.

> I am a man living in a world not of my making. I am filled with the quiet desperation of the undecided. I may extrapolate, draw conclusions upon little evidence and much fiction, but I can never know the truth of the situation, the value of the action or the desirability of the consequences. I have done and will continue to do such things, in the name of duty, that I cannot entirely agree with. Until, that is, some basic moral principle of my own is compromised.

There is also such a thing as displaced patriotism which may verge on idealism. In the same novel Dennerson is a failed doctor who spied for the Germans. His downfall had been caused by alcoholism and chronic bronchitis. Oerter 'realized with something of shocked surprise that this man thought of himself as a German. It was clear why Intelligence considered him safe. He was unpaid. His loyalty was secured by his belief that he was one of an Aryan, intellectual, counter-revolutionary élite.' German discipline and self-admiration has always had an appeal for weak-minded people who feel they are not sufficiently valued in their own country. Some of them succumbed to the lure of Aryanism during the thirties and into the war period.

Idealism

Aryanism scarcely deserves the description of ideology. It is a projected form of egoism with only the slightest signs of altruism. The overwhelmingly attractive ideology of our time has been Socialism and its perversion, Soviet Communism. The Establishment often found this difficult to understand. When Gouzenko defected in Canada, Norman Robertson, the Permanent Secretary for External Affairs, told Prime Minister Mackenzie King that it was doubtful if those who were suspected of giving information to the Russians did it for money. 'There was a sort of idealism of the Russian Revolution which sought to get human rights for the masses of the people and this became a religion with some persons and they were prepared to do anything to further the movement', King wrote in his diary. Gouzenko, who had lived and worked in Russia, could be more realistic. He said the freedom of elections in Canada surprised him. 'In comparison with them the system of elections in Russia appear as a mockery of the conception of free elections', he told the Royal Commission which examined his case.

Another one who was disillusioned, though he had to learn the hard way, was Dr Allan Nunn May. 'The whole affair was extremely painful to me and I only embarked on it because I felt this was a contribution I could make to the safety of mankind. I certainly did not do it for gain', he wrote in his confession. This is a very honourable sentiment and it compares with the absolute conviction of patriots like Hannay (and, of course, the real ones who often died or risked their lives *pro patria*). Ideology and patriotic loyalty were once more or less the same thing. Today the ideology has hived off from most patriotic sentiments, though not all. But not everyone could be so forgiving to Nunn May. After he was sentenced, the independent and former Labour M.P., W.J. Brown, asked the Home Secretary, Chuter Ede, to review the sentence. The whole issue of atom bomb secrecy, he said, 'constituted an extremely doubtful ethical area.' Incidentally, the other prominent academic spy, Fuchs, once accepted £100 in bank notes. Before that he had only taken small sums to cover expenses, mainly from Harry Gold in the U.S.A. Afterwards he said he took the money as a symbol, as a formal act to bind himself to the cause. After that there could be no going back. There seems no reason to doubt his sincerity.

Only one of the spy novelists has really discussed this aspect of motivation. Most of them are too much concerned with the development of the story to concern themselves overmuch with reasons for spying. Le Carré is the exception. In *Call for the Dead* Smiley tries to explain why two Germans, Dieter Frey and Elsa

Fennan, became spies for the G.D.R. Was Elsa a communist? 'I don't think she liked labels. I think she wanted to help build one society which could live without conflict. Peace is a dirty word now, isn't it? I think she wanted peace.' One of the most fascinating areas of modern politics is the semantic, as Orwell knew and illustrated so vividly in *1984*. It seems outrageous that 'peace' should ever be a dirty word, yet the peace movements and organizations of the time were often communist fronts and were not interested at all in peace but in Soviet domination. The Labour Party used to issue a list of proscribed organizations, which meant that they were either controlled by or infiltrated by Marxist opponents of democratic socialism: the list included the British Peace Committee, the Welsh Peace Council, People's Congress for Peace, West Yorkshire Federation of Peace Organizations, World Peace Council, Artists for Peace, Musician's Organizations for Peace, Authors' World Peace Appeal, Teachers for Peace and Scientists for Peace. It was inevitable that a number of innocent and sincere people should have been ensnared by these movements. What about Dieter? 'God knows what Dieter wanted. Honour, I think, and a socialist world. They dreamed of peace and freedom. Now they're murderers and spies.'

This reaches a level of thought and discussion that is rarely encountered in spy fiction. Deighton, for example, takes the line that most spies are merely professionals, in it for excitement or money. Smiley recognized Dieter's good intentions but hated him for his folly. He had 'the fabulous impertinence of renouncing the individual in favour of the mass. When had mass philosophies ever brought benefit or wisdom? Dieter cared nothing for human life: dreamed only of armies of faceless men bound by their lowest common denominators; he wanted to shape the world as if it were a tree, cutting off what did not fit the regular image; for this he fashioned blank, soulless automatons like Mundt. Mundt was faceless like Dieter's army, a trained killer born of the finest killer breed.'

Smiley kills Dieter. Far from being pleased with himself, he experiences a tremendous revulsion. 'They had come from different hemispheres of the night, from different worlds of thought and conduct. Dieter, mercurial, absolute, had fought to build a civilization. Smiley, rationalistic, protective, had fought to prevent him.' He had negated his own beliefs in his attempt to protect them. Apart from flashes like this, *Call For the Dead* is a rather wooden novel, no better than the average crime detection novel. But these moments transcend the workaday level of crime fiction and give us a foretaste of the much superior *Spy Who Came in from the Cold.*

Broken Careers

The spy may be hiding from the respectable world. 'How do you think an organization such as ours finds its rank and file?' asks Simmons in *The Spy Who Sat and Waited.* 'From the failures, the malcontents, the whiners, the fools. Those who are easily puffed up with small secrets and empty honours. The childish who long desperately to destroy the father figure. The cynical, the cowardly, the self-seekers, the greedy.'

Wilhelm actually became a spy by default. Another kind of failure, perhaps. Without ambition or drive, with nothing to look back on with pride, and no concern for the future, he had forsaken home and his loved ones and replaced them with a fiction called duty and love of country. For patriotism may be no more than a cover for something rather ugly.

This type of spy usually belongs to the ranks, as Simmons says. One of the rare exceptions is Marston-Gore in Valentine Williams's *The Crouching Beast.* He is cashiered from the Army and joins the Secret Service under the name of Nigel Druce. Williams is attracted by this type of recruit, especially as it is usually possible to rehabilitate him at the end of the story. (He didn't steal, kill, rape or whatever—it was a case of mistaken identity. Sometimes he is shielding someone else, which eventually makes him a hero. There is no doubt of Marston-Gore's fundamental goodness). In *The Gold Comfit Box*, by the same author, a German spy, who worked for the British, had been an officer in the German Army. He had killed a brother officer in a duel over a woman. This novel appeared in 1932, that is, only fifty years ago. In atmosphere it seems to be five centuries distant. But it is only the outward events that change. Inwardly things remain pretty much as they were. 'The Secret Service is the refuge of all broken careers', reflects Clavering.

Money

I imagine no-one ever made a fortune from spying. Even if he did, there must have been easier and less nerve-racking ways of doing it. Money is certainly important, as many writers assert, but it is usually accompanied by something else the agent demands: constant excitement, perhaps, or a complete rejection of the nine-to-five day.

Histories of espionage usually emphasize the financial side. It was acknowledged that certain posts in the Service had financial perks attached to them. Sir James Croft, one of England's major spies, was appointed to Berwick largely because it had solid advantages for the intelligencer (spymaster). Burn writes in *The Debatable Land* that 'the English were poorer than the French, but the Scots much poorer than the English and that much easier to bribe.' Croft, in a letter to Cecil about William Kirkcaldy, wrote: 'The man is poor . . . They be all poor, and you know in all practices money must be one part.' Philip of Spain sent Mendoza as ambassador to London with money to suborn spies. Mendoza reported: 'This is the only way Englishmen are kept faithful, for if they do not actually see the reward before their eyes they forget all past favours . . . We shall keep him longer by giving him the money in two payments.' The person referred to is none other than Croft! Burn's comment was: 'Put charitably it is possibly the story of one among many men who have entered into secret relations with a foreign power in the belief, or on the pretext, that what they were doing was in the interest of peace. Looked at less charitably, he did it for money.'

The lure of money is fully illustrated in Williams's *The Gold Comfit Box.* Sergeant Brandweiss of a Jäger regiment arranged to show Clavering a new type of rifle the German army was experimenting with. 'Probably Brandweiss was in financial difficulties—that is the way most traitors are made.' Clavering is contemptuous of him (in 1932 people could still be contemptuous of what they called filthy lucre): 'the thought of this unsavoury scoundrel selling the honour of the regiment to a foreign power was almost more than I could stomach. Instead of giving this Judas his shekels into his hand, I flung the envelope with the money on the table.' Not even the fact that Brandweiss was betraying the enemy could make his action acceptable.

It is well known that one of the more common ways of unmasking a spy lay in watching personal expenditure. This is illustrated in the same novel when a British naval spy was caught.

In those years immediately preceding the outbreak of the world war, when the counter-espionage on both sides of the North Sea was right on its toes, the spectacle of a petty officer laying fivers and tenners on the horses was one that merited the attention of sundry retiring individuals in plain clothes who kept unostentatious watch on comings and goings at our chief naval ports and dockyards.

But Clavering is shocked when Madeleine offers to sell a German spy for £200. 'Of course, transactions of this kind were no novelty to me, but I could never stomach them very well. If today middle age finds me cynical, it is because, during my years in the secret service, I saw so much of loyalties thus bought and sold over the counter. But in those days I still retained some ideals . . .' Madeleine was a Serb whose brother was a Pan-Slav nationalist and thus a plotter against the Austro–Hungarian Empire. He was held prisoner in a German military prison and this was the hold that Grundt (the famous Clubfoot) had over his sister. Madeleine discovered she could gain his release with a £200 bribe. The spy she shopped was an ex-lover. Very murky, and the environment has become murkier ever since.

General Vozdvishensky in Fleming's *From Russia, with Love* says that 'Americans try to do everything with money. Good spies will not work for money alone—only bad ones, of which the Americans have several divisions.' It is the bad ones who probably put the money to better use. In the same novel we are told of a spy who says he has a secret army in the Ukraine. The Americans load him with money to buy boots; he goes to Paris and buys women. And when Strange asks Jonathan (Dr Hemlock) why he worked for the C.I.I. (in Trevanian's *The Loo Sanction*) the following snatch of conversation leaves no doubt about motive.

> 'Money'.
> 'No slight tug of patriotism?'
> 'My sin was greed, not stupidity.'

The Manipulation of Love

Love is a two-edged weapon. It is used to recruit and entrap.

A French phrase, *cherchez la femme*, attributed to the notorious spymaster Joseph Fouché, used to be very popular in this country, providing a quick solution, requiring no thought, to any problem involving human error or perversity. It suggested the Higher Wisdom and was often accompanied by the Knowing Wink. It was just the kind of philosophy-cum-psychology that would impress a writer like William Le Queux. It operated forcefully in *Her Majesty's Minister* which, published in 1901, was probably one of the spy novels that roused Childers's contempt. A 'Chancelleries of Europe' secret is out—we don't know what it is or who is responsible. 'I tell you, Ingram', the Ambassador cried angrily, 'I tell you that this dastardly piece of trickery is some woman's work.' Edith ('pure, honest and upright') had had a 'pash' on her Italian master at school, Paolo Bertini. He persuaded her to steal from another girl's locker a letter addressed to her by her father, a high official at the War Office. This was to obtain the signature for the purpose of forgery. From that moment Edith was in Paolo's power, for he threatened to denounce her as a thief. Although she was a rich girl her eccentric aunt insisted that she should earn her own living. Bertini made her choose telegraphy and compelled her to act as telegraphist in an unassuming little cottage which became the HQ of French spies in England. (It was always England, never Britain. And note the enemy: France. This occurred before the *entente* of 1904.) Poor Edith has to confess: 'In my ignorance of the world and its ways I took one false step long ago while still at school, and then could not draw back.'

It sounds odd and stilted but more because Le Queux's supposedly civilized mind was undeniably coarse than from any inherent implausibility. The entry into espionage through the gates of love (even a schoolgirl infatuation) has provided copy for many writers after Le Queux. Modern writers, when they are not treating sex as light relief (which many do), sometimes describe the problems and difficulties which the relation between the sexes can bring in its train. No foreseeable risks can be taken in espionage—there will be sufficient unforeseeable ones to keep the organization occupied. Len Deighton is aware of this and paid especial attention to it in *Twinkle, Twinkle, Little Spy.* If the spy is known to be in love, then the loved ones must be checked. There are no secrets between lovers. Anthony realizes he is falling in love with Red Bancroft. He himself realizes how dangerous this can be and is obviously worried. Mann tells him it is unnecessary. 'She's been checked by the F.B.I., by the C.I.A. and her hometown police department. That girl is OK. There is good security: she'll be safe. It will all be OK.' Or it may be that the agent (or defector) is married. Professor Bekuv, an astrophysicist in the same novel, is recruited from the Russians. He is very upset because there had been a promise to bring his wife out too but so far she hasn't turned up. His new loyalty is at stake so long as this situation remains. In the end Mrs Bekuv does come out but she is a double agent. Castle in Greene's *The Human Factor* went through a similar trial. His defection is the other way (he goes to Moscow). There has been a promise to send Sarah out but there was a delay. When the novel ends she is told that it would be easy without the child but very difficult with. The espionage scene seems to run contrary to the fulfilment of love.

The Imponderables

Wilhelm in *The Spy Who Sat and Waited* trained himself to keep the many aspects of his life in separate compartments. 'He had become a good secret agent'. This in itself could explain why it is so difficult for a spy to enjoy a normally satisfying relationship with a woman. It is probable that most agents (in any case, the more successful ones) are complex personalities who may not even themselves have a very good idea of why they behave as they do. No-one gets closer to the psychological truth of a spy, with the separate strands of money and love and idealism and vanity all going to make up a densely organized whole, than Somerset Maugham. He asks why Caypor had become a spy. Ashenden did not think it was for the money. He earned enough in his shipping office to cover his family expenses. During the war there was no lack of work for men over military age. He probably did it to gain some devious psychological satisfaction—fooling big-wigs who had not even heard of him. It could have been vanity, showing off his talents, or simply a perverse desire to do mischief.

Maugham stresses the mischievous aspect—scoring off big-wigs, getting a private laugh out of their discomfiture, enjoying a huge joke at the expense of others. Leonard in Amis's *The Anti-Death League* comes close to this but without the humour. It is the skill of a mastered discipline that fascinates him. He works out a philosophy of spying. We read a conversation between two officers engaged on Operation Apollo. Naidu is an Indian, the operation being directed at the Chinese which leads to co-operation with India. He is puzzled because Leonard says quite openly that he is looking for a spy. He is so engrossed in the expertise of the job he seems to forget its original characteristic, secrecy. Hunter explains Leonard's attitude.

> Apparently what's called the philosophy of phylactology —spy-catching to you—has been transformed. Keeping dead mum until the final pounce is old hat now. You go round saying how near you're getting and wait for somebody along the line to get anxious enough to show a break in their behaviour-pattern. The new method works better except with very brave spies and there are figures to prove that only nine per cent or something are that.

Leonard's cover is his appointment as a captain in the 17th Dragoons, but he gave strong periodic hints of his real job on the principle that a security system works best when the opposition know it to be at work and may react significantly to that knowledge. 'Many of the officers and men in the camp had heard that Leonard was not really a soldier at all but some sort of agent of military counter-intelligence assigned to prevent anyone outside from learning what No. 6 Headquarters Administration Battalion was actually up to.'

At first sight Caypor and Leonard seem to have little in common but in fact they both belong to the intelligentsia of espionage. It is neither greed nor lust nor idealism or any other emotional outlet that drives them but a sort of *furor academicus*. Each feels that espionage presents a problem demanding solution and each seeks to solve it by his wits and native intelligence. Caypor could still have felt that a spy was a spy in his own right but Leonard was operating in a period when a spy was more and more maintaining some kind of identity with the aid of the machine. There was still an emotional element in Caypor's decision but Leonard resembled the teacher who is not a teacher without his visual aids or a salesman who is not a salesman without his mini-computer. The human element is declining. Marcel d'Agneau takes advantage of this in his amusing *Eeny,Meeny, Miny,Mole*. The so-called Stationmaster is saddened by the gradual elimination of the personal. 'It was all satellites now, but a satellite couldn't tell you about the rumours, it wasn't an ear on the ground.' Now they had to rely on scraps tossed by the Americans, and most of these came through young Oosty's 'steamy affair' with a male secretary. The coming man was Simon Caw, because he was so heartless. His maxim was: Machines don't leak, discs do not play back to all comers for a few ounces of cocaine and a paltry thousand pounds strapped to the back of an instant blonde. His successors would become spies because they had been advised by a computer rating.

Or would they? Perhaps it is the mood engendered by reading too many spy-thrillers which play to the trendy gallery rather than consider agents as human beings under stress but still answering the basic human drives. Michael Burn in his *The Debatable Land* writes that 'individuals for a long time to come will take to spying out of greed, or revenge, or because the open paths of opposition bore them, or do not suit their ambitions, or from a passion for intrigue, or from any other private motive.' These at any rate are the major motives but they can be inextricably mixed.

15: SOMERSET MAUGHAM

The general reader may think automatically of John Buchan when the spy story is mentioned but to the professional spy writer Somerset Maugham is a kind of father-figure, as Wells was for Science Fiction and Zane Grey for the Western. Maugham's work (which simply means *Ashenden*, 1928) has a high degree of authenticity, which must be related to the fact that he worked in Intelligence in the first World War. It does not follow however that everyone who has been in Intelligence can write convincingly about it. McCormick quotes Ambler as saying that *Ashenden* was the 'first fictional work on the subject (the life of the secret agent) by a writer of stature with first-hand knowledge of what he is writing about.' Ashenden himself has another claim to fame, for he can be seen as the first of the anti-heroes, though he was never so unpleasant (and deliberately so) as later models.

One does not have to be a spy to know that these stories are the real thing. Maugham in fact destroyed fourteen unpublished stories after Winston Churchill had seen the manuscripts and informed him that they violated the Official Secrets Act. Ted Morgan, Maugham's biographer, says he anticipated the work of Ambler, Greene and Le Carré—in other words, the three writers who surpass all others for their fidelity to the world of espionage. Le Carré told Morgan that 'the Ashenden stories were certainly an influence on my work. I suppose Maugham was the first person to write about espionage in a mood of disenchantment and almost prosaic reality.' This is an interesting comment for, as has been noted, espionage had always been regarded as a cad's game which the demands of patriotism rendered acceptable. But in *Ashenden* it is shown to be a very sordid affair. The *Times Literary Supplement* reviewer made no bones about this (12 April 1928): 'Never before or since has it been so categorically demonstrated that counter-intelligence work consists often of morally indefensible jobs not to be undertaken by the squeamish or the conscience-stricken.' But the most emphatic accolade came from Raymond Chandler:

There are no other great spy stories—none at all. I have been
searching and I know. It's a strange thing. The form does not
appear so very difficult. Evidently it's impossible. There are
a few tales of adventure with a spying element or something
of the sort, but they always overplay their hand. Too much
bravura, the tenor sings too loud. They are as much like
Ashenden as the opera *Carmen* is like the deadly little tale that
Merimée wrote. (Maugham Papers in Humanities Research
Center, University of Texas at Austin, 13 January 1950).

The Spy

Maugham's first assignment as a secret agent during the first World
War was in Lucerne to investigate an Englishman who was living
there with a German wife. He used this incident in 'The Traitor', one
of the Ashenden stories. It is always tempting, and frequently unwise,
to identify the hero of fiction with the author. We are given additional
cause to do this with Maugham when we consider that the narrator in
Cakes and Ale was also called Ashenden. Anthony Curtis makes the
unflattering remark that Maugham 'was clever at spotting traitors
because he was himself an arch-traitor.' Curtis presumably meant to
his friends and acquaintances.

In 1917 Maugham was sent to Petrograd to report on the situation
in the early days of the Revolution. He cooperated there with the
Czech patriots. His work was not espionage but could be classed as
Intelligence. For example, he used codes, which is admission that the
information being passed is secret. He used to send dispatches to
William Wiseman in New York from the British Embassy, using a
cypher that was not known to the Embassy officials. (He called
himself Somerville, as in *Ashenden*, Masaryk was Marcus, Kerensky
was Lane, Lenin was Davis and Trotsky Cole.) This was before Lenin
seized power. Maugham sincerely believed that if he had gone six
months earlier the Bolshevik Revolution might have been averted!
The British Ambassador, Sir George Buchanan, was displeased by
Maugham's secrecy and David Bruce, the first secretary, passed the
information on to Maugham. The story 'His Excellency' drew on this
material. It is likely that most people believe that embassies are
naturally espionage centres. It is obvious that the Iranian students
held this view in the American hostage case. In the past this was rarely

true because embassies were contemptuous of espionage, especially as they on the whole suffered from it rather than operated it.

Most of the Ashenden stories were set in Switzerland. Geneva was a centre of intrigue, its hotels were full of nationals from every country in Europe, and even beyond. One of Ashenden's agents was a Bulgarian, to whom he had never spoken in Geneva! A little German prostitute, with the face of a doll, frequently journeyed along the lake up to Berne. Her bits of information were undoubtedly pondered over very seriously in Berlin.

Maugham one day realized that he was participating in what he used to call 'a shilling shocker'. He mentions this in *The Summing Up* (1938). He was taught how to throw persons who were following him off the track; how to conduct secret interviews with agents in unlikely places; how to convey messages in mysterious fashion; how to smuggle reports over a frontier. The result was that the war became unreal to him—in fact, it became the source of material for writing his fiction. He realized that there were some people who adapted to the unreality without difficulty; in one of the stories, for example, it appealed to Gomez's 'sense of the absurd to play a part in a shilling shocker'.

The way Maugham joined the Service sounds like an incident from Greene or Le Carré. Maugham wanted to contribute to the war effort. His wife, Syrie, arranged dinners with a man in Intelligence, whom Maugham found 'ordinary and middle class' (according to Morgan). This man (called R by Maugham) was the lover of one of Syrie's friends. Apparently R met Maugham largely to please his mistress—yet another motive for recruiting to the Service! The meeting took place in a red brick house with a For Sale notice. Here R (in fact, Sir John Wallinger) made the classic promise to Maugham: 'if you do well you'll get no thanks and if you get into trouble you'll get no help.' It is interesting to recall that Compton Mackenzie was recruited at about the same time and served in Greece and Syria. A novel called *Extremes Meet*, based on his espionage activities, appeared in 1928, the same year as *Ashenden*, which overshadowed it. Mackenzie was peeved as he didn't think much of Maugham's work.

One of Maugham's cherished principles was that one can get used to anything, including treachery. As a spy (although it would be more accurate to call him a go-between) he condemned people he had nothing against, turning very few hairs in the process, if any. He seems to have been well paid. According to his nephew Robin he was given a vast sum of money for his secret mission to Russia in 1917 'because they thought that I could stop the Bolshevik Revolution'. (I never cease to be amazed by the naivety of people who are immersed in politics.) The authorities thought the writer's life was excellent cover. Superficially, he went to Russia to write articles for the *Daily Telegraph*.

He found his stammer was a tremendous disadvantage. In *The Summing Up* he relates how Kerensky gave him a message for Lloyd George that was so secret it could not be written down. In London, however, he did write it down because he knew he would not be able to enunciate it. Lloyd George was in a hurry and merely glanced at the note. Maugham was naive enough to think that history might have been altered if he could have spoken!

In the second World War Maugham went to America and possibly felt history was repeating itself although in different surroundings. Britain was at war with Germany, Maugham could revive his espionage activities. Sir William Stevenson (the Man Called Intrepid) was head of the British Secret Service in America and indicated in a letter to Ted Morgan that Maugham was under his orders. He sounded less than enthusiastic about the old man's services. 'With regard to Somerset Maugham, he is typical of a problem we had . . . Quite a large number of volunteers in warfare against Nazism were loath to be known as part of any intelligence agency, arguing that their services were given in a period of desperate emergency. Few had much taste for the business and became involved because they saw no alternatives . . .' Not a very illuminating comment.

The Stories

Ashenden, or The British Agent is usually referred to as a volume of short stories but there is sufficient continuity to regard it as a loosely constructed novel. It is greatly admired by most spy writers because it is accurate, unsentimental and unpretentious. Most of the important aspects of the spy's life are illustrated and Maugham draws his conclusions in a way that would not be out of place in a spy's manual. For example, Ashenden made a few enquiries about the past of the Baroness von Higgins. He knew her private income did not permit her to live on the lavish scale she exhibited in Geneva. 'Since she had so many advantages for espionage, it was fairly safe to suppose that an alert secret service had enlisted her services . . .'

He stresses the absence of glamour in the spy's life, thus controverting the popular writers like Le Queux and Oppenheim. In fact, it was a monotonous existence.

The public thought espionage was an adventurous business. It was nothing of the kind. Ashenden lived the life of a senior clerk, paying wages, engaging staff, sending them out on projects, receiving information and going into France for a weekly conference and to receive orders from London. The work was necessary but boring.

The spy was called upon to do dirty work. If he objected to this he had better try something else. The Germans had blown up factories in Allied countries and there was no reason why the same should not be done to them. It was a legitimate act of war, it hindered the manufacture of arms and munitions, and it shook the morale of the non-combatants. 'It was not of course a thing that the big-wigs cared to have anything to do with. Though ready enough to profit by the activities of obscure agents of whom they had never heard, they shut their eyes to dirty work so that they could put their clean hands on their hearts and congratulate themselves that they had never done anything that was unbecoming to men of honour.' This attack on the politicians is much more effective than some of the shrill outbursts made by later writers.

When Herbatus, the Pole, wants to know if he should go ahead with the sabotage of a factory in Galicia, which would incidentally involve the death and mutilation of a good many Poles, R pretends to be indignant that such an idea would be put to him. It was the same with the suggested assassination of King B. It would have been a damned good thing for the Allies if he were put out of the way, but R himself couldn't possibly advocate such a measure. 'They were all like that', thought Ashenden. 'They desired the end but hesitated at the means. They were willing to take advantage of an accomplished fact, but wanted to shift on to someone else the responsibility of bringing it about.'

This volume of stories brings in most of the moral dilemmas encountered in espionage, which is probably why it is so warmly admired by those who want something more than invisible ink and stolen naval designs. Maugham is often charged with cynicism though I cannot understand how anyone could read *Ashenden* and hold this view. The stance Maugham takes seems to be admirable:

dirty work is done, and has to be done if there is to be espionage, and the writer must narrate it without surrendering to moral qualms. On the other hand, it is this very directness of narration which provokes feelings of compassion in the reader. But wherever Maugham is discussed there is the taste of sour grapes and perhaps of whatever fruit signifies bewilderment. For Maugham, like Evelyn Waugh, could be utterly objectionable and apparently inhuman and yet display immense understanding of his fellow-creatures.

Two stories in particular illustrate the extreme agony and heartbreak that the espionage situation can land one in. The most fearful alternatives are presented—usually between sacrificing oneself or betraying the loved one. 'Giulia Lazzari' is one example. The love of two people is used to destroy one of them, perhaps both, so far as any possible peace of mind is concerned. Ashenden's utterly rock-like avoidance of showing any signs of the compassion he must have felt is brilliantly portrayed. 'The Traitor' is another example. When Mrs Caypor finally realizes that she will never see her husband again, she is completely destroyed.

> She turned away, the tears streaming from her weary eyes, and for a moment she stood there like a blind man groping and not knowing which way to go. Then a fearful thing happened, Fritzi, the bull-terrier, sat down on his haunches and threw back his head and gave a long, long melancholy howl. Mrs Caypor looked at him with terror; her eyes seemed really to start from her head. The doubt, the gnawing doubt that had tortured her during those dreadful days of suspense, was a doubt no longer. She knew. She staggered blindly into the street.

This passage is as powerful and as terrible as the unforgettable last sentence in *The Spy Who Came in from the Cold*. It is an aspect of the Spy 'Game' that is rarely mentioned in fiction.

16: THE WORLD OF JOHN LE CARRÉ

Le Carré (born David John Moore Cornwell) attracted a serious readership because he provided relief from the unreality and snobbishness of the Bond books, and also gave a much more accurate interpretation of the rival Secret Services during the cold war period. He is one of the few spy writers who can be read as a novelist pure and simple—or, to put it in another way, he can be read and enjoyed by people who take no interest in espionage. He and Graham Greene, with whom he has a good deal in common, ring true in a way that Deighton, for example, for all his skill, does not. It is possible, however, to over-praise him. The note of doom and pessimism which floods his work may at times be too shrill. McCormick makes the interesting remark that his characters are so busy pretending to be different from their real selves that they make a career of deceiving people. He feels that Le Carré has over-reacted to a civilization's decline, 'that he is a kind of Solzhenitsyn in reverse'.

A Novelist, not just a Spy Writer

It is commonplace for reviewers, enthusing about the latest recruit to spy writing (and they come apace these days) to say that he has joined the 'Le Carré bracket'. It is hardly ever true. There is a sterile sameness about nearly all the spy writers of today. Le Carré has sometimes been accused of being 'too much like Greene'. This is in fact his strength: his best spy novels are also mainstream novels, not patchwork affairs. In any case, the criticism is an odd one. If each writer has to deploy a new originality and sensibility, then fiction will dry up. Only a very few are capable of doing this and we should be grateful when new writers imitate Greene rather than Harold Robbins.

Greene's major contribution to the novel, at least stylistically, has been his habit of describing people and their dilemmas obliquely. The head-on description of Bennett and Galsworthy suited an age of splendid certainties. Greene grew up in an age of doubt and expressed the general uncertainty by what can be called a tangential approach.

Any sensitive reader would note the change and numerous young writers would try to emulate it, just as they had tried to emulate Lawrence. But it requires a certain degree of genius—a lesser degree, perhaps, but still a sort of genius—to adopt and adapt the qualities of genius. Most imitators make a mess of imitation. One who did not was Eric Ambler. He assimilated part of Greene, especially the narrative, suspense part. Le Carré went further and appeared to appropriate the spirit of Greene. It would make a nice parlour game to decide who was responsible for the following quotation and others like it: 'The Major's accent slipped from time to time like a made-up tie.' It is Le Carré, in *The Looking-Glass War* (1965). Or this, from the same novel. Avery has helped build the index, which had originally meant nothing to him, whereas for Leclerc it was a beautiful structure. Avery 'could believe in it, like love'. It suggests the growth of love, from an inauspicious start. I repeat, this is not mere imitation. It is assimilation and it is always going on. It is how James Joyce developed out of Henry Fielding.

It has often been stated that Greene has made failure his major subject. He led the way to the anti-hero. Le Carré peoples his work with anti-heroes like Leamas and Smiley. This is not simply a vogue, it is an extremely accurate observation of the world we live in. There seems to have been a twist in the tragic event which Le Carré has chronicled. No longer is the tragic victim a Prince of Denmark or a King of Scotland; he is a little man, even at times an anonymous man, and he is tragic because Fate has obviously singled him out for destruction. It reflects the feeling of helplessness in the face of big guns—mass parties and atomic bombs, roaming psychopaths and soulless unions—that characterizes our age and society. Thus Bruce Merry, in his thoughtful *Anatomy of the Spy Thriller*, writes that 'Le Carré's thrillers are tragic novels precisely because the small fish which is ventured becomes sympathetic to the reader, shows unusual integrity and is then coldly sacrificed to the power game'. It is the unusual integrity that makes him worth the writer's trouble.

Most thriller writers like to pare their work to the thriller bone. (If they don't, one of the new breed of 'editors' in the publisher's office will do it for them!) It is interesting to note, however, that the one writer you might have expected to have done this, Ian Fleming, was in fact quite liberal with 'irrelevant' material about fishing, gold, gambling, plants and Creole accents. But Fleming's sales and reputation were so great he could afford to break the rules. These passages were really set-pieces and could have been transferred from book to book without comment from the reader. Le Carré, on the other hand, transcends the thriller. He bursts the bounds of the spy story, which is humanized in the process. Take Peter Guillam, Smiley's chief assistant, for instance. He lives with a strange girl named Camilla. She contributes nothing to the espionage story but she reminds the reader that people, real people, not just what Carlyle used to call 'similitudes', have errant emotions, strange quirks, rum feelings—that they are 'funny that way'. This familiar little phrase from the vernacular expresses the human essence perfectly, as the vernacular (with its aeons of experience!) usually does. Camilla is very quiet and undemonstrative, even in her love-making. As the search for the mole gets going Guillam's mind becomes more and more contorted and suspicious. Camilla is a spy! She's employed by the opposition! She's having an affair with her music teacher, a mystery man named Saul! Saul is an enemy agent! All of this is complete fantasy, of course. The 'realistic' phase in the novel did so much to weaken the realism of fantasy.

Le Carré also has superb descriptive power, especially of a decaying world. Whether the reader agrees with his interpretation or not, it's what he sees. His description of a decayed holiday area, near the East German border, with its rotting boats and broken jetty, where Smiley found Otto's dead body in *Smiley's People* (1979) is one of the most striking in modern fiction. Over a wide canvas its horrifying brutality by Karla's men is contrasted with Karla's own sentimentality in his private affairs. The people who gather to watch Smiley as he investigates are dehumanized and pitilessly violent. They know what has happened but not one of them is prepared to intervene. 'They were police', one woman called out. 'When police go about their business it is the duty of the citizen to keep his trap shut'. An old man says, 'He was scum. They all are. Look at them. Polacks, criminals, subhumans.' Two boys dressed in jeans and black boots studded with love-daisies beat the lid of Smiley's boot with hammers. They demand money for repairs. Finally one breaks off a windscreen wiper. 'Smiley looked at the boy's face and saw no human instinct that he understood'. The desperation and hopelessness that caught the reading world's fancy in *The Spy Who Came in from the Cold* (1963) are back again, but they have spread from mere espionage through to the uncommitted world.

If all Le Carré's writing were on this level we would soon cease to admire it and regard it as a trick. In *The Honourable Schoolboy* (1977) the tone is lightened by a kind of residual romanticism which seems to fight within him as well as within society. But this novel is also remarkable for its organization. There is a point at which it falters (the meetings with Marshall and Ricardo, not in the writing, which is always excellent, but in the clarity that has to be maintained in the midst of complexity.) But the complexity is valid for it is of the situation and not imposed by the author's desire to mystify. It is an organic complexity, not super-added.

Le Carré adopts a stance that is unusual among spy writers. He writes as if the case is known, is even historical, only he is clearing up some of its darker corners. He corrects false impressions, refers to public anxieties. 'Certain people do still ask why no anxious word about Jerry's whereabouts had reached the Circus before take-off . . . Once more they look for ways of blaming Smiley.' Despite the obituary Fleming once wrote for Bond, I doubt if any serious reader ever believed that Bond had walked the earth. There is so much earnestness packed into Le Carré's writing, that there are probably quite a number of people who find Smiley as 'real' as William Whitelaw or Len Murray.

Le Carré proved everything he needed to prove in this book. In addition to his power of organizing a very complex story, his compassion (one of the major needs of the good novelist) had already been exhibited. In human terms what makes this novel outstanding is the fact that Jerry falls genuinely in love—real love, not the superficialities of Bonded sex or even the sincere yet unimpressive affirmations of Deighton or Freemantle. Le Carré manages to persuade the reader. There are probably times when he feels he would like to shake off the demands of espionage, find a theme that will give him the freedom of the mainline novelist. He obviously tried this in *The Naive and Sentimental Lover* (1971) but it was undermined by the intrinsic triviality of the characters. However well he writes a spy novel it will always appear to the reader (who is unwittingly brainwashed) to be on the periphery of human experience. But if you can forget labels like spy or crime or thriller you will realize that *The Looking-Glass War* is about human beings and not about agents or 'tecs or gunmen.

It is interesting to find Le Carré presenting an aristocratic hero in *The Honourable Schoolboy*, even if he is a very scruffy one. But this is entirely integral to his purpose. The day of the aristocrat is over yet there are aspects of it we may look back to with nostalgia. They not only sent poachers to Australia but they also established a code of good manners, or decent behaviour, among equals. Now we are all equal it is sad to find the behaviour of equals so frequently repulsive. Hannay would not have cared for Jerry Westerby but (like his creator) he was a man of considerable tolerance and would probably have recognized that Jerry was doing the best he could with what was left to him.

Antagonisms, rivalries and bitterness between British and Americans surface from time to time in all modern spy writing. The Americans ratted on Suez (according to the Establishment) and the British ratted on Vietnam. The Americans also felt they were entitled to a large degree of mistrust due to the shortcomings of British security, which leaked so much more than American. There is no writing in modern fiction which compares in emotional force with the episode where an American officer vents his bitterness, humiliation and sense of utter desertion on Jerry after the pull-out from Vietnam. Once again, Le Carré is writing about what was conceived as the most complete moral delinquency. The American thought he was defending civilization. The British had callously deserted him. We get the other side of the story in *Soldier No More*, by Anthony Price. Bill Ballance gives Captain Roche the low-down on Suez. That was when it was the Americans who betrayed their allies. Eden and Mollet knew the Russians were bluffing, with Hungary on their hands. 'What Eden really *needed* to know was not what the Russians would do, but what the Americans would do—our friends and allies—not Mr K., but John Foster Dulles and Dwight D. Eisenhower.'

Certainly betrayal is the hallmark of modern espionage to an extent unknown in the days of Hannay. And Le Carré is its chronicler.

Things Fall Apart . . .

In an interview with Miriam Gross published in *The Observer* ('The Secret World of John Le Carré', 3 February 1980) Le Carré said that no middle way is permissible these days and that it is necessary to commit oneself one way or the other. Smiley 'has a sense of decency but he's not sure where to invest it.' The use of the word 'decency' is Orwellian. Later in the interview Le Carré said he always voted Socialist but wished he could vote Social Democrat. There is a good deal of political history embedded in this remark. Like Orwell, and like more and more people since Orwell, Le Carré wishes to support the traditional decency that had always been the hallmark of Socialism. Socialism demanded decent treatment for those who had rarely had it. It has been a cruel irony that this century has spawned numerous perversions of the Socialist ideal, whether they call themselves Communist or Trotskyite, Militant or simply 'the Left', but all making use of the Socialist name and confusing large numbers of voters into the bargain.

Le Carré illustrates this whirlpool. He deals in treachery. Behind the treachery of the spies and the agents and the double agents (no matter how 'honest' they are they are trained in deception) lies the duplicity of our political life. Treachery is like an ineradicable stain. Its stigma can never be removed. Even men who had undergone a complete ideological reversal, who had found a new creed and had managed, alone and compelled by the internal power of their convictions, to betray their calling, their families and their countries—even they had to struggle against the stigma. 'Even they wrestled with the almost physical anguish of saying that which they had been trained never, never to reveal. Like apostates who feared to burn the Cross, they hesitated between the instinctive and the material.' (*The Spy Who Came in From the Cold*). Peters, who interrogates Leamas after his 'defection', is aware of this.

In this, the novel which made his name, Le Carré gives a depressing picture of post-war Berlin. It is not a tourist's picture, it is the one that lies behind the political exterior.

At first the city was full of second-rate agents. You could recruit one at a cocktail party, brief him over dinner and lose him by breakfast. It was a chaotic situation—too many agencies, too much penetration by the other side, too little space. By 1956 every Service department demanded high-grade intelligence which the agencies could not supply. They had to wait three years to get it.

The wages of treachery is very often death, and death can occur in numerous ironical ways. Life's little ironies, Hardy would have called them, but these are very deadly ironies. Think of *The Honourable Schoolboy*, with its public school title ('Well played, our side!' Sandy cried as he and Hannay outwitted and outfought the foreign scoundrels) and think of the nastiness that is revealed when the school cap is taken off. Frost: tortured and killed for helping Jerry, who had blackmailed him. Luke: killed in mistake for Jerry. Jerry: shot dead by his own side in the person of the hired killer, Fawn. Another author has resuscitated Flashman, the cad, as a worthy hero of our time. But Le Carré is not joking: Flashman really is making the grade these days.

Who, or what, sends out the agents? A decaying Empire. There are no real complaints today in an extraordinary world where the only people to practise nineteenth century imperialism, while covering the name with vituperation, are the Soviet oligarchs. But where the imperialism has gone there seems to have been nothing to take its place. It should have been Socialism but Socialism has been betrayed. Imperialism had a faith, and it was not a bad one for its time—those who trouble to read Marx's *Communist Manifesto* will understand what a worthy achievement it was in the historical process. So there is a vacuum. Instead of faith there is doubt, and doubt very soon attacks the individual himself. Once you begin to doubt the faith you once held you very soon begin to doubt your own personal worth. And because this situation cannot be allowed to last long a new emotion rushes in —it isn't really important what it is so long as it provides a vehicle for injured feelings. In our case it has been envy and fear of America.

Le Carré doesn't lecture. He reveals all through his characters. In *The Honourable Schoolboy* Craw gave a talk at Sarratt, the agents' training school. He told his audience about a half-caste agent in Hong Kong. She worked for the Circus. But who did she *think* she was working for?

For her the Circus was like a father. It was a kind of St. George, purging overseas Chinese communities. It broke the Triads, the rice cartels, the opium gangs, child prostitution. It had the interest of all *good* Chinese at heart. Part of her knew it was nonsense, but it was a pretence that served both her and the Circus. The faith might be crackpot but it would be folly to despise it. The Circus has precious little else to offer.

It's not an easy job, finding people to instil faith from a community that has largely lost it. And beyond that, instilling faith in qualities that you yourself no longer believe in! Smiley requires *will* from his fieldmen. But are you likely to find will among people who see doubt as a legitimate philosophical posture? Such people like to think of themselves as being in the middle, performing a skilled and necessary balancing act. Smiley doesn't believe this. In the middle is nowhere. No battle was ever won by spectators and he thinks there's a battle that needs winning. But what is the battle? 'Our present war began in 1917, with the Bolshevik Revolution. It hasn't changed yet' (*The Honourable Schoolboy*.) This is probably the reason why the spy novel did not reach flood proportions in 1910 or in 1933 but waited until the fifties. There was virtually no investigative spying to be done against Imperial Germany or Nazi Germany—they were obvious enemies and when there was spying it usually concerned those ubiquitous submarine designs. It was when Soviet Russia betrayed the hopes of Socialism that it became clear that the enemy was partly inside the gates, and an espionage situation was set up. Of course, the Soviet betrayal began very soon after the Revolution but in the early days it was not important. It signified disappointment, not danger. But treachery could still exist on a wide scale because some people rejected the disappointment and pretended the situation that caused it did not exist. The number of people who were prepared to commit treason on behalf of Germany at any time has been small because Germany has never projected an acceptable ideology.

The Honourable Schoolboy is an impressive novel because it describes this climate through the disarray of Smiley's Circus. The defection of Haydon had put the whole network at risk—it was in disgrace and was put out of action. Agents were called in, many paid off, some killed off before they could escape. 'They were stood down and not spoken of again. To injustice belongs injustice! Though tarnished, they might have been useful, but Smiley would not hear their names; not then, not later; not ever. Of the immediate post-fall period, that was the lowest point. There were those who seriously believed—inside the Circus as well as out—that they had heard the last beat of the secret English heart.' Smiley's instinct was to get rid of everything—the safe houses, for example, for they were no longer safe; Sarratt, the training school; the experimental audio laboratories in Harlow; the chemistry outfit in Argyll; the small-boat section in the Helford estuary; and the radio transmission base at Canterbury. They all had to go. He even wanted to do away with the code-breaking place in Bath but Lacon of the Cabinet Office persuaded him not to be so drastic. He pointed out that 'these outstations are gilt-edged stock.' Nevertheless, the Circus had pulled out of Hong Kong, Bangkok, Singapore, Saigon, Tokyo, Manila and Djakarta and Seoul—even Taiwan was depleted. 'A hoods' Dunkirk', Craw called it. The circus appeared to be broken. It was shorn of three-quarters of its staff, the networks had been blown to smithereens, leaving just 'a few old biddies to brew up tea'. Operational accounts (the 'reptile fund') were frozen by the Treasury. It sounds like a paraphrase of the Old Country.

Espionage and Ideology

Le Carré articulated a kind of credo for Miriam Gross that would probably be echoed by many of his contemporaries.

> If I knew exactly where I stood I wouldn't write. I do believe, reluctantly, that we must combat Communism. Very decisively. Of course, our own engagement in the cold war is a rather well-kept British secret. I don't think many British people are aware of the extent to which we are harnessed to the anti-Communist effort. Perhaps Mrs Thatcher is making us more aware of it.
>
> That doesn't mean I necessarily think that the goodies are all on one side and the baddies on the other. I detest dogma, institutionalized prejudice, even party politics. And even if the baddies *were* all on one side, I think Smiley is far too aware of the element of humanity in everybody to be able to hate them as they perhaps should be hated.

From the very beginning, or at least from *The Spy Who Came in from the Cold*, Le Carre's work has been full of political implication. Many other spy writers also make their political views known but nearly always at a much more superficial, daily-press level than Le Carré. He knows that the views a man wears on his shirt-front may not be what he really believes at all. Ideology can be a badge as meaningless as those that used to be worn so casually by teenagers—it was the badge that was important, not the message. When Leamas (in *The Spy Who Came in from the Cold*) was approached with an invitation to defect there was a progression in quality and authority which seemed axiomatic in the hierarchy of an intelligence network. 'It was, he suspected, a progression in ideology. Ashe, the mercenary, Kiever the fellow traveller, and now Peters, for whom the end and the means were identical.' Control told Leamas they would want to deal with a man they had bought. It was no good pretending ideology, they didn't want that. 'They want the clash of opposites, Alec, not some half-cock convert.'

Fiedler wanted to know something about the philosophy of the people at the Circus. This was a difficult question for Leamas. 'What do you mean, a philosophy? We're not Marxists, we're nothing, just people.' Fiedler couldn't understand this. People needed a philosophy to make them act. If they hadn't one, what was the justification for their work? 'The *Abteilung* and the organizations like it are the natural extension of the Party's arm. They are in the vanguard of the fight for Peace and Progress. They are to the Party what the Party is to Socialism: they *are* the vanguard.' The wardress who accompanies Liz to and from the tribunal has no doubts whatsoever. The prisoners are spies, and she knows they are spies because the Party says so. There is a combination of complete confidence and ignorance. At the end Leamas says it was a 'foul operation, but it's paid off and that's the only rule.' When Liz complains about the inhumanity of such an operation, he goes for her. 'What the hell are you complaining about? Your Party's always at war, isn't it? Sacrificing the individual to the mass. That's what it says. Socialist reality: fighting night and day—the relentless battle —that's what they say, isn't it? At least you've survived. I never heard that Communists preached the sanctity of human life.'

It is obviously a very muddled situation. Smiley (or Le Carré) tries to make sense of it, to find a way through the maze, by distinguishing between ideology and philosophy. Ideology is largely a matter of unquestioned and unchanging ends, and it is governed by strict authority; philosophy means looking straight at life and deciding, as an individual and with only individual sanction, what steps to take. The purpose and task of an Intelligence service, said Smiley, was not to play chess games but to deliver intelligence to its customers. If it failed to do this, those customers would resort to other, less scrupulous sellers or, worse, indulge in amateurish self-help. In *The Observer* interview Le Carré, after listing his literary influences as Greene, Conrad, Balzac, Wodehouse and Conan Doyle, said that 'the strongest literary influence was all that German literature that I devoured either compulsorily or voluntarily.' Which reminds one of the similar German literary influence admitted by Somerset Maugham, Le Carré's most distinguished predecessor in spy writing and of the conviction, expressed by both Maugham and Smiley, that the philosophical approach was the only valid one in human relations. In normal everyday language I think this means that you should always have a clear idea why you are doing what you are doing. This measures the distance between Smiley and Bond, who was virtually a robot activated by a writer named Fleming or a bureaucrat named M, whichever way you look at him.

Le Carré's agents are professionals and his subject is treachery. There had been a time when the Secret Service was the preserve of young men of good family recruited while still at one of the old universities. In the early *Call for the Dead* (1961) the whole nature of Smiley's work had been changed by NATO and American insistence. It was no longer a relaxed, amateur business, conducted over a glass of port. The efficiency of highly qualified, under-paid men had been replaced by bureaucratic efficiency and official intrigue.

The point that had to be learnt was that overt patriotism was no defence against treachery. Generations of Englishmen had been brought up to believe that an Englishman's word is his bond, that he will always play up, play up and play the game and that never under any circumstances would he fail his King and country. The lower classes would, of course, do all these things. But something odd happened to human nature, or at least English human nature, for quite suddenly these things were no longer true. (It is significant that C.P. Snow's single essay into espionage fiction was called *The New Men*. The treachery in this novel, however, does not belong to the Maclean–Philby–Blunt social area.) Indeed, there was a suspicion that things had even been reversed, that the young man who had not been to a Public School might be more dependable than one who had. Buchan could not have believed this, nor could Oppenheim or Le Queux, and it is extremely doubtful if Fleming could. But Le Carré knew it, and so did dozens of new spy writers belonging to his generation. Leamas in *The Spy Who Came in from the Cold* is one of the new men. He waits for a definite approach from the other side. He has prepared the ground carefully. He knows the kind of obstacles that might be encountered. They would expect him, for instance, to be afraid for 'his Service pursued traitors as the eye of God followed Cain across the desert.'

They would know the whole thing was a gamble. The best-laid plan can be shattered; cheats, liars and criminals could resist the most attractive offers and respectable gentlemen could stoop to the most appalling treasons for no convincing reason.

One thinks of Maclean. Le Carré gives us Haydon. Bill Haydon, the Circus traitor, who spied for the Russians and carried on a love affair with Smiley's Ann. The authentic mingling of private and public is something at which Le Carré excels. Others try to master this area but they do it gauchely, sticking on pieces at intervals to show their story is part of real life and not simply invention. But it needs a special skill. Ann wants to come back to Smiley, or says she does in *Smiley's People*: 'To be together again, as she sometimes called it. To forget the hurts, the list of lovers; to forget Bill Haydon, the Circus traitor, whose shadow still fell across her face each time he reached for her, whose memory he carried in him like a constant pain. Bill his friend, Bill the flower of their generation, the jester, the enchanter, the iconoclastic informer; Bill the born deceiver, whose quest for the ultimate betrayal led him into the Russians' bed, and Ann's.'

How can one have a sense of triumph in such a world? It may not be easy to win over the traitor at first. He may have remarkable powers of resistance. But when he finally gives way there may be no stopping him. The secrets may pour out as from a burst dyke. When Grigoriev finally decided to cooperate he enjoyed the 'luxury' of one confession so much that he was eager to follow with others. Success for Smiley! He must be radiant with joy. And then Karla, his great opponent, walks across the bridge and defects to the West. 'George, you won', said Guillam as they walked slowly towards the car. 'Did I?' said Smiley, 'Yes. Yes, well, I suppose I did', and the novel ends. He had achieved his purpose. He knew, more than anyone, the degraded ingredients that went to make up his victory: the ruthlessness employed in catching Karla, and the awareness that it was only possible because Karla was a victim of the weakness of love. Smiley knew how that felt.

The Man Smiley

When Sir Maurice Oldfield died on 11 March 1981 *The Guardian* reported that he was said to be the model for Le Carré's Smiley and Ian Fleming's M. They obviously thought he was a chameleon. In *The Observer* interview Le Carré denied the Smiley identification. He sounded rather weary of the subject, as well he might, for nothing is more stupid in literary discussion than the eternal search for models. There was no truth in the rumour, said Le Carré. 'I have said this repeatedly and it has made absolutely no difference: the Press believes what it wants to believe.' If you can pin a fictional character to a living person, there is no need to decide what kind of a person the character is. You point at the living man and say: That's he.

George Smiley appears, although sometimes peripherally, in all Le Carré's novels except *The Naive and Sentimental Lover*. 'Short, fat and of a quiet disposition, he appeared to spend a lot of money on really bad clothes, which hung about his squat frame like skin on a shrunken toad' (*Call for the Dead*, 1961). He was once likened to 'a bullfrog in a sou'wester'. Next year, in *A Murder of Quality* (1962) Miss Brimley used to think of him as 'the most forgettable man she had ever met; short and plump, with heavy spectacles and thinning hair, he was at first sight the very prototype of an unsuccessful middle-aged bachelor in a sedentary occupation.' The last paragraph of *Call for the Dead* shows Smiley on the midnight plane to Zurich.

> Smiley presented an odd figure to his fellow-passengers—a little, fat man, rather gloomy, suddenly smiling, ordering a drink. The young, fair-haired man beside him examined him closely out of the corner of his eye. He knew the type well—the tired executive out for a bit of fun. He found it rather disgusting.'

The best spy does not call attention to himself. But there is also a concealed comment here on a social change that has occurred since the war. More and more ordinary people have adopted an outrageous appearance, perhaps as compensation for their failure to make a creative or intellectual or administrative mark. Fifty years ago it was the odd character who dressed oddly—now he often takes refuge in apparent sobriety. The quoted paragraph also contains a sharp dig at the knowingness of those people, frequently journalists, who categorize the human race and then apply facile labels. This wouldn't matter if it were not the reflection of many political and social attitudes which appear to be taken seriously in some quarters.

Smiley's favourite relaxation was not golf or sharpshooting or military history but reading lesser German poets. 'Some time in the twenties when Smiley had emerged from his unimpressive school and lumbered blinking into the murky cloisters of his unimpressive Oxford College, he had dreamed of Fellowships and a life devoted to the literary obscurities of seventeenth century Germany' (*Call for the Dead*). Sometimes these interests would intrude into his daily routine, as when he felt tempted to tell the policeman, Mendel, how he had wrestled with Goethe's metamorphoses of plants and animals in the hope of discovering, like Faust, 'what sustains the world at its inmost level'. He also wanted to explain why it was impossible to understand nineteenth century Europe without a working knowledge of the naturalistic sciences . . .

Smiley is what some people call faceless. The face is so dull, so uninteresting, it isn't really a face at all. The young man on the plane, who apparently has a sturdy and biassed idea of business men, knows Smiley for what he is—or should be, according to the conventional wisdom. But Toby Esterhase knows exactly what the style implies and how essential it is for the job in hand. Flamboyance will not get results in this trade. 'Smiley's faceless style, his manner of regretful bureaucratic necessity, were by now not merely established, they were perfected: Grigoriev had adopted them wholesale, with philosophic, and very Russian, pessimism' (*Smiley's People*). In other words, Smiley doesn't get results by bullying or browbeating but by establishing a mood of inevitability which his victim feels obliged to adopt. In the end Griegoriev becomes quite relaxed and even jovial, and volunteers information before he is asked. Really a very jolly type of interrogation. You'd have to be an awful kind of bounder to reject it.

The Reverse Image

The reflected image is immensely important in European culture. One thinks of Narcissus, of Velazquez's *Venus and Cupid*, *The Arnolfinis* by van Eyck, *Alice Through the Looking-Glass*—each of these bears a comment on itself and takes the reader or viewer to a deeper level of perception. I feel that *The Looking-Glass War* performs a similar action in the limited field of espionage fiction. It is the most desperate and despairing of all Le Carré's works. It is his most thoughtful comment on the world he is describing.

This is not the Circus at work. It is an outfit run by a man named Leclerc and they are a gang of bunglers, utterly amateur and inefficient. Most of them had served together in the war and nostalgic, sentimental memories of their war service hang over the novel like a cloud. The title expresses this: their espionage is a kind of reverse image of wartime action. All the time they try to create situations as close to a war atmosphere as possible. But there is a big

difference in the result: the war was the last time the British
population could be proud of what they were doing. Since then there
has been defeat, treachery and dishonesty paraded as ideology.

There is a club near Charing Cross where the survivors meet and
indulge in their nostalgia, laced with crummy jokes.

> Woodford glanced round the bar and asked quietly, a note
> of mystery in his voice, 'What did dad do in the war?'
>
> A bewildered silence. They had been drinking for some
> time.
>
> 'Kept Mum, of course', said Major Dell uncertainly and
> they all laughed.
>
> Woodford laughed with them, savouring the conspiracy,
> reliving the half-forgotten ritual of secret mess nights
> somewhere in England.
>
> 'And where did he keep her?' he demanded, still in the
> same confiding tone: this time two or three voices called in
> unison, 'Under his blooming hat!'
>
> They were louder, happier.

John Avery is odd man out. He is younger and never knew the war.
Haldane dislikes him intensely, probably for this reason, feeling he's
an intruder. Leclerc speaks kindly to Avery: 'You didn't fight in the
war, John. You don't understand how these things take people. You
don't understand what real duty is.' Avery is apologetic.

Leclerc is possibly clinically insane. When the project of putting a
man into East Germany fails miserably, every possible mistake has
been made, virtually no information has been obtained, and the man
himself has been caught and will certainly be executed, Avery cannot
control his tears. But Leclerc immediately moves to what he
obviously thinks are highly urgent matters: 'There's something else I
want to discuss with you, Adrian—Smiley, you won't mind this, I'm
sure, you're practically one of the family—the question of Registry.
The system of library files is really out of date. Bruce was on to me
about it just before I left. Poor Miss Courtney can hardly keep pace. I
fear the answer is more copies . . . top copy to the case officer,
carbons for information. There's a new machine on the market,
cheap photostats, threepence halfpenny a copy . . .'

The astute reader is not surprised. The very idea of putting a man
into East Germany excited Leclerc immensely. It is clear that he is not
really concerned with the purpose; the important thing for him is that

there is an enemy and they are going to score some points in the Great Game. He can hardly contain himself. He babbles like a man possessed.

> We're putting a man in. The Minister's given his consent. We go to work at once. I want to see Heads of Sections first thing tomorrow. Adrian, I'll give you Woodford and Avery. Bruce, you keep in touch with the boys; get on to the old training people. The Minister will support three-month contracts for temporary staff. No peripheral liabilities, of course. The usual programme: wireless, weapon training, cyphers, observation, unarmed combat and cover. Adrian, we'll need a house. Perhaps Avery could go into that when he comes back. I'll approach Control about documentation; the forgers all went over to him. We'll want frontier records for the Lübeck area, refugee reports, details of minefields and operations.

All very impressive, and no doubt these are the things that must be done—but Leclerc lives in the past and is determined to organize it like a wartime operation.

When Leiser goes in he takes Polish shoes, because the East Germans import them—but they are new and this is noticed when he arrives. There is enormous attention to detail. In his wallet he carries an identity card, fingered and stamped, an authority to travel and a written offer of employment from the State Co-operative for shipbuilding in Rostock. He has a food registration card, a driving licence, a Party card, the photograph of a woman, some love letters. He has a Union card and a cutting from a Magdeburg newspaper about production figures at a local engineering plant and a tattered testimonial from a former employer. Then there were the odds and ends which Hartbeck (Leiser's assumed name) would plausibly have about him: a bunch of keys on a chain, a comb, a khaki handkerchief stained with oil, a couple of ounces of substitute coffee in a twist of newspaper, a screwdriver, a length of fine wire, some fragments of metal newly turned—'the meaningless rubble of a working man's pockets.' But Leiser makes every conceivable mistake. He is certainly the wrong man for the job. But he was not chosen for his suitability; he was chosen for his membership of a wartime companionship.

Just before Leiser left, Leclerc gave him a final briefing, especially about his assumed identity. 'There is just one thing that *I* might add about cover. Never *volunteer* information. People don't *expect* you to explain yourself. If you are cornered, play it by ear. Stick as closely to the truth as you can. Cover should never be *fabricated* but only an extension of the truth.' And with this excellent advice, culled from the training manual. Leiser goes out into the looking-glass world, where he will always mistake right for left and forget to scuff his shiny shoes.

The Mole

Le Carré popularized the mole who burrowed from within. Although he is usually associated with *Tinker, Tailor, Soldier, Spy* (1974) he makes his first appearance in *Call for the Dead.* Samuel Fennan of the Foreign Office is interrogated by Smiley after being accused in an anonymous letter.

Fennan had naturally been Left Wing at Oxford. There seemed no choice: the rise of Fascism, the Japanese in Manchuria, Franco in Spain, the American slump and the wave of anti-semitism sweeping across Europe, what else could he do but join the Party? Intellectuals were convinced that the Communists were the only people who could turn the tide. It turned out that Fennan was not a spy but was married to one. This virtually turned him into a Mole, even if an unconscious one.

It's no easy matter, unmasking a Mole. Lacon pointed this out in *Tinker, Tailor.* If the Mole operated inside the Circus, as he apparently did, how were they to find him? 'We can't interrogate, we can't take steps to limit a particular person's access to delicate secrets. To do any of these things would be to run the risk of alarming the mole. It's the oldest question of all, George. Who can spy on the spies? Who can smell out the fox without running with him?' Imagine, for instance, that the person chosen to smell out the fox was the fox himself! For fox, of course, read mole.

The only clues seemed to be contained in the homosexual pink tie-up. The careers of Burgess, Maclean and Blunt substantiate this. In *Tinker, Tailor* doubts were expressed about Prideaux, especially his time at Oxford. They were dismissed by Lacon. 'We're all entitled to be a bit pink at that age.' But Prideaux and Haydon 'were really very close indeed.' The Oxford don Fanshawe had been a talent-spotter for the Circus. He recommended Haydon, who was True Blue until Suez when he changed sides, not because the action was wrong, but because Britain's weakness was shown up. Haydon recommended Prideaux, whom he found 'irresistible', to Fanshawe. Haydon's suspected homosexuality was confirmed by the girl he was living with at the time of his unmasking. He was having an affair with a sailor.

When *Tinker, Tailor* was dramatized for television there was a tremendous brouhaha about the Mole, who he was, and how he operated, which was never generated by the book. Le Carré himself obviously had enormous fun out of all this nonsense and wrote a mocking letter to *The Guardian* in which he said there had never been a Mole and that all the errors of British Intelligence could be traced to the incompetence of Control. This is certainly not the place to revive the controversy. It is, however, the place to declare that this is not one of Le Carré's better books. It was over-sensational in a way that Le Carré usually avoided.

The opening, especially, where Prideaux is throwing watchers and followers off the scent, would have been acceptable in a Bond novel but falls below what we expect from Le Carré. Prideaux said it was easy to throw off tails. The security services which organized the tails knew next to nothing about street watching, probably because no administration in living memory had to feel shy about it. He realized that he was being watched by three women, one pushing a pram, another with a red plastic handbag and the third walking a dog on a lead. Ten minutes later he saw two others, arm in arm. You can always pick up watchers, even when they change their garments—they haven't time to change footwear. When he saw these women again, their top clothes had changed but their shoes were the same. Prideaux was in Prague and was catching a train for Brno, but it was cancelled. He took a football train which stopped at every station. There were watchers (or hoods) at every station. 'If there's one thing that distinguishes a good watcher from a bad one it's the gentle art of doing damn all convincingly.' In Brno they were working teams of seven on foot. Overall direction came from a green van. The cars could be detected because in one a woman's handbag had been carefully placed on the gloveboard and in the other a passenger sun visor had been needlessly turned down. Prideaux bought things in a store, stole a fur hat and white plastic raincoat, and a carrier bag to put them in. In the men's lavatory he pulled a white raincoat over his overcoat, stuffed the carrier bag in his pocket and put on the fur hat. Then he ran down the emergency staircase, down an alley, stuffed the white raincoat into a carrier bag and bought a black raincoat to replace the white.

Le Carré is just showing off here. Prideaux ran round a corner and went bang into the arms of Dr No—I mean Irma la Douce—no, wrong novel. The point is, none of Prideaux's antics here, apart from his eventual fate, is relevant to the plot of *Tinker, Tailor*. We read Le Carré for his psychology not for rousing Stevensonian adventure.

Agent Types

There is an impressive cast of characters in Le Carré's work. The weakness of most genre novels is the flatness and predictability of their characters. When this is avoided the author scores a triumph. Dorothy Sayers managed to create a living character out of Lord Peter Wimsey and the public took to him. Many people feel that Conan Doyle did the same for Sherlock Holmes, leading to the greatest success ever recorded in the history of the genre novel. Smiley should join this gallery. But he is not the only one who can transmit the sense of reality. In *The Honourable Schoolboy*, the most comprehensive of all his novels, we are presented with a Group of Five who discussed strategy in the 'rumpus' room. There was, of course, Smiley. Then there was 'his cupbearer', Peter Guillam. 'Big, flowing Connie Sachs, the Moscow-gazer' progressively saddens the reader in her decline. Doc di Salis was known as 'the Mad Jesuit, the Circus's head China-watcher.' And last, least and least likeable was Fawn, 'the dark-eyed factotum, who wore black gym-shoes and manned the Russian-style copper samovar and gave out biscuits'—and was also a vicious killer.

I have already discussed Smiley at some length but we still have not discovered why this nondescript little man impressed acquaintances so much, and still impresses the reader. The truth came to Jerry when it dawned on him that 'he was talking not from the textbook but from experience: that this owlish little pedant with the diffident voice and the blinking, apologetic manner had sweated out three years in some benighted German town, holding the threads of a very respectable network, while he waited for the boot through the door panel or the pistol butt across the face that would introduce him to the pleasures of interrogation.' And Smiley had once explained his dilemma to Peter Guillam: 'To be inhuman in the defence of our humanity, harsh

in defence of compassion, single-minded in defence of our disparity.'
Life seen in a mirror, in fact.

Smiley wondered, in a letter written to his estranged wife, Ann,
how he had ever got into his present position. Looking back, he
believed it had been the best way to serve his country. In those days
the enemy had been clear and obvious. But things had changed, now
life had to be interpreted in terms of conspiracy. Sometimes he felt
terrified. But if he was stabbed in the back he would at least know that
it was the judgement of his peers. Smiley in fact represents a
generation. It is a generation that was compelled to adjust to
uncertainty, treachery and second-rateness. The situation is too
bewildering for him or anyone else to say exactly how it has arrived;
the only certainty is that it is there. Has it in fact been a subtle kind of
Americanization? Smiley, who is very tolerant, hated Americanisms
but not Americans. He knew it was possible to tolerate the man who
possessed intolerable qualities; that it is possible to respect the
Fascist, despite his violence, or the Left Winger, despite his treachery.
If anyone used an Americanism in his presence he would look pained
or puzzled and perhaps ask for an explanation. For example, if he
heard such expressions as 'meet with' or 'snafu' he would react with
bristling irritation, beneath it the suspicion that he was being got at.

But Smiley was his own man. He was certainly not a typical agent.
Some people were agents from birth, congenital agents. Craw used to
give a talk that he entitled *Agents Who Recruit Themselves.* They were
appointed to their work 'by the period of history, the place, and their
own natural dispositions. In their cases it was simply a question of
who got to them first . . . Whether it's us; whether it's the opposition;
or whether it's the bloody missionaries.' Phoebe was an example.
'Codename Susan toiled and span and she was worth a little less each
day, because agents are only ever as good as the target they're pointed
at . . .' Sarratt, the training centre, was clear on the point. 'They have
a very worldly and relaxed attitude to the motives of a fieldman, and
no patience at all for the fiery-eyed zealot who grinds his teeth and
says "I hate Communism".' If he hates it that much, they argue, he's
most likely in love with it already. What they really like—and what
Jerry possessed, what he *was*, in effect—was the fellow who hadn't a
lot of time for flannel but loved the service and knew—though God
forbid that he should make a fuss of it—that *we* were right. *We* being a
necessarily flexible notion, but to Jerry it meant Smiley and that was
that.

And then there was the other kind of agent, the defector, the man who had come in from the other side, the biggest headache in the whole business. Was he genuine? How could he best be used? Modern spy literature bristles with defectors but, as usual, it is Le Carré who really goes to the heart of the defector situation. (It must be admitted, however, that some very sensitive work has been done on the British defector, ebbing his life away in Moscow, by various writers, among them Greene, Bennett and Alan Williams.) *The Honourable Schoolboy*, which touches all the major aspects of the spy's experience, includes the defector in its haul. What, for instance, would happen to Nelson Ko, who was being picked up: 'stateless, homeless, a fish to be devoured or thrown back into the sea at will.' It is a striking and accurate metaphor. Ko was not really a defector but he would be interrogated, probably taken back across the border for hasty *recycling*, as the Sarratt jargon called it—'quick before they notice he has left home'. But suppose they didn't push him back, suppose they kept him? 'Then after the years of his debriefing—two, three even—he had heard some ran for five—Nelson would become one more Wandering Jew of the spy trade, to be hidden, and moved again, and hidden, to be loved not even by those to whom he had betrayed his trust.' It is not surprising that the defector, who is always welcomed triumphantly by the press and the innocent, should be seen by Le Carré to be often nothing but a huge embarrassment. It may be pleasant to know that the rival régime lacks charm for so many of its citizens, but this is not sufficient reason for supporting them in large numbers. Spy writers in general recognize the unhappiness of the average defector.

18: GRAHAM GREENE

Like Maugham, Greene is, for want of a better term, a 'mainline' novelist who has turned his hand to spy writing and has done it successfully. Such switches are not always happy ones, although the results in this area are not as disappointing as they are in, say, science fiction. Greene's influence has been profound. First of all, his unsentimental approach to some of the less attractive aspects of modern life, such as failure, has had considerable appeal for the more serious spy writers. It was his writing in general, not merely his spy writing, that impressed—in fact, his most ambitious spy novel, *The Human Factor* (1978), appeared between *The Honourable Schoolboy* and *Smiley's People*, that is, quite late in the Le Carré canon to date. And Le Carré is the spy writer who is most frequently related to Greene. Then another point that goes in Greene's favour is his early championship of Eric Ambler as someone worthy of attention. Ambler must be included in any count of the best spy novelists in English.

Greene worked in Intelligence (with Philby) during the war. He has infuriated some people by his sympathy with Philby and his apparent justification of Philby's defection. Philby shocked most people but Greene is not a person who is likely to be shocked by any external action. A large part of his fiction is devoted to describing how and why people behave in a way that others may consider false or treacherous. It is this tone that Le Carré has picked up so well. Another writer who served in Intelligence during the war is Malcolm Muggeridge. He never chose espionage as a subject for his fiction but he also felt the disenchantment with the contemporary world that is so evident in the work of the other two. Here, for instance, is a snatch of conversation from *Affairs of the Heart*, which appeared as early as 1949:

> 'Don't even your nostrils catch the stench of decay, everywhere and in everything?'
> 'Yes', she said, 'as a matter of fact, they do.'

One gets the feeling at times that Greene was specially created for an
espionage situation, one where no-one can trust anyone else.
Whereas most enlightened people these days are disgusted by the
record of the Soviet Union, Greene appears to go out of his way to
justify it. Evelyn Waugh thought this was just part of a vast master-
plan. In a letter to Ann Fleming, 5 September 1960, he wrote: 'I think
he is a secret agent on our side and all his buttering up of the Russians
is "cover".'

Apart from *Brighton Rock* (1938), Greene's fiction never fulfilled
its potentiality until *The Power and the Glory* (1940). Passages of deep
human understanding would alternate with others that were jejune
and superficial. *The Confidential Agent* (1939) was a conspiracy novel,
if not a spy novel, and was not one of his best, although Philby quoted
it with approval in *My Silent War* for the agent's choosing his side,
once and for all, and letting history judge. But it did highlight, long
before it became fashionable, the complete lack of trust that lies at the
heart of espionage. This is reiterated again and again. 'The one
person that you trusted was yourself.' 'Nobody trusts a confidential
agent.' And so on. But as a novel it suffers from Greene's early
portentousness. *The Ministry of Fear* (1943) was a wartime
production; it belongs to his lesser work (he called it an Entertainment, though this was never a satisfactory classification), and it
was definitely concerned with espionage. In it Greene makes a
statement that has been reiterated many times since: life today
imitates, not art, but the adventure story. This new perception first
arose during the war when people began to regard the surrealist
movement as prophetic. Reports of nuns floating down by parachute,
grasping automatic weapons, turned out to be untrue, but they were
widely believed, because this was exactly the kind of thing we might
expect. And today one hears repeated, again and again, the
conviction that the extraordinary things that happen in thrillers do
actually happen in the 'real', non-fictional world.

Arthur Rowe accidentally gets involved with a spy ring which has
photographed some important plans and is trying to get them
through to the enemy. He dreams he is with his mother, who is now
dead. He is trying to explain to her how the world has changed. 'You
used to laugh at the books Miss Savage read—about spies, and
murders, and violence, and wild motor-car chases, but, dear, that's
real life: it's what we've all made of the world since you died.' He says
the world has been remade by William Le Queux. But (and we still

come across the same thing later in Deighton) there are still some who cannot accept the change and get irritated by what they feel is play-acting. The detective goes into a tailor's shop; after five minutes Rowe is to follow and ask for him; and Davis is to count a hundred and then follow Rowe. Davis gets angry, saying he is 'a plain man', and doesn't want to participate in this sort of foolery. But Rowe has learnt to accept the strange new world.

Espionage during the war seemed to bear little relationship to ideology, which appears to have dominated it since. (Bearing in mind, of course, that ideology can sometimes be a cover.) In *The Ministry of Fear* Digby asks Johns what is a Fifth Column, and concludes it refers to people who are in enemy pay. Johns says, 'There's this difference. In the last war—except for Irishmen like Casement—the pay was always cash. Only a certain class was attracted. In this war there are all sorts of ideologies. The man who thinks gold is evil . . . He's naturally attracted to the German economic system. And the men who for years have talked against nationalism . . . well, they are seeing all the old national boundaries obliterated.' The English members of the spy-ring, like Dr Forester, were anti-nationalist. Digby found a book of his by Tolstoy where passages expressing hatred of nations and their systems had been marked.

Our Man in Havana

Elsa Fennan, the spy in Le Carré's *Call for the Dead*, attacks Smiley for playing his spy-game. She has seen many many victims of the same sickness. The mind is separated from the body, loses reality, contemplates the ruin of others without emotion. But sometimes this does not happen: 'the files grow heads and arms and legs, and that's a terrible moment, isn't it?' There are families to be considered as well as records. Human motives are involved. Elsa is in fact hiding her own involvement in the 'spy-game'. But this outburst sounds very much like a description of what actually happens in *Our Man in Havana* (1958), which appeared three years before *Call for the Dead*.

Our Man in Havana contains a good deal of comedy and when it first appeared the comic side was stressed by reviewers and readers. Greene called it an Entertainment. In fact, it is an extremely sad novel. In its mingling of the traditional tears-and-laughter theme it is one of Greene's most professional jobs. Both the tears and the laughter revolve around the recruitment of agents. Wormold himself is simply appointed by Hawthorne with neither explanation nor consultation. Hawthorne is the perfect stage spy, as there have been stage Irishmen and stage Cockneys. Hawthorne takes Wormold to a men's toilet and turns on a tap before he speaks. This is more 'natural', he says, and will confuse the mike. He has chosen Wormold because he is a 'patriotic Englishman. Been here for years. Respected member of the European Traders' Association.' The patriotism is pure assumption. Hawthorne obviously lives in the past, created by Le Queux.

Having been appointed, Wormold now has to find his own agents. He invents them, although their names are of real people. This is the great joke at the heart of the book, and it turns sour when the people behind the names are attacked and even killed. There is Raul, the drunken airline pilot; Engineer Cifuentes; Professor Sanchez; the dancer Teresa. Lopez, Wormold's assistant, is unknowingly recruited, that is, he goes on Wormold's payroll. When Wormold asks Hasselbacher how he can recruit agents, the German is drawn into the conspiracy as if by fate. Each of Wormold's proposed agents has to be investigated for 'traces'. Vincent C. Parkman is rejected because he is already being used by the Americans. Lopez's job is to buy Government publications (on open sale, naturally) with information on the sugar and tobacco industries. (It is well known that one of the most important jobs of the Intelligence agent is the collection and collation of technological material available to anyone who is interested in specialist publications.)

Greene is fascinated not so much by espionage as by the prestige it has gained in our society. He tries, both in this novel and in *The Human Factor*, to fit it into its precise slot in contemporary mythology. Wormold's daughter Milly could accept fairy stories: as a Catholic she was aware of the virgin who bore a child and of pictures that wept or spoke of love in the dark. 'Hawthorne and his kind were equally credulous, but what they swallowed were nightmares, grotesque stories out of science fiction.' Beatrice tells Wormold that they're back in the *Boy's Own Paper* world. It might have been the *Sunday Mirror*. 'The world is modelled after the popular magazines nowadays'. She adds that her husband came out of *Encounter*, a world of earnest cultural do-gooders attending international conferences.

The idea that behaviour in the 'real' world is always being affected by the various mythologies that are illustrated in the fantasy world of the press is very strong in Greene. In a previous chapter I drew attention to the misgivings that had occasionally been felt by diplomats when confronted by the needs and acts of espionage. Today a definite cleavage has been set up and it is illustrated by *Our Man In Havana*, and also in the novels of Warren Tute. Both embassies and spy-rings are in the business of collecting information. The disagreement arises over method. The embassies have a tradition of 'gentlemanly' behaviour whereas the spy agencies are prepared to do anything, including 'dirty tricks', to gain their ends—and information. The Havana Embassy rejected Wormold and stressed that Hawthorne was not employed by them. 'Wormold came away from the Consulate Department carrying a cable in his breast pocket. It had been shoved rudely at him, and when he tried to speak he had been checked. "We don't want to know anything about it. A temporary arrangement. The sooner it's over the better we shall be pleased".'

It is fashionable, and often reasonable, to be amused by the pretensions of modern embassies, but in this case they have a great deal on their side. Even Wormold realizes the enormity of what he has done when the final count is made. He has behaved with the utmost callousness without being aware of it. Yet this is a characteristic mark of the spy novel and, by implication, of the spy-world, and then, by further implication, of our society. At the end of the novel the Chief discusses the situation in Havana with the Permanent Under-Secretary. He refers to the death of one agent and an attack on another. He says placidly that they must expect casualties at the beginning of an operation. He persists in seeing Wormold as an old-fashioned merchant venturer—thus can the reality be disguised. By now Wormold is obstinate, the fun has disappeared for him. 'Perhaps it was worth a few casualties to open his eyes. Cigar?'

The Human Factor

As in all Greene's later work, one is impressed by the maturity of his discussion, which rises well above the level of the political weeklies. The distinction lies between writers whose view of human nature is formed by their political opinions and Greene whose view of the political scene is formed by his knowledge of human nature.

The Human Factor (1978) is a splendidly mature novel and understandably annoyed many reviewers on that account. Old Mr Halliday, for instance, confesses to being a spy for Russia. He had been a member of the Communist Party since he was seventeen. He volunteered for the Army and spent four years as a prisoner in Archangel.

He is asked if he has never wavered a bit. Stalin, Hungary, Czechoslovakia—had they meant nothing? He dismisses them as insignificant. He would set Hamburg, Dresden, Hiroshima in the balance against them. In his opinion the Russians and their supporters had been at war since 1917.

You may not agree with Halliday but at least this discussion is on an intelligent and mature level, unlike the crude goodies and baddies that a writer like Deighton tends to give us. Several attempts have been made to explain the Fellow Traveller phenomenon. It could not be given more clearly than it is here. The fact that Halliday was a Party member means nothing. Many were encouraged *not* to join the Party.

The story is developed with great subtlety. Castle is its 'hero', to use an outmoded but convenient term (and one that is possibly justifiable in this context) and it is only slowly that we realize that he is the spy, that is, in conventional terms, the villain. There is some resemblance here to the development of *The Riddle of the Sands* which begins with two Englishmen setting out to catch a spy working for a foreign power and eventually being revealed as spies themselves—but admirable ones. Is Castle admirable?

In his mother's eyes, no. He is a traitor, the worst of men. If she knew where he was she would inform the police immediately. But among those in the business the term 'traitor' is no longer used. It is a case of conflicting loyalties. Percival, answering Sarah, when she asks him if he thinks she is also a traitor, replies: 'Oh, in the firm, you know, we don't use a word like traitor. That's for the newspapers. You are African—I don't say *South* African—and so is your child. Maurice must have been a good deal influenced by that. Let's say—he chose a different loyalty.' The issues have become very complex and interwoven. Our sympathies are with Castle. Greene never casts villains. (Who would 'scape whipping?) Castle works for Africa, not for Communism.

This novel pre-dated the Blunt affair. Blunt said he passed secrets to the Russians because he obeyed his conscience, which told him that

GRAHAM GREENE   197

Communism was just. Others have passed through the phase without following Blunt's path or, of course, being tempted. Percival, who is in charge of the Castle investigation, questions the whole ethical background of political loyalties when his boss, ['C', Head of the Secret Service ('Legends Spies Tell', by Robert Cecil, *Encounter*, April 1978.)] tells him he cannot admire treachery. 'Thirty years ago when I was a student I rather fancied myself as a kind of Communist. Now . . .? Who is the traitor—me or Davis? I really believed in internationalism, and now I'm fighting an underground war for nationalism.'

There are two kinds of spies: patriots and traitors. What label you use depends on which side of the fence you are on. The traitors used to shock—they still can shock the older generation, like Castle's mother, who would willingly have handed him over to the police. Percival has learnt to adopt a broader view. They are all players in a game. (Perhaps the Great Game was an accurate description after all!) 'The player is as important as the game. I wouldn't enjoy the game with a bad player across the table.' No-one in *The Riddle of the Sands* could have expressed himself like that. There is probably a moral advance involved here, something that is so rare in our society that it should be celebrated.

Greene describes a conference about the relative tasks of MI5 and MI6. When it is over and MI5 retire, there is an extraordinarily English discussion about the contrasted roles of espionage and counter-espionage. C says: 'I'm never quite happy with those MI5 types. Somehow they always seem to carry with them a kind of police atmosphere. It's natural, of course, dealing as they do with counter-espionage. To me espionage is more of a gentleman's job, but of course I'm old-fashioned.' It would be completely wrong to sneer at such a statement. The gentleman may be outmoded and in some ways he may appear ridiculous, but he did value standards of conduct.

The truth is involved and the truth can be a very nasty customer. Castle was being checked by Daintry. He told him that Davis was a member of the Labour Party and that he himself didn't trouble to vote. Daintry said it was an interesting point of view when Castle called most modern political issues parish pump. 'Castle could see telling the truth this time had been an error of judgment, yet, except on really important occasions, he always preferred the truth. The truth can be double-checked.' This seems a pretty cynical statement. When he rang up the office to say he would be late because he was taking his dog to the vet, he wondered if he should actually visit the vet to sustain the alibi, but decided against it: 'taking too much care could sometimes be as dangerous as taking too little—simplicity was always best, just as it paid to speak the truth whenever possible, for the truth is so much easier to memorize than a lie.' And again, what a cynical reason for recommending the truth! At first sight this advice follows Carruthers's principle (in *The Riddle of the Sands*), always to tell the truth. But Carruthers acted on moral grounds, Castle on grounds of expedience. Also Carruthers would have been surprised by Castle's proviso: 'except on really important occasions.' It is hard to say where the development is the more remarkable: in the novelist's more acute understanding of human duplicity, or in the adoption of virtue as a cover for mendacity.

Percival thought it would be better to close their eyes to the leak and draft by whoever was responsible to some innocuous department, rather than make the case public through a trial, which would be held *in camera* and would therefore be believed to be more important than it actually was. Daintry demurred to abetment of a crime. Percival reminded him that they all committed crimes, it was their job. Percival and his boss (C) discuss elimination. This is done so coolly as to shock Daintry. But C is not concerned with morality. 'I know that elimination is rather a new thing for us. More in the K.G.B. line or the C.I.A.'s.' He had brought in Percival because he was a medical man and could do the job scientifically and without undue fuss. In fact, Davis is murdered on the merest assumption—and he is the wrong man. C does show a few scruples when he realizes that Davis may have been innocent. (They are not sure at first.) But Percival has no remorse. 'You shouldn't worry so much about Davis. He's no loss to the firm. He should never have been recruited.' There is a world of difference between these people and Carruthers and Davies in *The Riddle of the Sands*. My repeated comparison of these two novels is not because they are in any way alike but because they are virtually the first and the last good specimens of a genre. They are the two ends of an extension. It is not only the acts of Percival that Carruthers would have shunned but even more so the callousness with which they were conceived and later considered.

Greene, like Le Carré, is fascinated by treachery but even more by duplicity. Castle in Moscow is visited by Boris, who had been his Control in London. Boris tells him the bits of information that Castle had been handing over had had no value in themselves at all.

> I know I am not very clear. I am not used to whisky. Let me
> try to explain. Your people imagined they had an agent in
> place, here in Moscow. But it was we who had planted him
> on them. What you gave us he gave back to them. Your
> reports authenticated him in the eyes of your service, they
> could check them and all the time he was passing them other
> information which we wanted them to believe . . .

It may be said that this sort of situation is incidental to the spy-
situation but is not fundamental. Some spy writers seize on it and
make it central to their work. This is perhaps an excess of ardour.
There is a vast amount of duplicity, deception and double-crossing
in espionage but the essential act is still the acquisition of
information. The best spy writers perform a delicate balancing act, in
which they give duplicity its due but do not allow it to rule the roost. It
is the film that encourages this. Cinema audiences are not concerned
with the causes of action. It is the action *per se* they are after. Some
spy writers are in fact turning out film scripts, with the emphasis on
confusion. It is the major weakness of that very talented writer, Len
Deighton.

19: THE ENEMY

Espionage occurs in such a murky area of human relationships that it is often genuinely difficult to know who is an enemy and who isn't. Then again, once the enemy has been established there is a powerful tendency to admire and respect and, finally, even to love him. People who are paid to hate and kill others, that is to say professionals, have a way of getting on the best of terms with those they are supposed to hate and kill. After all, they understand each other. They do the same job. They resemble the eighteenth century generals who used to mess together before and after they set to work to eliminate each other. We are told that victims sometimes grow uncannily fond of their torturers. It is the civilians who manage to keep their hate at white heat.

Before launching into the intricacies of who hates who in the spy world, I would like to outline three scenarios from modern spy novels. First, Len Deighton's *Horse Under Water*. Lieut. B.T. Peterson, R.N., was court-martialled for espionage—he supported the enemy during the war. He had met, as a P.O.W., another spy who possessed a *Weiss List* (a sort of code name for a Black List), with the names of English collaborators. The British authorities were strongly against its publication, especially as one of those named was Henry Smith, now a cabinet minister, who was being blackmailed. Peterson also possessed a letter from Smith, written in January 1941, with this passage: 'I am forming a Brains Trust (as they say these days) of people who see eye to eye with me on these points so that when the country finally comes to its senses we will be in a position to do something about it.' Deighton's lead (codenamed Zayat) thought Smith should be arrested because he was 'a corner-stone of an international Fascist movement dedicated to the overthrow of democratic government.' Dawlish said: 'You surely don't imagine that they can put everyone who answers that description in jail. Where would we find room for them, and besides, where would the Bonn government get another Civil Service?'

That's one complication in the friend–enemy set-up.

Another is suggested in Chapman Pincher's *The Four Horses*. This is an international conspiracy novel, with a group of Arab and

German terrorists threatening to blow up the famous Four Horses monument in Venice. Who is to say which of these men and women are ideologically motivated? (Ideology is itself a cover at times.) Most of the book is devoted to the chequered history of the sculptures, with the emphasis on repeated plotting, espionage and violence. It is a fast-moving tale but told in a flat, insensitive style, cheapened by alliterative section titles. There is a prophetic element when the terrorists seize the cardinal who is expected to be the next Pope. (It was published in 1978.) Although not a spy novel, the constant factors of the spy's condition are stated: that it is the world's second oldest profession (put into the mouth of Nero); that spies are always unpopular with diplomats, though their tasks overlap; and that a spy whose cover is broken is useless. But who is the enemy? Who are the terrorists working for?

The most profoundly pessimistic novel in the whole genre is surely John Simpson's *Moscow Requiem* (1981). It is most accurately called a political thriller but it is barely a novel: there are characters and now and again attempts are made to individualize them, but the whole is overcast by political manoeuvring, affairs of state and the reporting of mass events. One gets a sensation of despair from many thriller writers but from none so strongly as Simpson. This may account for the vaguely sad look he used to wear when he read the BBC news. He takes the view that the West must succumb to a more ruthless system, never a better one. The story ends with the West in disarray on the political level and Britain an unimportant pawn in the Big Power game—a view rather similar to William Haggard's. On the more personal but also political level, a Russian defector is shot dead as he imagines he has got away and a Russian girl, also trying to escape, is caught in front of her English lover and whisked away—to where? To some fuliginous area, bequeathed by the medieval Christians to the modern Humanists, and reserved for unsuccessful spies, agents and defectors. There are no *sides* in the Buchanesque sense here, all are enemies and friends and no-one knows which is which.

Who Are the Enemy?

I probably maligned Buchan in the last paragraph. There have been far less sensitive cases than his among spy authors. Buchan recognized that there were 'good' Germans, although they might be

202   THE BRITISH SPY NOVEL

actively engaged in fighting against you. Although Buchan was a patriot he was also greatly concerned with moral values. Therefore the enemy is the man who deliberately wills evil. He may be on your side, even entrenched in the Establishment. Janet Adam-Smith quotes a letter from Edward Sheldon to Buchan in her biography: 'Your best villains were always the ones with a magnificent streak of perverted nobility running neck-to-neck with their villainy.' One feels that Williams slowly developed this kind of feeling about Clubfoot. Although Buchan was influenced by Oppenheim he surpassed him in seriousness of approach. He certainly went far beyond Sapper's jingo patriotism, with its unquestioning presentation of 'goodies' and 'baddies'.

The most clear-cut case of the author/agent who had no doubts about the identity of the enemy is of course Fleming/Bond. There is not a single enemy, it is true, but the organizations can be counted on the fingers of one hand and, so far as the United Kingdom is concerned, they constitute a single enemy. We learn in *Diamonds are Forever* that the groups that worry M are SMERSH, the German cypher-breakers, the Chinese opium ring, the Mafia and the big American gangs. Now only two of these are essentially political and, apart from the industrial spy who is rarely celebrated in fiction, the spy is a political animal. Opium rings and protection rackets are the concern of Raymond Chandler and the private eye. But Bond finds himself constantly being involved with these non-political groups, which is another way of saying that the boundaries between political and non-political are rapidly fading. It is this sort of thing that can confuse a Smiley, who wants the mud to settle so that he can analyse it. But this doesn't worry Bond. A man has a gun and he's trying to shoot you: where's the complication?

At first he was contemptuous of the gangs. 'They're not Americans. Mostly a lot of Italian bums with monogrammed shirts who spend the day eating spaghetti and meat-balls and squirting scent over themselves.' They had read too many horror-comics and seen too many films. Bond felt depressed to think that, as a cover, he was actually serving them, eating their dinner and sleeping in their beds, while *they* watched *him*. The more he tangled with them the less respect he had. There was only room for contempt and dislike. But later he modified this view. I think this was probably much more of a subjective change than one based on facts. So long as they were just common criminals they didn't really rate his attention. As soon as they gave signs of being connected with the political enemy (Dr No certainly, and some of the others probably) he began to revise his opinion. 'I used to think your gangsters were just a bunch of Italian greaseballs who filled themselves up with pizza pie and beer all the week and on Saturdays knocked off a garage or a drug store so as to pay their way at the races. But they've certainly got plenty of violence on the payroll.' Replace a garage with a nuclear bomb and Bond immediately saw red—or SMERSH.

Fleming had considerable justification for seeing the Enemy in simplistic terms as Communism or the Soviet Union. The Radcliffe Report on *Security Procedures in the Public Service* declared the most formidable subversive organization in this country to be the Communist Party of Great Britain, with its fringe of associated bodies and sympathizers. The Report also stated that 'for the sake of brevity we have followed the common practice of using the phrase "Communist" throughout to include Fascists.' How this must have infuriated the comrades—yet recent history and common practices support such identification (from the Hitler–Stalin agreement to invade Poland to Ken Livingstone's kind words on behalf of the Galtieri régime). Most fiction in the current wave of spy-writing is directed against 'Communism' rather than 'Fascism' but this is because the three major Fascist régimes (German, Italian and Japanese) have been eliminated whereas the major Communist régime is still active.

It is natural to find uncertainty about the identity of the real enemy clearly expressed by Graham Greene. Not even a spy can be treated as a puppet by Greene—he too, like anyone else, will have his doubts and evasions, his mendacities and uncertainties. Greene was quick to notice the moral misgivings in Buchan. By 1959, and the publication of *Our Man in Havana*, with a world-shaking war intervening, the uncertainties had become practical as well as moral. The principals in the spy drama don't know who they are acting against, or who is trying to thwart them. (It had been perfectly clear in *The Riddle of the Sands*). When Wormold asks what will happen to Dr Braun, an enemy agent, he suggests that he will have a passage booked to Moscow. But Segura doesn't know. 'Not necessarily. Perhaps Bonn. Or Washington. Or even Bucharest. I don't know.' Who *was* he working for?

This aspect is always stressed by Warren Tute in his spy novels set in Greece. Here no-one is ever sure. Suspicions sway back and forth. Paul Tarnham of the Foreign Office defected to the Russians and is now (*The Powder Train*) working in Prague. The year is 1968. Saul

Kretzer, a young American who is apparently trying to organize students in the powder train (which will ignite Russia) is not sure if he is really working for the other side. There are doubts about Kretzer himself. And so on. Marides, the Greek millionaire, has a very large finger in the pie but no-one is sure what he's up to. 'Capitalists like me and the Communist *élite* are brothers under the skin', he says. They are both interested in power. He also has a hobby: money. Dr Novacek, ex-Czech ambassador to the Lebanon, and Paul Tarnham were both Marides men. Each differed in basic outlook and neither trusted anyone at all. 'Marides believed firmly in the right hand not knowing what the left was up to.' Dr Novacek, for example, knew nothing of the organization to which both his wife and daughter belonged, though it was inspired and paid for by Marides.

Double Agents

The natural result of this confusion is the existence of the double agent, a man who works for both sides and whose priorities of loyalty are unknown, often even to himself. Is there any other field of human activity where a double agent (or its equivalent, a Yes/No man or a Black/White star) is taken for granted?

There is nothing new about the double agent. He is as old as espionage. Espionage, by its very nature, must produce him. Roche, in Anthony Price's *Soldier No More* (1981) was a double agent who was at first committed to the Russians but then returned disillusioned to the Western fold. He felt tainted. He longed for the sixteenth century when a man could change sides two or three times and be thought none the worse for it. (He is a *soi-disant* soldier-scholar) 'That was *his* century, which he had studied most and enjoyed most; when there were two rival faiths, just like now, but with just enough elbow-room for the same man to make honest mistakes and learn from them without being damned, unlike now . . .' Times were not so good for the turncoat now. *'Those were the days!* He could have prospered then, in those days. He could have served his own interest, and saved his own skin, and kept his self-respect as well.' Roche, of course, does know his own mind, even if he tends to change it. This means that he knows which of two loyalties has priority at any given moment.

Deighton describes in *XPD* how a double agent may be made. It

may start with blackmail. Kleiber worked for the Russians because
they had evidence of his membership of the Nazi SS. When the CIA
got him, with details of the various murders he had committed, they
proposed making him an illegal resident for the Russians but
controlled by the CIA. Kleiber was afraid the Russians would
become suspicious but they assured him they would pass on material
the Russians desperately needed: such items as undersea water
technology, computer advances and cruise missile data. The C.I.A.
project chairman assumed it would be easy to put the Russians in a
situation where they would naturally appoint Kleiber illegal resident.

This type of double agent was probably, against all appearances,
the most reliable. As early as *Casino Royale* (1953) Fleming was
pointing out that the ideological defector was often useless. Russian
colonels had a habit of coming over and then turning double after a
few months' 'asylum'. But this double act was usually to the advantage
of the Russians. The best-known Russian colonel in spy fiction is
probably Deighton's Skok, who destroys the credibility of every
book he appears in, being a one hundred per cent formula figure.
(Naturally, Fleming knew nothing of him at the time). Skok is not a
defector but he confuses everybody by pretending to be on the verge
of coming over. So he is almost a double agent, perhaps a one point
seven five agent. In this extraordinary world this is not a joking matter.

Le Carré seems to agree about the uselessness of the double agent.
The Wise Men (the political masters) composed a *codex*, a catalogue
of proscribed practice. The use of double agents (they called it
'obsession') was one of them. This had nothing to do with reliability.
Being British in the post-war world, it was purely and simply a
financial consideration. Was the taxpayer expected to maintain those
planeloads of defectors *and* their families, all earnestly passing on
useless and outmoded information? Lacon said to Smiley, 'The old
games of coat-trailing—turning and playing back our enemies'
spies—in your day the very meat and drink of counter-intelligence,
George, in the collective opinion of the Wise Men—today they are
ruled obsolete. Uneconomic.' The exile groups were ruled provocative, anti-detente and inflammatory. They were an expensive
indulgence. Toby Esterhase was contemptuous of Otto Leipzig. His
information was fabrication or even a rewrite from *Stern* magazine.
But some of his stuff was rather good, protested Smiley. You could
count it on one finger, said Toby. But what about his Moscow Centre
material? 'Okay! So Centre gave him some decent chicken-feed

occasionally, so he could pass us the other crap! How else does anyone play a double, for God's sake?'

The role of the double agent becomes more and more farcical. Both his employers distrust him. His employment does seem a luxury. Perhaps the next step will have to be the use of a treble agent. There are actually hints of this in Deighton's *The Ipcress File*. Jay, the master-spy, was a Pole. During the war he served in the Polish Underground, which had many different political origins. He was a member of the National Armed Forces, who were Right-wing extremists and he probably did a deal with the German Abwehr. For this he was regarded as a hero by the Communist-dominated A.L. (or People's Army) for reducing Fascist power. 'A massive treble-cross', says Deighton.

A Fellowship of Spies

Spies of opposing factions develop respect and even liking for each other. They are doing the same job. This development might also be partly a defensive reaction to the inconclusiveness of their situation.

The camaraderie is not sexual—with the expected exception. Bond has orders to kill a sniper. Discovering it is an attractive girl, he only wounds her! (*The Living Daylights*) Greater love hath no spy than this, that he spare the life of his enemy. When the mission was completed Bond didn't want to leave the little flat from which, for three days, 'he had this long-range, one-sided romance with an unknown girl—an unknown enemy agent with much the same job in her outfit as he had in his. Poor little bitch . . .!' Bond also falls in love with the opposing female spy in *From Russia with Love* but then he has been programmed to do just this.

The notion of fellowship grows stronger as the spy novel develops. The fellow-feeling between Smiley and the Russian Karla in *Tinker, Tailor, Soldier, Spy* hinted at possible treacheries! They met in Delhi where Smiley tried to persuade Karla to defect. His approach was sentimental.

They were both getting old. They had spent their whole lives looking for weaknesses in the other's system. Their trade produced a negative vision. The great visions of youth had evaporated. In conversation with his most trusted friend, Guillam, he expanded on this. He had suggested to Karla that, although they had followed different routes, they had reached similar conclusions about life.

What he called 'the political generality' was probably meaningless. The politicians do no more than achieve new forms of the old misery by their grand designs.

The most full-blooded respect for the enemy is to be found in William Haggard's novels, especially the suggestively titled *Yesterday's Enemy* (1976). Haggard's hero (his Smiley, one might say) was Charles Russell, at one time Head of British Security. He 'had never regarded the Colonel-General as in any sense a personal enemy. They had too much in common for private malice, in particular a respect for reality. Power would survive the humanist fallacy, the pipedreams of the new reformers with their comfortable private incomes behind them. It wasn't love which made the world go round and it wasn't, for that matter, naked hate. It was the ability to think politically and to see that one's orders were carried out. The General possessed these and Russell the first of them. Being in retirement, he could not possess the second. It was the basis of their mutual respect and sometimes for something quite close to affection.' He tells the Colonel-General that he is a 'trusted enemy'.

> 'You have the highest reputation and your interest is basically just like mine, to stop us all destroying ourselves. You have just the same motives to tell the truth and my masters, though jumpy, are far from fools. I'd believe what you said and so would they. I mean in these rather special circumstances.'

The special circumstances are that the Colonel-General is afraid that some people in Germany may be planning a nuclear attack on Russia or, which is almost as bad, giving that impression so that the Russians will strike first.

Russell loathed the soft Left, that is, the Western Left. This caused him to swing to what he called the hard Right, that is, orthodox Russian Communism, which was feared and hated by the new elite. But Russell had begun to believe in its ultimate victory. It had discipline, which the new lot lacked. 'It had an empire and a real foreign policy; it thought, as men should, from accepted premises, unblinded by a cloudy humanism.' Russell, of course, is ultra Right Wing, or ultramontane, to revive and adapt a valuable old term, and recognizes his kinship with the Communists in Russia sixty years after their Revolution. And so Yesterday's Enemy became today's collaborator.

Another author who celebrates the brotherhood of spies is Brian

Freemantle, whose vulgar, lower class Charlie Muffin detests the public school element in Security. Charlie is in many ways a highly representative modern Englishman: he deplores the divisiveness of our class-based society but sees no attraction in the political alternatives that are offered him. His attitude to the enemy is therefore extremely ambivalent. The enemy is personified by General Berenkov of the K.G.B. who has been sentenced to forty years in Wormwood Scrubs (*Charlie Muffin*, 1977). Charlie visits him, officially to gain information, but he is hampered by the awkward fact of liking him. Berenkov reciprocates the feeling and says, 'Apart from being born in different countries and being absolutely committed to opposite sides, we're practically identical.'

Marcel d'Agneau, in his brilliant parody of Le Carré (*Eeny, Meeny, Miny, Mole*, 1980) naturally seizes on this aspect of the spy-situation. It is meat and drink to the satirist. Grimly (an agent, not an adverb!) speaks feelingly of his Soviet opposite number, Larianov, code-named Tinkabelle. 'With sadness, I realized there was little between us. We had become the same man, taken different routes, but we had arrived at the same destination and time, in an identical frame of mind. Our devotion to duty, honour, political and ideological commitment was nothing more than habit. The world we had fought for, dreamt of, had been cut off in its prime by politicians and purges, weaknesses and sheer stupidity.'

Once the mind starts romancing about espionage one begins to envisage a situation where Spies of the World Unite and hive off from their parent bodies. The germ of this intriguing idea might be found in Antony Melville-Ross's *Tightrope* (1981), though it is certainly not a suggestion made by the author. A personal K.G.B. contact warns Rafferty that a nuclear explosive device is being placed somewhere in the Greater London area. The Minister asks if such contacts are commonplace. He is obviously worried: where might it lead to? Rafferty says they are not regular occurrences but, on the other hand, not uncommon when mutual interest is involved. 'Rafferty thought of the many times he had walked, talked and drunk with members of the official opposition in different places round the globe, but he didn't think it would help his present case to develop that theme.' Yet there is an implication that if the animosities and threats of the politicians become too dangerous Smiley, Russell, Muffin, Rafferty and even Grimly will be there to keep the finger off the button and remind the world that the cost of having your own way can be too high.

20: LOYALTIES

Bond meets Felix Leiter in Royale (*Casino Royale*). 'Bond soon noticed that he never spoke of his American colleagues in Europe or in Washington and he guessed that Leiter held the interests of his own organization far above the mutual concerns of the North Atlantic Allies. Bond sympathized with him.' The claims of the organization are beginning to override those of patriotism and ideology.

After Bond had recovered from his savage beating and is recuperating in hospital, he becomes philosophical about his role. He talks to Mathis, who does not take him seriously. Bond has killed two men and has nearly been killed by Le Chiffre. Now things get muddled, he says. First the hero kills two villains, but then is cast in the role of villain—but he knows he isn't a villain. 'Of course, patriotism comes along and makes it seem fairly all right, but this country-right-or-wrong business is getting a little out-of-date.' He points out that today we are fighting Communism. Fifty years ago the brand of conservatism we endure today would have been considered pretty near to Communism, and we would have been urged to fight it. The organization has a fixed quality about it. Patriotism and ideology seem to drift from something that seems fixed to something that won't keep still.

Supposing Le Chiffre could come back. Bond would kill him. But why? Out of personal revenge, and not for some high moral reason or for the sake of the country.

This is Fleming's most thoughtful novel. Chapter XX is called 'The Nature of Evil' and contains some pretty jejune philosophizing, but the mere fact that it is there is interesting. Mathis, the down-to-earth member of the Deuxième Bureau (who hasn't been beaten up—in this instance, anyway) tries to straighten Bond out. 'When you get back to London you will find there are other Le Chiffres seeking to destroy you and your friends and your country. M will tell you about them. And now that you have seen a really evil man, you will know how evil they can be and you will go after them to destroy them in order to protect yourself and the people you love. You won't wait to argue about it.'

Ostensibly Bond is a patriot. In fact his first loyalty is to himself, the second to his friends (ideology, both positive—for conservatism—and negative—against Communism) and the third to his country (patriotism). This is an honest statement and probably true for most agents, however they like to dress it up. The organization itself manages to contain all three loyalties without being too explicit about it. There is no doubt about the loyalty of most members of British Security. Chapman Pincher dedicated his *Their Trade is Treachery* to 'the loyal members of the Security and Intelligence Services, on whom so much depends'.

Patriotism

This emotion remained relatively unmixed and unsullied during the early stages of spy-fiction: Childers, Buchan, Valentine Williams and Sapper. When Bond begins to question its nature we can be sure that the old certainties are really breaking down. But a more profound writer, Eric Ambler, had already drawn attention to what was happening.

Graham, in *Journey Into Fear* (1940) on board ship sailing from Istanbul to Genoa, is at the mercy of Moeller, the German agent. Moeller says a man might be tempted to talk of his 'duty to his country' but Graham is in a business (armaments) which is highly sceptical of such heroics.

> 'Love of country!' There's a curious phrase. Put a German down in a field in Northern France, tell him that it is Hanover, and he cannot contradict you. Love of fellow-countrymen? Surely not. A man will like some of them and dislike others. Love of the country's culture? The men who know most of their countries' cultures are usually the most intelligent and the least patriotic. Love of the country's government? But governments are usually disliked by the people they govern. Love of country, we see, is merely a sloppy mysticism based on ignorance and fear.

The peoples who have suffered most are the most patriotic. Therefore it is the Poles who take first prize in this league. In Geoffrey Household's *A Rough Shoot* (1951), the Pole Sandorski reproves Taine. 'Good God, man, are you going to put your miserable private affairs before service to your country?' Taine reflects that never in his life had he heard such a lousy argument. Of course, there are other factors to take into consideration in this very complex psychological matter. Buchan would not have considered it a lousy argument but since his time Englishmen had become reticent about patriotism. It is even doubtful if Taine was any less patriotic at heart than Sandorski. One cannot put aside easily memory of the generation that resisted Hitler after several declarations, both public and private, that the country was not worth a sacrifice. But was this patriotism?

As Bond gets older he becomes less philosophical. His public want action, not doubts. *Diamonds are Forever* is not an orthodox spy novel, for no-one is trying to worm out another's secrets. But Bond is still 007 and he is still working for the British Secret Service, and now, only three years after Royale, he and M bang the patriotic drum. M says that the diamond smuggling they are out to uncover damages England. They are working for the protection of England. 'It's only England that's the loser'. The pipeline ends in America and as America is outside the jurisdiction of the police and MI5 only the Secret Service can handle the job.

One would expect the French to be very realistic about patriotism. Len Deighton shows how it works across the Channel in *An Expensive Place to Die* (1967). Monique had worked occasionally at Datt's clinic. She wasn't an agent but she was on the edge of the espionage world, probably without knowing it. She is a typical girl of the French lower class, always ready to take advantage of a situation. She expresses herself on the subject of patriotism with characteristic frankness.

> At the Ritz a man friend of mine paid nine francs a day to them for looking after his dog. That's just about half the pension my father gets for being blown up in the war. So when you people come snooping around here, flashing your money and protecting the Republique Française's rocket programme, atomic plants, supersonic bombers and nuclear submarines or whatever it is you're protecting, don't expect too much from my patriotism.

Warren Tute's Mado is frankly puzzled. Like Smiley, he's not exactly enraptured with what his country offers—but what's going to be put in its place? The Dream of Brezhnev? Chinese regimentation? Reaganomics? A system organized by the P.L.O. and I.R.A. acting jointly? None of this is on. Marides tells Mado he is a man of integrity (*The Powder Train*, 1970). Mado reflects that no-one in London would have believed that. Styles keep changing. Perhaps the modern man of integrity is as hard-bitten as the old-time gangster. 'Because cynical though you like to imagine you are', says Marides, 'patriotism is still not a dirty word to you.' Perhaps we are encountering a little semantic difficulty. Did patriotism ever become a dirty word? Wasn't Dr Johnson's 'last refuge' merely an indication that there are hypocrites about and they don't all choose the Church? Isn't it, after all, nationalism that is the dirty word, as Orwell recognized so clearly? Mado denies that he is a patriot because he hasn't really thought about it and follows a fashion, but later he wonders if perhaps Marides hadn't been right after all. He socked Tarnham on the jaw. Why? For the Queen of England? Could be.

With John Braine we come full circle, right back to the old patriotic ideal of Queen and Country, and a blind faith in their rightness—or at least betterness, if I may be allowed the word. The Director of Counter-Espionage in *The Pious Agent* (1975) wanted 'intelligent patriots . . . who know that dirty jobs have to be done quickly and efficiently'. But they are to be killers, not sadists. Flynn saw his role as preventing people from 'committing the grave sin of harming my country'. A Catholic, his final prayer was 'O God let me know how best to serve You and my country.'

This new wave of patriotism characterizes an important section of the spy fiction of the seventies. One may not agree with it but it is at least refreshing to find a writer who has managed to make a successful career for himself show gratitude to the society that made it possible, rather than bombard it with sneers and jeers, as have some others. Braine is not an intellectual, and Le Carré is, which may explain why the former is far more forthright than the latter. Le Carré's line is: I know we're bad but we're not as bad as they are. It recalls the poet C. Day Lewis's statement on the outbreak of the last World War: We must support the bad against the worse. It may not be very satisfying but at least it's honourable. Our new patriotism cannot be idealistic, like Buchan's. It's a matter of cutting losses. The ideal of a duty to one's country returns. Flynn's words to Vanessa after she was unmasked were: 'You've harmed my country. My duty is to protect my country.'

This is not a spy novel in the accepted sense, but it presents certain security characteristics clearly if crudely. It is an imagined spy-sabotage world, having little contact with reality. Thus, although it has points of interest, as suggested in the foregoing (just as Le Queux had), it is a thoroughly bad novel. The puerility of the sex passages makes Bond's adventures sound sophisticated. The recurring insistence on professionals and professionalism results in raw B.O.P. stuff. It is extremely crude: 'How many Russians have you killed, Xavier?'—'Fifty', he said, 'and various other odds and sods.'— 'Fifty,' she said. 'May God spare you to kill fifty more.' This is combined with literaryness in the worst sense—for example, there are descriptions of Xavier working out in exact hundredths of a second each stage in a knife attack. As I said, it is all imagined, without reality. It is not a good advertisement for the new-style patriotism. One is advised to stick to Mado.

Traitors

Sir Walter Ralegh knew what a traitor was, which is more than most of us do, although new definitions are being worked out. Ralegh wrote an account of the last fight of the *Revenge* entitled 'A Report of the trueth of the fight about the Isles of Açores'. When I was a boy we were expected to read all about this great action and also Tennyson's ballad and, if we could get hold of it, Kingsley's *Westward Ho!* It was gripping stuff and it taught us that one Englishman was worth fifty Spaniards (on examination, the number was later reduced to fifteen). Ralegh accused the Spaniards of distorting history and also warned Englishmen against succumbing to Spanish offers to serve His Most Catholic Majesty. If they acceded they would be traitors, 'onely assured to be imployed in all desperate enterprises, to bee helde in scorne and disdaine ever among those whome they serve. And that ever traitor was either trusted or advanced I could never yet reade, neither can I at this time remember any example.' A solemn warning, which Guy Burgess would have done well to note.

Modern spy fiction introduces characters who are half way to becoming traitors and then have second thoughts. Understanding and sympathy are not withheld. After all, the Worker's Paradise is a wonderful target. One only rejects Paradise when it turns out to be something else. Andrea Eckersley in Warren Tute's *The Resident* (1973) is reporting the East European Trade Fair at Athens for a Sunday paper. She has also been given a minor intelligence job. She is an Earl's daughter. She keeps this in the background and persuades her fellow-journalists, 'who daily sold their souls to the capitalist press', that she had the full quota of necessary Left-wing bias. British Security was well aware of her Maoist ideas but knew she was not a 'tatty little King Street traitor. She was loyal—if not to her Queen and country—at least to her ideas of English civilization, freedom and to the general way of life which her socialist friends seemed so anxious to modify and even destroy without apparently realizing what they were really doing'. Le Carré's Connie Sachs might have approved of her. There is a similar character in Haggard's *Yesterday's Enemy*. And there is a good example of this point of view in Household's *Arabesque*, where Montagne, a Free French officer, refers scornfully to the Vichy men as 'rats who put politics before their country'.

Defection is a risky game. The defectors do not give the impression of happiness or fulfilment. Brian Freemantle illustrates this in his *Face Me When You Walk Away* (1974). Pamela, an English girl married to a Russian, is lonely in Moscow. She had some contact with the expatriate British colony, although she despised them as traitors.

> She had found them grubby, insecure little men, like junior clerks lost on a firm's outing to the seaside. Their slang vocabulary was of a decade ago, their conversation meaningless trivia involving nostalgia about favoured restaurants that weren't really very good or plays that had long ceased to run or prompt comment. Most retained their old-school ties, she noticed, and wore suits shiny with grease and over-wear, just because there was a London or New York label inside the jacket. There was not one whom she had met whom she did not feel secretly regretted the activity that had forced them into exile.

This is not objective comment, of course. It is interesting, however, because it is put into the mind of a woman who has thrown in her lot with the Russians, but for romantic and personal reasons, not political and collective.

I have already drawn attention to the fact that for some people it is no easy matter to say who is a defector because there is no overriding agreement about which loyalty should have priority. Pol, the French financier who plays a dubious part in the action of Alan Williams's *Gentleman Traitor* (1974) says 'traitor' has become a senseless word. It is impossible to decide what his own opinions are, if he has any settled ones beyond self-interest. On one occasion he is provoked into exclaiming, 'Who are the great traitors? Pétain? Salan? De Gaulle? Perhaps your Mr Smith in Rhodesia?' But one of the best examples of a person who gets hopelessly confused in his conception of loyalty is to be found in Deighton's *Yesterday's Spy* (1975). Serge Frankel, an ex-communist, is part of the spy ring based on Marseille during the war. He tells how he began as an idealist, which led to police beatings, bullets in the leg and pneumonia caught in the Spanish War. He didn't regret it—a youth must have something to offer his life to.

> When they told me about this Stalin–Hitler pact I went round explaining it to men of lesser faith. The war you know about. Czechoslovakia—well, I'd never liked the Czechs, and when the Russian tanks invaded Hungary . . . well, they were asking for it, those Hungarians—I ask you, who ever met an honest Hungarian? . . . But I am a Jew. They are putting my people into concentration camps, starving them, withdrawing the right to work from anyone who asks to go to Israel. When these pigs who call themselves socialists went to the aid of the Arabs—then I knew that no matter what kind of Communist I was, I was first and foremost a Jew.

What starts as a case of simple idealism, good versus evil, right versus wrong, gets hopelessly mixed up. Note, too, how Frankel is prepared to put up with even the most deplorable acts of the Soviet régime, until they touch his own people and interests—then he is jolted into some aspect of reality.

It is not only Frankel in this novel who has learnt to distrust everybody. Security agents were professional betrayers. You might be shopped by anyone. Champion had told Charlie again and again that a spy should trust no-one. Claude sees the irony of it all. 'The battle-lines have been drawn afresh'. Frankel, the ex-communist, is revealed as a racist; Claude himself, once a German nationalist, has become a champion of parliamentary government; Charlie, who once fought with the Communists, now works to defeat them; and Champion has become an active anti-Semite. There is no guarantee that these later loyalties are any more respectable than the former ones.

These are depressing conclusions. It is left to Marcel d'Agneau to extract humour out of them. The talk goes on in El Vino's (*Eeny, Meeny, Miny, Mole*). Eleven men had been convicted of working for the

Russians, but you must trust them. They're cads, bounders, rotters, but 'they have given their word as gentlemen. My God, man, of course, their word is good, as old Etonians then, will that do? And come off it, old chap, not so much traitor; it was ideals, more sneak than traitor.' There is caustic repetition of this 'tolerance' for the traitors (as sound public school men) throughout. You've got to be realistic. 'But tell me this, is there one man, is there one man in the whole British Secret Service who doesn't work for the Russians?' asks Croc rhetorically. (Croc, by the way, is an 'Outfielder'. The really trustworthy men, men who can be depended on to be in touch with Moscow, are in the slips.) Grimly, who is called in to clear up the mess, wonders why the English make 'such keen traitors'.

Tradition

Behind the choreography of idealists, traitors and defectors lies the unhappy feeling that this country is going downhill and has been going downhill for a long time. Indeed, this feeling has sometimes been held to be actually responsible for the transfer of loyalties. It has been suggested that Burgess and Maclean, for example, had no admiration for the Soviet régime but were simply getting on to a craft that appeared to be more seaworthy than the decaying Empire.

It is never easy to notice fundamental changes which are taking place in a society and it is even more difficult to accept them. Six years after the war Geoffrey Household brought out his novella, *A Rough Shoot* in which it is suggested that Pink has shot Hiart (they are both members of a subversive group). Taine protests to a Polish friend: 'Good Lord, Peter, this is England!' (Compare D. in Greene's *The Confidential Agent*. He certainly hadn't been followed into the train. Would something happen at Hyde Park Corner? or was he exaggerating the whole thing? This was England.) It was still possible in those days to believe that England was still the safe and secure haven that Gladstone and even Baldwin had known. But there were novelists who had sensed the slow change from a traditional and peaceful society to one in which sudden death and outbreaks of violence, in continental style, might occur. A few writers issued warnings. Perhaps the best example came from America, with Sinclair Lewis's *It Can't Happen Here*. All the same, America wasn't Britain.

Warren Tute's *The Golden Greek* (1960) which wasn't a spy novel, is heavy with the same kind of pessimism. Others are filling gaps left by the retiring English. The world had left Christopher Sandbrooke behind. He was too 'nice', too much of a gentleman. 'He was fighting for something he knew and understood. He was proud of the R.A.F., proud of England, proud of everything he'd been brought up to believe. Now it's all turned to ashes and he doesn't know why.' This is the feeling that motivates many of the fictional agents and counter-agents, especially perhaps the latter. Christopher was neither but they belonged to the same world. His younger brother Paddy comes to terms with the new ways, distressing their father. 'You were all brought up to respect the big things in life—don't they mean anything to you now?—the greatness of England, pride in your country's achievements, all the things your brother risked his life for in the war . . .' To some it was a decline in decency (this underlined Orwell's attitude), fair play and tolerance. For others it was expressed politically in loss of Empire, power and prestige. 'To both of them (father and son) the British Empire would always remain the Empire and not the Commonwealth.' For such people the Commonwealth is a fake, an attempt to disguise an unpleasant truth.

William Haggard's Security chief, Charles Russell, is seen against a background of decadence. Here is a portrait of him taken from *The Hard Sell* (1965).

> He was a pillar of the establishment but its values were quite alien. It could make him laugh sardonically lest otherwise he weep, and it could often make him angry. He knew that the young felt a shadow they feared and hated and that they reasonably blamed their elders for a life which might end tomorrow. Charles Russell seldom apportioned blame but his own view wasn't dissimilar. It was his private conviction that Europe as he understood the word had committed suicide when he himself had been nine years old. Everything that had followed had been merely the obsequies, the best one could hope for that they be conducted with decorum.

This must be a reference to 1914. There have been many others who have expressed the view that Europe never recovered from the mauling it received over those four dreadful years, and some (such as J.B. Priestley) very forcibly. Le Carré's Smiley probably belongs to the number only he is not so vehement; he is a divided man, unable to hide his irritation with the messiness of a beloved country.

Again, in *A Cool Day for Killing* (1968) Haggard makes no bones about his dislike of the contemporary world. He is less grumpy than Le Carré, whose mood stems from the gentleness of nostalgia. Haggard's mood is one of downright detestation. He sees an England that has lost its guts and is soft at the centre. He compares English society unfavourably with the French. 'Can you imagine a Frenchman in a Bunny Club? The civilization where they thrive deserves the bomb on it tomorrow. I'd rather see a daughter in a brothel.' This dimension gives Haggard's work an added interest but at the same time the commentary he cannot resist slows it down. There is little flow in his writing. Even more than Anthony Price, another writer with strong feelings, he holds up the action by posing hypotheses and setting forth his characters' ratiocination. Len Deighton never makes this mistake and yet, although he writes like a man perfectly adjusted to his time, he also expresses his dissatisfaction with what has happened to his homeland. He does it, however, through vital and stark imagery. In *XPD* (1981), Stuart looks through the window. 'Beyond the canal, the rusting tracks and ruined shed were the remains of a railway system which had once made the world gasp with envy.' This novel emphasizes the grotty side of London life.

Philip Gibbs, one of the relatively gentle old school of political thriller writers, lived on into the post-World War Two maelstrom and even wrote a book called *Behind the Curtain* (1948). In it Vladimir asks his English mother if an ambassador is a spy, because he has to send back reports about trade and politics. Her answer is revealing—of a world that was fast disappearing. 'Good heavens, no . . . An Ambassador is a most honourable man. It's one of the best jobs a man can have in England.' (The novel was set in the early twenties. Writers like Tute and Freemantle tend to be contemptuous of the diplomatic breed.) But Vladimir mentioned trade. The commercial aspect of spying is rarely exploited or even mentioned in fiction, although Ken Follett treated it in his novels, e.g., *The Shakeout* and *The Bear Raid*. The change of scene is interesting but they are marred by carelessness over detail. Colonel Pemberton, head of Diversified Corporate Services Ltd., was reported in *The Guardian* as saying, 'There is not much evidence of bugs being used in British industrial operations' (4 January, 1982). It is taken for granted in Tute's *The Golden Greek* that the big companies employ agents to spy on each other, but the activity is only mentioned in passing. Susan assumed that Kraskewitz was employed by Kostas and Levantikos International to spy on Sandbrooke and Duvinicoles. Kalamakis, Kostas's father-in-law, employed Skoufarides as a spy.

One of the few novels where even a minor reference is made to the practice is d'Agneau's *Eeny, Meeny, Miny, Mole*. Hallam meets Lord Leech in a Paris hotel. He ran 'a small but highly effective industrial espionage company, mostly selling new product developments to rival companies.' After he leaves Leech, Hallam sees him talking to the Soviet agent. It seems likely that commercial espionage lacks glamour when compared with political. There is certainly scope for the dames but the weaponry is on a smaller scale and nuclear warheads have greater appeal these days than old-fashioned orgasms.

21: SPIES AND THE CLASS WAR

The class issue has been one of the major concerns of British fiction this century. It is so powerful that hardly any writers have been able to avoid it. On the one side they attack it, openly and consciously, and on the other side they illustrate it, instinctively and secretly. The novel has been written largely by middle-class authors and its orientation has been what you might expect. Most British readers (also, until the fifties, largely middle-class) like to establish the hero's social status. It is a large part of his reality. Thus we have fictional figures such as Lord Peter Wimsey and Richard Hannay who acquire almost mythological status because, like mythological heroes, they stand for a recognizable type.

It was inevitable, as social changes occurred, that the lower class (virtually the 'other' class) would hit back. This became apparent in the Northern and kitchen-sink novels that appeared after the Second World War, but the spy novel has become the chosen vehicle for some writers in this movement. Reaction against the public school conventions of Buchan (who never went to public school) gave impetus to this.

John Le Carré's *A Small Town in Germany* can be seen to a considerable extent as a case of Turner versus the Embassy. Turner is common, vulgar, free with his language and accusations and the complete antithesis of the famous 'old school tie'. He expresses his contempt for the Embassy officials and they express theirs for him. Before Turner even gets to Bonn he is irritated by Shawn. Turner finds Shawn slow-witted and inefficient; Shawn hears 'a Yorkshire voice, and common as a mongrel'. After a tiff, Shawn stares after Turner as he goes down the corridor. 'That's what happens, he decided, when you open your doors to the other ranks. They leave their wives and children, use filthy language in the corridors and play ducks and drakes with all the common courtesies.' Shawn wore a 'Brigade of Guards jacket'; he travelled First class, Turner Second.

Lumley tells Turner he has to go to Bonn to find an apparent defector. He tells him to get a suit, to look as if he belonged. But I don't, do I? says Turner. 'All right', says Lumley, 'Wear the cloth cap. Christ, I'd have thought your class was suffering from too much recognition already.' Which is what Lumley hopes for, as he finds Turner's self-assertion embarrassing. Once in Bonn, at the Embassy, Turner encounters the same antagonism when he meets Bradfield: 'They were glaring at one another across centuries of suspicion: Turner clever, predatory and vulgar, with the hard eye of the upstart . . .' And Turner has the advantage of a biting sarcasm denied to the others, as when someone tells him 'Steed-Asprey's got Lima'.—'Yes, we're all thrilled about it', says Turner, who was never less thrilled in his life.

Public School Spy

Recruiting spies from Cambridge (which until recently meant in effect from the public schools) is a tradition that goes back to Elizabethan times. Sir Francis Walsingham wanted to plant an agent in the Jesuit seminary at Rheims, which was training young men in the conspiracy against Elizabeth. In February 1587 Christopher Marlowe was selected to go there as a potential (and bogus) Catholic student. At that time, of course, the class system as we know it had not yet come into existence. Marlowe was the son of a shoemaker.

We don't hate these public school and Oxbridge heroes. In fact, we have a very soft spot in our hearts for them. They are much more attractive than some of the agents who have superseded them. The only thing we have against them is that their entrance into the charmed circles they adorned was too easy. This is envy, not hate, and it is based on reason, not emotion. It is not easy to say which is the best spy novel to have been written—whether it is the pukka *Riddle of the Sands* or the sordid *Spy Who Came in from the Cold*—but there is no doubt at all that *Clubland Heroes*, by Richard Usborne, is the best book to have come *out* of the genre, although there is a considerable overlap with detection and the sheer physical adventure yarn. This book lauds the three great club writers (Buchan, Dornford Yates and Sapper) and their heroes. It is a remarkable piece of work for there can hardly have been a more unpleasant character than Bulldog Drummond or a sillier one than Berry and yet Usborne manages to envelop them in a charm that he dredges up from the most unpromising material. It is really another way of illustrating how literature can transmute pain into pleasure and ugliness into beauty.

First published in 1953, the 1974 edition has a useful Introduction by the author. He obviously writes out of nostalgia. Clubland itself has changed, even disappeared. He points out that Wodehouse's Psmith, just down from Cambridge, was a member of six West End clubs. 'Some of today's heroes don't have clubs at all. I doubt if Le Carré's and Len Deighton's favourites possess dinner jackets.' I'm sure Bond had one and I think Usborne is probably wrong about some of Le Carré's people, especially when they sit down and moan about decline. But it doesn't seem likely that Charlie Muffin even sports a tie.

Leaving fiction for a while and looking at the actual security organization in this country, it becomes clear that the unquestioning trust in the public school product eventually led to disaster. Sir Percy Sillitoe, head of MI5 when Maclean and Burgess defected in May 1951, complained that he had not been told that they were under investigation by his own organization. David Wise and Thomas B. Ross wrote in *The Espionage Establishment:* 'A former police official, Sillitoe apparently felt his background was resented by the Oxbridge types in MI5, who could not believe the two Cambridge men had committed treason.' Class tensions of this type have undeniably contributed to Britain's bad record in the area of treachery, especially during the 1960s, involving MI5, MI6, the Foreign Office, the Admiralty and the Defence ministry. British Security was a nineteenth century virtue which has become a twentieth century fault. The recruitment of Intelligence was too deeply rooted in Oxbridge and the London club world. This may have been satisfactory during the *Clubland Heroes* era, say 1900–1930, but it constituted a considerable disadvantage in the context of high-speed communications, insistent news media and K.G.B. aggressiveness.

Allen Dulles, the C.I.A. boss, said on television that British Intelligence had suffered from 'too much of the old-school tie. If you went to Oxford or Cambridge you were all right. Well, it didn't turn out that way.' Harold Wilson made a similar charge in a Commons debate over the Vassall case in May 1963. 'Were our authorities too easily reassured by the school the man went to, the fact that he came of a good family . . . the fact that he was personable, had a good accent and manner, and was a member of the Conservative and Bath clubs, as Vassall was? I wonder if the positive vetting of Vassall would have been so casual if he had been a boilermaker's son and gone to an elementary school.' Among the fiction writers no-one stresses this opposition more strongly than Warren Tute.

The public school spies and collaborationists were a mixed bunch and came from two main backgrounds. There were those from very rich families, usually aristocratic and possessing large landed interests. These were prominent during the years leading up to the Second World War and usually had Nazi sympathies. They do not figure to any marked degree in spy fiction because the genre did not seem to attract a large readership; there is, broadly speaking, a gap between Sapper (say the early thirties) and the first Bond (the early fifties). Admittedly this is only the secondary reason for the comparative absence of fiction about Nazi espionage. The primary reason is a social one, and it is not in my present frame of reference, though we can speculate: perhaps a contributory cause was the fact that the English novel is decidedly middle-class in origin and readership, and this class of writer and reader was not anxious to reveal the less pleasant face of the Establishment. But there was another type of spy who came from a much poorer family, which had often had to make large sacrifices to send their young to public schools, who tended to be disgruntled and dissatisfied with the paucity of opportunity which life after university offered them—and their sympathies frequently lay with the Communists. Among them were the Macleans and Philbies and out of their histories and experience came the new-style spy novel.

These ex-public schoolboys often had close links with British security and in some cases were actually employed by MI5 and similar organizations. Of course, the majority of security officials were honest and loyal but they could not escape the stigma which the traitors laid upon their class. Nothing, absolutely nothing, is clear in the jungle world of Intelligence, as I have stressed until the reader is probably sick of it—but at times it does seem the only certainty one can discover. I have referred to Tute's strong antipathy towards the public school security man but having said that it is necessary to make a qualification. 'Mado had a long-standing prejudice against upper-class public schoolboys and the way they carried on, but there were times when that casual style could achieve results he doubted could be obtained in any other way' (*The Resident* 1973). This was in interrogation rather than field activity. On the whole, however, the

Security organizations in much recent spy fiction are characterized by a class division, with attendant animosities, that is scarcely calculated to improve efficiency. Here is one last example from one of the lesser known writers, N.J. Crisp. In *The Gotland Deal* (1976) Kenyon, a policeman, is not particularly class-conscious. He knew that crime was not confined to one income bracket. But Lance Everitt, an Establishment officer in the Foreign and Commonwealth Office, irritated him. His cordiality was patronizing. Kenyon thought of him as 'an upper-class creep.' Kenyon's father was a retired taxi-driver.

One would not accuse Le Carré of any powerful class prejudices, judging by his writing. Rather than bitterness one finds nostalgia for a lost paradise, and such a paradise could only have been upper-class and aristocratic. Nevertheless, according to his interview with Miriam Gross, his opinion of the upper classes is abysmal. There is no inconsistency here, of course—they are a wretched crew because they have fallen so far below the level of their forebears. Le Carré told Gross how he taught at Eton.

> It was an absolutely fascinating time. I had never had any experience of the British ruling class before and it probably coloured my later writing more than any other experience. People who rail against the English upper classes don't know how awful they really are—the way they talk, the way they function. Their prejudices are absolutely stunning.

It is certain (another certainty at last!) that some of these prejudices have cost the country dear. Appointments have been made that have been based exclusively on the kind of family the recruit came from. Sir Roger Hollis, one-time Director of MI5, and widely suspected of having been a spy for Russia, was the son of a bishop: 'in all probability, sufficient evidence of his loyalty', comments Chapman Pincher in *Their Trade is Treachery*. (Blunt was a vicar's son.) But this pathetic faith dies hard. Stuart Hood, reviewing Montgomery Hyde's *Secret Intelligence Agent* in *The Guardian*, 22 July 1982, complains that Hyde regards the new head of MI6 as well fitted 'by birth, education and professional background for a difficult and exacting job'. This highly satisfactory background was Eton and the Guards.

Grammar School Spy

The new-style spy novel usually has a fellow of no social account as its lead. Brian Freemantle's Charlie Muffin is their model. But he is not alone, though he is certainly the cheekiest.

Anthony Price's Colonel Butler is of humble East Lancashire origin. His loyalty to his organization (and also the old-fashioned loyalty to country) are never suspect. He is solid, rather unimaginative (this meant in the good sense, i.e., not flighty!), utterly and absolutely dependable. Richard Hannay would have regarded him as the ideal lieutenant—or perhaps sergeant-major, for although he was a colonel he had risen from the ranks. He represents the new grammar school product which is slowly replacing the public school model. He is aware of the class tensions which disturb the efficiency of security procedures but he does his best to ignore them. In *Colonel Butler's Wolf* he is given the job of masquerading as an academic but he believes this is only because the more suitable (because of his public school accent) Hugh Roskill is injured. Butler feels ashamed of his personal bitterness. He is a highly disciplined military man. (The good soldier is on the highest level in Price's pantheon.) He acknowledges that suitability for a job is all that matters, irrespective of the reasons for it. His irritation is kept under, not flourished like Charlie Muffin's.

His time has come because there is now a new breed of politician who wants to promote the under-dog of the old dispensation. His father was a Regimental Sergeant Major who became a prominent trade unionist after leaving the Army. Butler's real qualification (i.e., he is being considered for promotion) is that 'the bloody politicians won't be able to resist him. Ex-grammar school scholarship boy, risen from the ranks by merit—son of a prominent trade unionist, a friend of Ernie Bevin's—still with a touch of Lancashire in his accent too. Which he can turn on when he wants, when he needs to . . . no Labour minister can resist *that*. Not for the power behind the throne in Intelligence!' (*Tomorrow's Ghost* 1979).

Deighton doesn't stress the class angle but nor does he hide it. In *Spy Story* the wealthy Ferdy Foxwell turns up in a swagger car, dark blue with matching upholstery. 'The car cost more than my father earned from the railway for ten years' conscientious service ', Pat Armstrong reflects but he (or Deighton) immediately makes a comment which puts the class war in its place: '. . . but Ferdy buying

a small Ford wasn't going to help my father', which is very much the
kind of reaction one would have expected from Colonel Butler. Steve
Champion in *Yesterday's Spy* was certainly spurred on by class
resentment. He got to Sandhurst on merit and scholarships. 'Don't
ask me to say thank you', he said. 'By God, Charlie, you're a working
class boy. You know what I mean.'

Braine's *The Pious Agent* (1975) again catches the mood. (It is not
always the best novels which are the most representative.) The
Director of Counter-Espionage is looking for an agent of a particular
kind. The ones he had been offered are no good: 'They're public-
school muttonheads, decent chaps, gentlemen—which is the last
thing I want.' He says he wants 'agents who can go anywhere, and
an agreeable young grammar-school boy holding Her Majesty's
commission is just the ticket.' It turned out to be Xavier Flynn. 'His
father is a working-class boy who made good—*his* father was a dock
labourer—and he got a scholarship to the grammar school and
eventually became an accountant.' Origins are reflected in faces:
Droylsden had an upper-middle class face, while Flynn's was a
navvy's or bookie's face. (One is reminded of one of Evelyn Waugh's
characters who was said to have working-class hair.) Behind all this
rather superficial discussion of class origin lies a much more
important question which is certainly exercising the minds of many
modern spy writers. Who does the country belong to anyway? Who
has a stake in it, and what kind of stake? It used to be assumed that the
country 'belonged' to the upper classes, who spoke with a special
accent to differentiate themselves and denote possession. Flynn
spoke Seventies Classless.

All of this is excellent material for Marcel d'Agneau. John Welland
(in *Eeny, Meeny, Miney, Mole*) should never have been recruited. He
was a commoner. Strawson (the boss who defected) had said: 'The
service is going to the dogs if we let in Grammar schoolboys, sons of
butchers and spotwelders. The popular classes have no inherent
loyalties, they have been weakened by social security, no moral fibre,
no backbone when it comes to the crunch. They will squeal at the first
sign of interrogation. No butchers' boys in the Service, blackball the
bastard who lets them in.' Sandy Bleak, who had been to a second-
class public school and whose father was director of only two
companies, considered himself lucky to get into the Service. Strawson
never met Welland but he had a nose for proles. ' "X", he said, "our
man X is a prole, Hugh. You're infiltrating the proles into the Service

I know it." He knew that anyone who needed a scholarship wasn't one of his crowd. Couldn't afford to buy his way in, like the rest of them.' (This is Willy, who recalls that Welland got a scholarship to Cambridge.)

Gallant agrees with Strawson. While he was being trained at Easton a bunch of graduates came in from Bristol and some northern universities. Hopeless. Recruitment was being done by Jerry Rattle, who came from Sussex University. 'Red brick', said Gallant. 'Knew there was something second class and flaky about him. Red brick would fit.' Simon Caw is worried that he might be under suspicion. No, says Grimly: 'you didn't go to Eton or Harrow, Newcastle University is not noted for its left wing politics, you were never really socially important enough . . .' When Grimly finally obtains the Second Eleven list he is disgusted to find seven Cambridge men on it and five red brick—a travesty, he says. He was presumably disgusted that the Cambridge men were in the *second* eleven.

Charlie Muffin

Spies have four main targets. The first is the original, the enemy. The object is information. The second is counter-espionage; the object, the spy himself. Then it starts getting complicated and progressively more nasty. The spy spies on his allies. In Brian Freemantle's *Charlie Muffin* an American operative in Moscow has been ordered to keep Snare under observation as soon as he arrives. After Snare had been arrested the Americans put the Moscow Embassy on full alert so that they could spot his replacement. The final stage comes when the spy spies on his fellow spies. There is complete absence of trust between administration and field operatives. The Director in this novel keeps Charlie under constant surveillance and this includes reports from Janet, his secretary and god-daughter, who was sleeping with Charlie: 'I want to know your pillow talk as well.' Charlie knew that while he was talking to her the electronic division were bugging her flat.

As if the espionage jungle is not complicated enough, Freemantle introduces class tension as a serious element. It wouldn't stop at murder so long as it could be arranged that the political enemy actually squeezed the trigger. There is a pleasing freshness about this novel, the first of the Charlie Muffin series. Perhaps it is a product of the cards-on-the-table approach that Freemantle adopts. He deliberately selects a man with a lower-middle class grammar school background as his spy, and uses him to point class distinctions and to satirize the Establishment. It is a direct challenge to the traditional social background of the spy novel, which was not only extremely well-heeled in the days of Buchan and Oppenheim but usually (as Maugham pointed out in *The Summing Up*) required the presence of aristocrats as well.

Snare is seen through Muffin's eyes. He is a colleague and a Cambridge graduate, and he utters obscenities with careful modulation.

> Had there still been National Service, thought Charlie, Snare would have rolled his own cigarettes in the barracks to prove he was an ordinary bloke and made up stories about N.A.A.F.I. girls he'd screwed. No he wouldn't, he corrected immediately. The man would have used his family connections to obtain a commission, just as he was invoking them to push himself in the service. He'd have still lied about the N.A.A.F.I. girls, though.

Charlie was irritated because the others called each other by their surnames. In his world they used Christian names. 'He knew they used the public school practice to annoy him.' Charlie didn't always come off best. When he retorted, 'I'd rather have a mate than a rich father and a public school accent', he was laughed down in derision. They accuse him of inverted snobbery. Who can doubt it? Snare knew Charlie was a professional but still regarded him as an out-of-date anachronism. (This seems odd, in espionage terms, because Charlie seems to represent a new presence to the reader.) 'Muffin was an oddity, like his name, a middle-aged field operative who had entered in the vacuum after the war, when manpower desperation had forced the service to reduce its standards to recruit from grammar schools and a class structure inherently suspect, and had risen to become one of the best-regarded officers in Whitehall.'

Charlie was particularly sensitive about money. He liked to pay his way and didn't like to owe anything to anybody. His wife had money and he was reluctant to depend on it. Why, she wondered, did he have to have 'that bloody grammar-school pride'?

Apart from the flat-vowelled accent, Charlie wore his fair hair too long and without any style, flopped back from his forehead. He perspired easily and thus rarely looked washed and the fading collars of his shirts sat uncomfortably over a haphazardly knotted tie, so it was possible to see the top button was missing. It was a department store suit, bagged and shapeless from daily wearing, the pockets bulging like a schoolboy's with unseen things stored in readiness for a use that never arose.

Cuthbertson, the Director, loathed him. He was not surprised to find that Charlie was having an affair with his secretary and god-daughter. 'Rutting always has been the pastime of the working class.' They used to call him Charles until he insisted on 'Charlie'.

The class angle is so heavily emphasized it suggests more than mere prejudice. Freemantle is seriously claiming that Manchester Grammar School is a far better training for espionage (and probably, by implication, for the labyrinth of modern life) than Eton, Oxford and the Guards. But Charlie is fair-minded—he is a great admirer of the previous Director, who came from the 'enemy' social group. If we bear this in mind, though it is easy to overlook amidst the welter of other antagonisms, Charlie Muffin is a plea for individual worth.

There is in fact much more than class prejudice to interest the reader in Freemantle's work. At his best he is one of the better spy writers of the second rank, but his work is uneven. It is noteworthy that Charlie's wife, like Bond's, was killed through involvement in his work. There is a strange fatality among the wives of fiction spies. Smiley's is estranged, and she is not the only one. But Charlie, although very unprepossessing by accepted social standards, attracted women easily. It was his revenge on the snobs, a bonus granted by the author. But sex wasn't really important to him. His god was expertise. It didn't matter who showed it, the Russians as much as the British—he was a fully paid-up member of the Fellowship of Spies. His deference to hoods and the skills they possessed was immense and at the same time distasteful. 'Professional' expressed his highest mark of esteem. Sometimes one feels that Freemantle may be having the reader on, as when *Charlie Muffin's Uncle Sam* ends with the greatest massacre in the history of Spy-Fi. Charlie manages to set the hoods, the FBI and Russian-trained Cubans against each other, with the police coming in to finish it off. What's more, as all the Cubans were killed, it was taken for granted that the C.I.A. had sent them in.

There is always the suggestion of satire in Freemantle, though it is not so overt as in Trevanian or d'Agneau. He likes to deploy his spies and agents in huge numbers so that the outcome often resembles a pitched battle rather than a small local engagement. In *Charlie Muffin* Charlie goes to the Austro-Czech frontier to meet Kalenin, who is believed to be defecting. 'One hundred and fifty British and American operatives had already been drafted into Vienna and three tons of mobile electrical equipment flown in and housed at the American Embassy. Fifty more men were being moved in that day.' The operation was planned on a map. If there was pursuit a decoy car would be used. If the crossing were unchallenged, Kalenin would be taken to Vienna through a corridor of operatives, all linked by radio, so that they could close in behind and surround the Russians in a circle of safety. Is it perhaps possible that this is the Finland Station in reverse? Unless my memory of the Ancient Egyptian language is playing me false, surely Kalenin means the Spirit of Lenin? There is a possibility that Lenin, if reincarnated, would get out of Eastern Europe as quickly as he could!

But on the more serious side, Freemantle is mainly concerned with treachery, including its causes and its effects. Defectors from either side are common enough in both life and fiction but it is rare to find a Russian openly declaring his treachery to another, as he does in *Face Me When You Walk Away* (1974). Illinivitch, a Deputy Minister of Culture, appears to be doing this when urging a certain line of action on Josef. Josef says he wants to make one thing absolutely clear—he is a good Russian and will do nothing to damage his country. Illinivitch tells him he is a fool. It is a trap but the method is unusual. Josef is confronted by many of the problems that are peculiar to the espionage milieu. He is married to the daughter of an English Tory M.P. The marriage was a failure sexually but it also made him especially vulnerable. It 'was an inconvenience. An inconvenience he was uncertain whether he could afford.' And it is not till the final pages that we realize that there is also another love, and of a different kind, in Josef's life that complicates his situation even further. But then, what spy in his right mind (or operative or defector) would ever complain about difficulties? Before leaving for Prague to meet Kalenin, who was apparently planning defection, Charlie called on his previous and admired boss, Sir Archibald Willoughby. He is in effect saying goodbye. He could be killed or caught. But it is an agent's goodbye. Sir Archibald says, 'The risk isn't new: it's been there on every job upon which you've ever been engaged.'

One of Freemantle's faults as a novelist is that he presents people saying what they think rather than what they actually say. If he had advertised this as a gimmick, in the avant garde manner, as a kind of god-nephew of Virginia Woolf, it would have excited the posh Sundays. But for a popular novelist it's a bit risky because it irritates. Another irritating habit is shared with Anthony Price, that of commenting on the cleverness or otherwise of his agents' procedures and thinking. But Freemantle's major contribution to the spy novel remains Charlie Muffin, the twisted little man from below-stairs. His most rounded portrait is to be found in *The Inscrutable Charlie Muffin*, (1979) where his particular vice, self-pity, was highlighted. He envied people with wives, mistresses and friends but concealed his feelings under a blanket of contempt. He dressed appallingly. 'Charlie wore the sort of concertina'ed suit he remembered from their every encounter, like a helper behind the second-hand clothes stall at a Salvation Army hostel. The thatch of strawish hair was still disordered about his face and the Hush Puppies were as scuffed and down-at-heel as ever.' Charlie once reflected that much of his life had been spent 'getting hold of the shitty end of the stick that nobody else wanted to touch.' Both his wife Edith and the one man he had admired, the former head of Security, Sir Archibald Willoughby, had drawn attention to his inverted snobbery and inferiority complex. He even descended to scoring off secretaries because they had posh accents. He resented his wife's wealth, feeling he was being patronized. 'You're a shit, Charlie, he thought' (speaking to himself). 'But he'd never made the pretence of being anything else.'

One last intriguing fact. He had been an aerial photographer in R.A.F. Intelligence. There couldn't be many of them around. Len Deighton had been one too.

22: LEN DEIGHTON: AN ENIGMA

The main puzzle about Len Deighton is that, while being such a good writer he is not even better. One feels he ought to be placed in the same class as Le Carré and Greene but just fails. If one were making out his school report it would be necessary to state that he 'could do better'.

He brought a lot of new ideas to spy fiction, prominent among them being his delight in gimmickry combined with a remarkable display of technical erudition. But when this is compounded with an array of footnotes and appendices it tends to irritate. He seems to be a very private person. I am told that you cannot phone him but must communicate through telex, although I discovered that a letter to him got through and produced a friendly reply. His hero is usually nameless, which may again hint at a desire for anonymity. Films demand names so the hero of *The Ipcress File* (1962) became Harry Palmer.

It occurred to me that spy fiction may not be his strongest point. Certainly none of his spy novels is as good as *Bomber* (1970) which is about war. It's on the grand scale, Tolstoyan in type, with masses of characters. Again, the technical knowledge is stupendous. Unlike the spy novels, it isn't confused by the urge to confuse. It is probably the gravity of the subject (a bombing raid on Germany which went tragically wrong, from every point of view) that caused Deighton to present his characters with understanding and pity rather than as vehicles for wisecracks. His Germans are as likeable and unlikeable as his British.

Information Man

His best spy novel is perhaps *Horse Under Water* (1963) (*Funeral in Berlin*, 1964) is its rival for the title), much superior to the over-praised *The Ipcress File*. It exhibits, as the best work usually does, all the merits and faults of his work, and more positively than elsewhere. It is immensely ingenious, full of detailed information and it is written with great verbal sensitivity and yet there are times when he strains credibility in a way that would rouse even Bond's admiration, as when the anonymous lead manages to hoodwink a professional criminal named Butcher and photograph a diary. This would have been possible if Butcher had been either hopelessly drunk or mentally subnormal or in some other way incapacitated, but there is no hint of this. Like so many novels that are mentioned in this book it is not spy fiction *sui generis*. Its subject is political conspiracy (which always fascinates Deighton) and narcotics control. The tone of ceaseless cynicism, which is present in all his spy fiction, irritates. It is one of those things which causes the reader to exclaim: Why does he do it?

I can't help feeling the absence of a name suggests another kind of unfinished business. (Just as the continuing recurrence in Greene of the name Davis must have a meaning, if one could only get to it.) The lead in this novel is in fact codenamed Zayat. *Spy Story* (1974) is an exception, for here the lead is Patrick Armstrong, but he appears to be the same man we have encountered elsewhere. He wears glasses; he reads military history; he is familiar with Dawlish, a civil servant in Intelligence whom we have met before; and he encounters an old enemy, the Russian Colonel Skok. (Skok tends to appear on the scene at critical moments; his presence always detracts from the sense of realism Deighton strives for, usually successfully, particularly through his technical detail.) But there is one inconsistency between Armstrong and the other leads, whoever they are: he dislikes modern music whereas elsewhere he (or they) has been observed enjoying Schoenberg.

Is the Unnamed Deighton? This possibility always agitates the critic and it is frequently rebutted by the author. In many cases, perhaps most cases, the lead *is* the author, whatever the author may say, because the author cannot help himself. He may take his lead into situations which he has never known but the inner man, and his reactions to hypothetical external situations, are his and no-one else's. Perhaps a chance remark in *Billion-Dollar Brain* may be relevant. The lead hears the third movement of the Mozart A Major Concerto 'which was working itself up to that frantic minor-key Turkish routine which I've never thought a good enough ending for such a great beginning; but then that complaint went for just about everything in my life.' Is this an authentic personal note? Would it tally with the decline in his spy fiction? A strong sense of dissatisfaction, even a lack of fulfilment, seems to drive Len Deighton. It is something more than the boy from below getting his own back, although that element is also present. Unlike Freemantle, he never stresses his origins but he does state from time to time that he is a grammar school product working with public schoolboys.

Then the masses of information which he supplies (quite unnecessarily, if we consider the traditional nature of the novel) may be a form of showing off. Let us look at *Horse Under Water* again. There are the footnotes. 'Friends', we are told, is jargon for the employees of MI5. There are actually three on one page: 'cut-outs', the construction of a network to ensure that one detected person doesn't lead to another; 'post box', a place where messages are deposited so that collector and depositor do not come face to face; 'superimposed system', a method of checking the network. There are six appendices: on Telephone Tapping, Operation Bernhard (counterfeit banknotes), Kurier (a signalling device used by the German navy) and the brief accounts of a couple of agents. Then on the flyleaf there are fifty-eight words, mainly of one syllable, arranged in two columns of twenty-nine each, headed *Solution*. No. 2 is Nostrum: at one point the lead is filling in a crossword and writes Sistrum, then changes it to Nostrum.

There are a lot more footnotes in *An Expensive Place To Die* (1967). One gets the impression that Deighton is at heart a very serious person who feels concern for the world and its unhappy millions but he can't be bothered to write the novel that lurks somewhere within him. But that statement is too stark: so far he hasn't written it but he is working towards it. He is certainly closer to it than the writer of many a pretentious campus novel. His one serious novel of civilian life, *Close-up* (1972), is a more satisfying performance than Le Carré's counterpart, *The Naive and Sentimental Lover*; it is less trivial. Whatever the result, Deighton must be aiming at the serious reader for no sex-crime addict is going to bother with footnotes. The footnotes are often interesting because they give information that is otherwise hard to come by—for instance, on the complexity of the French police system and details of the Sûreté Nationale, which attends to counter-espionage and economic espionage (involving the unions and potential strikes) as well as frontier policing, gaming and the normal standard police work.

The total effect of all this information gravitates against the human vitality that is so necessary to fiction. It is too mechanical, too efficient, too exact. It becomes impossible to care about the fate of his characters because they never show signs of breaking through the master's plan, as they usually do in Greene, Le Carré and Ambler and even Freemantle. So Deighton tries to compensate with some rather glib philosophy. At times he is guilty of a stark falsity which is the direct result of his desire to be clever or funny. In *Billion-Dollar Brain* Dawlish and the lead replace eggs from Porton that have been injected with a living virus with others that are non-injected. 'We got them from the canteen, but had a terrible job removing the little lion stamp-marks that guarantee purity.' In this novel the chapter heads are adorned with quotes from nursery rhymes. (Perhaps Deighton had a vague memory of a Graham Greene novel which had quotes from a Charlotte Yonge child's novel as chapter sub-heads.) There are three appendices. Espionage jargon is helped out by the usual footnotes. In one he explains that many modern espionage terms come from the German: *die Hosen herunterlassen*, to take one's trousers off, that is, to reveal you are an agent and attempt to recruit another. The older term had been 'the moment of truth'. You *come to rest* when you are sure that a person is no longer under surveillance. A man who is tailed or suspected is said to be *spitting blood*. Of course, all spy writers use such terms. What is different is that Deighton gives them a text-book effect. There seems to be a pedagogic intent. This is not entirely new. Robert Brain included an appendix in his *Kolonialagent* and the height of absurdity was reached by Ethel Mannin before the war with her *Ragged Banners: a Novel with an Index*. The truth is that Deighton is basically a documentary writer and his later works on war suggest that he realizes this. Le Carré, in contrast, never told his readers what 'to come in from the cold' meant. It was their job to pick up the meaning. The result is that the phrase has been used by others with varying implications. This may be a pity but it should not be regarded as a novelist's responsibility.

One picks out these faults reluctantly because Deighton is an extremely effective writer. In common with many other thriller writers (Chandler is the supreme example) he has a great gift of tangible imagery. Sometimes one gets the feeling (as one did with Chandler also) that the image is *forced* out of the material by the energy that must be expended on violent action. This can lead to misuse (one of Chandler's characters once squeezed another man's shoulder to a pulp!) but it can also be very successful. Only a writer who is also a poet could write that 'the air clung like a warm face-cloth. Men moved in the leisurely evening warmth like alligators across a mud-flat' (*Billion-Dollar Brain*). Deighton would have made (and may still make) a superb critic. The rewards of criticism are not commensurate with those of fiction. His thinking is positive and he has a firm grasp of detail, well illustrated in *Close-up*. Like Brian Aldiss, he is capable of coming from what the academics consider the 'lower levels' of literature to teach them their craft.

Strength and Weakness

The Ipcress File is ingenious but it is the kind of ingenuity that can exasperate the reader. To begin with, it groans with wisecracks. (Forsyth's strength, incidentally, is that he always resists the temptation to make the wisecrack which one feels he is perfectly capable of making.) Wisecracks are not wit. An occasional one relaxes tension; too many destroy concentration. 'She gave me a sour look, or perhaps I already had one'. That would be more at home with a TV comic than in a novel which is fundamentally serious. The obsession with objects and the exactness of his listing has the opposite effect because it buttons down the concentration. Thus a tension is set up and it is one that disturbs the required flow of the novel. 'Dalby moved one half-eaten egg and anchovy sandwich, toasted. A speciality of Wally's delicatessen downstairs in Charlotte Street. He then moved the SARS to SORC volume of the *Britannica* and *Barnes' History of the Regiments*, a Leica with the 13.5 cm and a bottle of Carbon Tetrachloride, and was able to sit down on the desk.' This keys up the reader's attention. It tells us something about Dalby. It is not used for snobbish purposes, as in Fleming. But the very exactness may set up a quibbling frame of mind in the reader. Was it not a mistake to put 'Barnes'' in italics?

The merit of *The Ipcress File* is that it emphasizes without fuss the quality of mistrust and trickery which the new generation of spy writers brought to their work. The older writers had of course been aware of mistrust and trickery, but these had been the prerogatives of the enemy, who were cowardly, villainous and deceitful. Reading Deighton and his contemporaries one is left in no doubt that British spies have nothing to learn about villainy and disloyalty from their enemies. The novel was catching up with life. After the Burgess-Maclean fiasco there could be no further pretence. Defectors came from the top drawer. Le Carré weighed in with Haydon. Deighton's contribution was Dalby, head of an Intelligence unit. The lead is told he was apparently under suspicion at one point 'to take the heat off a high-ranking subject, so they did a phase two on you so he'd stick his neck out helping to clobber you.' Ironically it is Dalby who passes on the information.

Whatever his faults, one enjoys the strength of positive personality that shines through his writing. His mastery of detail is both physical and ideational. Here is an encapsulation of his method. The lead in *Funeral in Berlin*, his best novel if *Horse Under Water* isn't, and an American named Harvey enter a room where a Czech army officer is standing. 'Harvey turned to me and began to relight his cigarette. Americans don't often relight an inch of cigarette so I watched Harvey's lips. He mouthed "O.B.Z." under the cloak of his cupped hands. I didn't nod.' And then there is the inevitable footnote: 'O.B.Z.: Obranne Zpravodajstvi—security police of the army'. On the other side of this coin is the fact that at times he tries too hard, so that his style becomes overblown. Ice can be *slammed* into Martinis, though so far I haven't found the accelerator being *gunned*, an old favourite of the thriller school. His love of detail sometimes leads to quite meaningless statements. They open a tin of Beluga: 'Inside the tin were the light-grey veiny spheres of caviare, almost as big as a tiny pea.' This kind of irrelevance becomes very irritating when repeated *ad nauseam*.

It is not surprising, in view of his verbal facility, that the dialogue all too often consists of a series of wisecracks, with very little resultant communication. This is where Le Carré is superior, he tells us what is happening without concealing it in a mist of verbiage. The irrelevance extends to the epigraphs accompanying the chapter titles. In *Funeral in Berlin* there is a quotation from a chess manual at the head of each chapter. This may sound good at first but it soon becomes apparent that the quotations bear little relevance to the action. There seems to be a lot of wasted effort and intelligence. The footnotes and appendices are often informative and interesting, as in Sir Walter Scott, but it doesn't seem the right way to get the message across in a work of fiction. The love of detail can also lead to triviality. Perhaps the real accusation that can be levelled at Deighton is that so far he has not selected his material with sufficient care. Consider this: ' "Cigarette?" she said and flicked the corner of a pack of Camels with a skill that I can never master. I took one and brought a loose Swan Vesta match from my pocket. I dug my thumbnail into the head and ignited it. She was impressed and stared into my eyes as I lit the cigarettes.' The reader says: 'Coo!'

The essence of a good spy, crime, adventure or detective novel is that, however complex the plot may be, the author should present it cleanly. Fleming usually managed this with Bond but it is a skill that often eludes Deighton. The complexity of his action can be unravelled but it demands more patience and concentration than the reader is likely to give it. This weakness is usually signalized by a lengthy chapter of explanation at the end. It is very obvious in *An Expensive Place to Die*. But this chapter is not really fiction, it is an essay in clarification.

Now and again he introduces conscience into his story. Perhaps it is to increase respectability, or to appeal to another class of reader in addition to the action-at-all-costs type. The conscience sits uneasily, it is portentous, it doesn't belong to the warp and weft as it does with Greene or Le Carré or Chandler in the crime story. For instance, towards the end of this novel the hero (his name is given for once, but perhaps grudgingly, for it is T. Davis and could be a borrow from Greene, who brings Davis into half the novels he writes) finds he has been exploited by Byrd.

> 'You used me, Byrd' I said. 'You sent Hudson to me, complete with pre-fabricated hard-luck story. You didn't care about blowing a hole in me as long as the overall plan was okay.'
> 'London decided', Byrd corrected me gently.
> 'All eight million of 'em?'
> 'Our department heads', he said patiently. 'I personally opposed it.'
> 'All over the world people are personally opposing things they think are bad, but they do them anyway because a corporate decision can take the blame.'

This leads to a brief reference to the Nuremberg Trials, and where responsibility lies, whether with the individual or with Coca-Cola or Murder Inc. or the Wehrmacht General Staff. This is the route by which Deighton approaches politics, but it is pop politics, making a quick appeal to the simple-minded, emphasizing the Chinese menace and accepting historicism as a substitute for ideology. Deighton is not fundamentally interested in politics. The poverty of his political thought is disguised by this sort of apparently thoughtful concern:

> Permissiveness is slavery. But so has history always been. Your jaded, overfed section of the world is comparable to the ancient city states of the Middle East. Outside the gates the hard nomads waited their chance to plunder the rich, decadent city-dwellers. And in their turn the nomads would conquer, settle into the newly-conquered city and grow soft, and new hard eyes watched from the barren stony desert . . .

and so on.

Yesterday's Spy (1975) is a fairly typical Deighton performance. It starts cleanly, crisply, one begins to hope for a new clarity compared with his middle works. But once again he gets bogged down in his own ingenuity. Once again one concludes that wisecracking doesn't make a novel. Clarity is the key, one cannot repeat it too often, to the best spy novel. *Riddle of the Sands* had it and Le Carré manages it through terrain as difficult and complicated as Deighton's, however much television manages to mess it up. (This is an interesting point which I will return to in a later section.) Buchan and Fleming, both inferior to Deighton in their verbal skills, also had it. Deighton used to be cookery correspondent for a Sunday paper. Using this analogy, he makes the mistake of the inexperienced cook and crams in too many ingredients without regard for their compatibility. The character of the American security man, Schlegel, has turned into a stock figure (like stock for the pot), just as the Russian Skok had done previously. Schlegel is ultimately the fool who thinks everyone else is a fool until things are put right in the final chapter.

Deighton's Spy World

Deighton's enormous popularity is the product of his complete oneness with the environment he lives in and describes. He is the truly contemporary writer. In a sense, he even creates contemporaneity as he goes along. Goodness knows what Oppenheim would have made of him. It is often the role of poet to represent his society, as Auden did his. If we were looking for a Mr Seventies we might well choose Len Deighton. Of course, fashions change, beauty dies and the contemporary becomes the out-dated but there was certainly a period when Deighton was a kind of psychological thermometer.

That is why *The Ipcress File*, despite its many faults, caught the imagination. It may come as a shock to realize that this novel appeared over twenty years ago; its representativeness may have faded. But in 1962 it served as a kind of paradigm of the big world outside the family parlour and the office party. The Home Office was worried sick about the disappearances of top biochemists. It turns out that they (and also personnel from other backgrounds) were not defecting but were being kidnapped and brainwashed, although 'thought reform' was the new term. IPCRESS was an acronym formed from Induction of Psycho-neuroses by Conditioned Reflex with Stress. The mastermind was Jay who said, 'One of these days brain-washing will be the acknowledged method of dealing with anti-social elements'. When the organization was broken up Jay survived and in fact was employed by British Intelligence. But Henry, an Establishment figure, who had been working with him, was not unmasked.

The agent's life is a dangerous one and is always at risk. 'People like Vulkan are in danger—physical danger—every moment of every day' (*Funeral in Berlin*). Vulkan was an agent working for the British in Germany. What must be the response? Certainly not flamboyance and absurd heroics. (The Scarlet Pimpernel once went into action defiantly singing 'God Save the King'.) The agent is as careful and painstaking as a first-class carpenter making a window frame. In *Horse Under Water* Giorgio and Joe were both murdered. The unnamed lead had been near both of them at the time. He did not think the attempts had been levelled at him 'but diligence brings more agents to pensionable age than bravery ever did' so he decided to make his own personal enquiries. The secret agent who makes a name for himself is virtually 'blown' already. It always amazed me how Bond used to go round the world announcing his presence to all who would listen. But not Zayat. 'The greatest tribute you can pay to a secret agent is to take him for a moron. All he has to do then is to make sure he doesn't act too exactly like one' (*Funeral in Berlin*). Talking to the agent Vulkan he says, 'Listen, Johnnie. One of my great advantages in this business is that I look a little simple-minded; but I don't stop there; I *act* a little simple-minded.' Vaclav said that the English agent seemed 'not very professional'. The Russian Skok replied, 'In our business that's the very height of professionalism.' What Old Etonian would have taken Charlie Muffin seriously? It's the only way he managed to survive. Spies who had been caught by Charlie Muffin reminded him of 'the grey anonymous people at rush-hour bus queues. Which was why, he supposed, they had made such good spies'. (*The Inscrutable Charlie Muffin*, by Brian Freemantle.) Compare Tommy Hambledon in Manning Coles's *They Tell No Tales*, 1940. He had his facial scars removed (unlike Bond, who kept his) by a plastic surgeon. Van Krug complained because they had given him a very distinguished appearance. 'That's why I had 'em removed', said Hambledon.

This apparent moron must have his wits continuously on call. Every agent will be followed and every agent must have a plan for throwing off the tail. Spy literature is chock-full of tailing. The agent usually manages to get away but in most cases it is because the author has decided he will get away. To hell with probability! Deighton's man has it worked out, as in *Billion-Dollar Brain*. 'In view of the razzle-dazzle these boys were going through it was reasonable to suppose they were having me followed, so I took a cab and waited till we got into a traffic jam, paid off the driver quickly and hailed a cab moving in the opposite direction. This tactic, well-handled, can throw off the average tail if it's using a private car.' The drawback to this method is that it doesn't please the film companies, who want a car chase, preferably through San Francisco.

Deighton is aware of one of the major dangers that keep politicians awake at night: the growth of private enterprise in espionage, subversion and terrorism. Hitler, Chancellor of the Third German Reich, may have started the last major blood-letting; the next could be primed by a relative of Lucky Luciano or even Mad Mike Hoare. *Billion-Dollar Brain* is about this sort of activity. (Of course, we have had it before in Fleming and even J.B. Priestley. The difference is that it has become much more feasible.) Harvey Newbegin (a nephew of that old terrorist Begin?) is recruiting the lead.

> We don't normally tell our operatives anything about the organization, but I'll make an exception for you under the old pals' act. This is a private intelligence unit financed by an old man named Midwinter. Calls himself General Midwinter. He's from one of those old Texan families that have a lot of German blood. Originally the family came from one of the Baltic states—Latvia or Lithuania—that the Russians now have and hold. This old guy Midwinter has dreams of liberating the territory. I guess he'd like to instal himself as king or something.

He has two radio stations on ships that beam into the Baltic states. It can be treated as a joke ('Stand by for freedom and coke.') but it's a joke that can have nasty consequences. They have a mass of computer equipment and a training school back in the States. Deighton cannot resist an appendix—No. 3 in this volume, entitled 'Privately Owned Intelligence Units'. Most of them, we are told, are emigré formations like the Ukrainian Socialist Party, an anti-Communist Russian group based in Munich.

Deighton is very careful about cover. It is not good enough just to adopt a name and a job and leave it at that. It must be convincing. (I am reminded of the Oppenheim agent who represented Bethlehem Steel—and that was the end of Bethlehem Steel so far as he was concerned.) The protagonist of *An Expensive Place to Die*, Davis, is classified as a 'travel agency director', and this is inscribed on his *carte de séjour*. But he is also supposedly employed by a German magazine, 'a piece of fiction that the office in London had invented for the rare times when they had to instruct me by mail.' Byrd, another English agent, poses as an artist. There is a strong temptation to adopt an artist's pose because of his relative freedom, but it is extremely easy for a bogus artist to give the game away. Byrd has strong views which he expresses loudly. He is very critical of the avant garde and gives the impression that he knows what he is talking about.

The Lure of the Film

Is it possible these days for a thriller writer to write a book without having the film of the book in mind? An answer to this question would throw much light on a lot of modern writing.

The best stories are simple in design and structure: *The Riddle of the Sands* and *The Human Factor*, at the two extremes of the espionage fiction extension, are excellent examples. The worst stories are immensely complicated. The complication, usually unnecessary, is probably intended to induce a sense of significance—wonder, awe, what a fantastic world!—in the unaware and especially the unsophisticated reader. This can frequently lead to incomprehensibility. It can also lead to impatience and the reader asking himself: is it really worth all the brain-puzzling I have to go through?

Such novels in fact bear all the marks of having been written primarily to be filmed. They belong to the category of Latent Film Script. Our minds have become so dulled by a continuing flow of nonsense—instant sex with the minimum of preliminaries, miraculous escapes, naked, brawling violence, impossible punishment, murder without finesse, in short, a world where the senses have been all but banished—that we tend to forget how silly it all is. It becomes acceptable simply because there is so much of it. Very often the author cannot even be bothered to establish a motive. The human element, so strong in Greene's carefully titled *The Human Factor*, is totally missing. The film demands action. When I wrote in the previous paragraph that the reader is subjected to much 'brain-puzzling', I was of course referring to the thoughtful reader. It seems very likely that the fans of action films do not want to think. They simply want action, and the author of the script is perfectly prepared to give them that and that alone. There has certainly been a noticeable development in this area. The things that Orwell objected to so strongly in James Hadley Chase have now become commonplace.

Both Fleming and Deighton are self-consciously filmic. With both of them there is always fast-moving action. Deighton also adds the complexity of plot that seems to be an inevitable part of the film thriller. Fleming goes in for striking visuals, a posing of the actor in his environment, such as the man crawling out of Marilyn Monroe's mouth on a giant hoarding (*From Russia with Love*) which makes superb film, or of the girl lying spreadeagled on a white-striped bathing wrap in the golden path of the setting sun streaming across a beach (*On Her Majesty's Secret Service*). This is not the sort of effect we get in Deighton. The effect he seeks constantly is dynamic.

One major weakness of the novel *The Ipcress File* is its basic incredibility. But the incredibility is a consequence of the telling rather than the plot. The Burgess-Maclean-Philby story is every bit as sensational as *The Ipcress File* but when written down soberly it becomes credible. Deighton hypes everything up so that what could be credible becomes incredible during the reading. It is this quality that makes me think he has an ultimate film in mind. The reader doesn't really care what happens so long as it happens. (It ain't what you do, it's the way that you do it.) In the end, despite the verbal skill, *The Ipcress File* doesn't rise above the good adventure-yarn level. When the lead tells Jean the plot she exclaims, 'A plan to brain-wash the entire framework of a nation. It's hardly credible.' In this mood Deighton can best be described as an extremely literate Hank Janson.

Of course, he is not the only offender. The same quality spoils Warren Tute's work. *The Tarnham Connection* is an unsatisfactory novel partly because it has no centre and gives the impression of forming a rather unco-ordinated link in a series of connected novels. To write a series in which each component part can stand on its own is not an easy task. Anthony Powell and C.P. Snow have succeeded but many have failed. But Tute's novel also provides a good example of what can cause or compound obscurity in any story which depends on mystery for its effect. Obscurity is not really caused by complexity of plot alone. Where the characters are strong and convincing, the story is fleshed out and credibility and understanding follow. Where the characterization is weak there are no human contrasts to make relationships clear. We are still waiting for Deighton to give us a character who will bring his story into our world as well as the film world.

23: DIRECTIONS

One of the attractions of the spy fiction scene is to observe the directions in which it seems to be going. I use the plural form advisedly because there is considerable variety in the forms the genre is taking.

Before considering some of the leading spirits (that is, in the wake of Fleming, Le Carré and Deighton) in more detail, let us dip into the post-war bag and see what comes out. There has been, for instance, Peter Cheyney, now dead, who used to write common-or-garden thrillers which were never highly rated by the critics but were devoured by the readers. Among these books were some spy stories, especially a series which made use of the epithet *dark*. They were purely and simply action stories, but very professional. *Dark Wanton* (1948), for example, is mainly concerned with 'the double double-cross used a million times in the war by "double agents"—those supreme beings who worked on two sides but gave loyalty only to one side.' This is the kind of complexity that is meat and drink to the thriller writer. The plot of this novel is infuriatingly yet expertly and legitimately tangled. Cheyney had nothing to learn from his successors, and despite the greater critical acceptance of writers like Deighton he gives us credible plotting and counter-plotting, not merely a criss-cross of cosmetic bewilderment. But, as might be expected, he nods on occasion—considering the speed at which he wrote, this was inevitable. Why did the two girls, who were colleagues, actually fight and indulge in face-slapping *when there was no-one there to witness it—except the reader*? This was cheating. But he wastes few words, which is a boon to the reader who only wants a story, without embellishment; his style may be called mixed laconic and semicolonic. Another interesting point about Cheyney is that he did not always throw sex at the reader, a device that has become automatic with some writers. One of his characters, an agent called Antoniette Brown, openly 'disliked sex'. Of course, Oppenheim's Miss Brown of X.Y.O., in the novel of that name, had the same kink!

That was shortly after the war, in 1948. If we move on to 1966 we find Kingsley Amis entering the field. Now this is a completely different kettle of fish. Amis is an intellectual who pretends he isn't, and on the whole this has proved a good thing, because he can devote his considerable intelligence to writing without showing off. Part of his ploy is to admire James Bond openly and another part was to actually write a spy novel, which Virginia Woolf never did. *The Anti-Death League* (1966) has Amis's recognizable flavour. It doesn't set out to be a human document, like Le Carré or Greene, but it is immensely cultured and it operates over a wide sweep of human experience. His wit, at times Waughesque (that is, off-hand but penetrating) separates him from most of the other spy writers. There is no perpetual straining for effect, as in those cases where the spy novel seems to be emulating the TV sit-com. There is great compassion at the heart of what appears at first sight to be just a thriller. Brian Leonard is the nearest approach to the funny spy figure that a serious writer could allow himself. In the end we feel sorry for Leonard because he has been so obviously duped by his colleagues. Dr Best, on the other hand, is a stock figure who never transcends the role; he imagines he is a spy who will save mankind. You don't have to be a spy to believe that, of course.

Almost a decade later came one of the most unusual spy novels in the whole canon: R. Wright Campbell's *The Spy Who Sat and Waited*. The title proclaims it as a spy novel but it is in fact a mainstream novel about espionage. It should really be classed with a very select group of novels which would include Conrad's *The Secret Agent*, Greene's *The Human Factor* and Ambler's *Judgment on Deltchev*. When McCormick contacted him for his *Who's Who in Spy Fiction* he received the kind of reply that we would not expect from the average thriller writer. 'I wanted to write a book that illustrated the existentialist quality of modern life, showing life as being quite absurd and the things we do or are asked to do being even more absurd. I can think of no character more apt to create hell because it is his duty than a spy or a government assassin. Oerter's finest hour is the moment he refuses to enter into the plot against Hitler.' The average Left Wing ranter would consider that his basest hour, for he would never understand Oerter's commitment to mankind.

Some of the work of Manning Coles deserves mention at this point. *Drink to Yesterday*, 1940, is notable because the emphasis is on the person, not on the spying. In all Coles's best work the hero is mortified by the death and destruction he causes. These authors (Manning Coles was a partnership between Adelaide Frances Oke Manning and Cyril

Henry Coles), who flourished during the 'forties and 'fifties, were far superior to Sapper but not quite in the Ambler class.

Eric Ambler

We probably owe more to Eric Ambler than to any other spy writer because he rescued the genre from the kind of slough into which the detective novel has fallen.

Without Ambler I think it unlikely that either Le Carré or Deighton would have emerged. At a time when most spy writers were congenital Tories he applied his enlightened intelligence to the political background of espionage. His *Judgment on Deltchev* (1951) almost ranks with Koestler's *Darkness at Noon*.

McCormick says that Ambler 'struck a note of neutralism' in the spy story, telling the reader that in espionage one side was as bad as the other and that spies and spy-catchers were not only not heroic but they were often unpleasant people. Although he has never been engaged personally in Intelligence or Security and contradicts the familiar notion that those who have been 'in the game' are the most accurate, he is very strong on the background to espionage. The chain of circumstance which he narrates is always rational and probable; his leading characters are ordinary people who become enmeshed in situations. McCormick quotes him as saying, 'I have to be very careful because I know so little, you see. But perhaps that isn't the same for everybody.' But because he himself takes great trouble with his facts, he is quick to point out errors in the work of others. As an example, Fleming, who had been in Naval Intelligence, confused the Golden Horn with the Bosphorus in *From Russia with Love*. If there has been an increase in the volume of spy fiction it is because there has been a corresponding increase in the amount of espionage itself. Kenton, a freelance journalist in the early *Uncommon Danger* (1941) tells us why.

> The trade in military secrets was, he knew well enough, a very busy one. With the nations arming as fast as they could, the professional spies were prospering. He himself knew of two cases of military attachés paying fabulous prices for what, to him, had seemed trifling pieces of information—in one case the maximum angle of elevation of a new field gun; in the

other case confirmation of a slight inaccuracy in a previous
report on the thickness of the armour plating on a new tank.

The excellent *Judgment on Deltchev* is not a spy novel, though at one
point the hero, a Foreign Correspondent named Foster, is accused by
the country where he is observing a show trial and is denounced as an
enemy agent. This novel appeared before treason became such an
irresistible property for the spy writer but the first sentence suggests,
coolly and pointedly, why its character had changed in our century.
'Where treason to the state is defined simply as opposition to the
government in power, the political leader convicted of it will not
necessarily lose credit with the people.' After that, no wonder loyalty
could no longer be defined accurately. When you read Ambler you
realize what is often wrong with Deighton. Deighton is too feverish.
Ambler handles a complicated story soberly and lucidly. Deighton
compounds the complication and ties both himself and the reader in
knots.

As a background to *The Schirmer Inheritance* (1953), Ambler
developed the idea that espionage was becoming more and more
unavoidable in our world. Moreton is trying to find the heir to a huge
American estate and his enquiries take him to Germany. 'In the
summer of nineteen-thirty-nine, any foreigner who travelled about the
Rhineland asking questions, checking official records and sending
cables in cypher was bound to become suspect . . . In Essen I was
interviewed by the police and asked to give an account of myself.'
Ambler had already pointed out that the political configuration of the
modern world, plus its technological skills, made espionage inevitable.
Here we have the other side of the picture—a certain kind of behaviour
will arouse suspicions which did not exist in an earlier, less jittery age.

As the activity gathered pace, so there were more practitioners and
more people who were attracted by the life. Although spying has
traditionally been condemned as a dirty game it has always exercised
its attraction on a certain type who probably thinks it will endow him
with mystery and glamour. In the same novel Arthur is a cockney who
served in Greece and Yugoslavia during the war and then stayed on
with the ELAS (communist) guerillas. He wasn't a communist but he
enjoyed the life. Terrorists, assassins, commandos and guerillas do not
keep office hours; the life has obvious allure. Now he and his band
deserted by the politicians, lived in the mountains and raided banks
and other institutions. There were always devoted communists on the

inside to help them. Carey, the American lawyer, is impressed by what he thinks must be their courage and devotion. Arthur doesn't agree.

> If you ask me, these political convictions that make it O.K. to play someone else a dirty trick behind their backs, have something pretty phoney about them . . . I'm not pretending to be better than I am. It's these phonies I can't stand. You should talk to some of them. Clever. Know all the answers. Prove anything you like. The sort you *don't* want with you if you're going out on a patrol because, if things get sticky, *they're* the ones who'll start looking round for a reason for everybody to chuck in their hands and go home.

This is hardly logical, but presents an interesting if unusual standpoint. (After all, it does recall the way the International Brigades were forsaken when the Communists lost in Spain.) One of the dilemmas of modern society is that we tend to admire people, reluctantly perhaps, who are anything but admirable. To put it in another way, we admire their loyalty and loathe their philosophy. Arthur thinks the loyalty is phoney. Criminals get rather more sympathy than victims these days. Ambler was also preparing the way for William Haggard's Colonel Russell.

It is unusual to find a writer of political thrillers who, in addition to the more usual qualities of clarity, readability and pace, can also create recognizable characters and is endowed with the kind of maturity one finds in novelists who do not confine themselves to a particular genre. Over-specialization has its dangers; it sharpens the mind in some respects and dulls it in others. One can never be quite sure how to classify an Ambler novel. *The Light of Day* (1962) is a good example. It is not until we reach the last few pages that we can decide whether we have been reading a spy novel, a political thriller or a crime story. This is surely all to the good. Life never hangs out labels. The novel turns out to centre on burglary, though of a very ambitious kind. The suspense is also maintained by another device which is rare—the leading character is not only rather pathetic but no attempt is made to rouse our partisanship. At least, this was rare in 1962 though since then many have followed suit. We have no idea whether the fellow will get his deserts or whether he will manage to save his skin. Imagine Le Queux on that kind of jag!

The novel is not about espionage but it is about security. For some time the Turkish police believe there may be a political plot. Arthur

Simpson, a petty crook who is blackmailed into assisting in a scheme far beyond his own ambitions, is aware of Intelligence and sees its agents from the opposition angle. He knows that the Army (for instance) prefer to give a suspected man the benefit of the doubt, to avoid trouble, and that the police are much more difficult because they want to get you. But Intelligence people are even worse. 'Nine times out of ten they don't even have to worry about building up a case against you to go into court. *They* are the court—judge, jury and prosecutor, all in one.'

> I think that if I were asked to single out one specific group of men, one type, one category, as being the most suspicious, unbelieving, unreasonable, petty, inhuman, sadistic, double-crossing set of bastards in any language, I would say without any hesitation 'the people who run counter-espionage departments'. With them, it is no use just having one story; and especially not a true story; they automatically disbelieve that. What you must have is a set of stories, so that when they knock the first one down you can bring out the second, and then, when they scrub that out, come up with a third. That way they think they are making progress and keep their hands off you, while you gradually find out the story they really want you to tell.'

Arthur Simpson is a pathetic little man. Ambler makes no attempt to give him any appeal whatsoever, but we feel sorry for him. There is one moment when he flares into a state of moral indignation which briefly transcends his general feebleness. It is a case of the worm turning—not for long, but it expresses the frustration that such a large proportion of the human race must experience. It occurs when, for once, he feels he has an advantage over a man who has grossly insulted him. 'I suddenly felt as if my whole life had been spent trying to defend myself against people compelling me to do this or that, and always succeeding because they had all the power on their side; and then, just as suddenly, I realized that for once the power was mine; for once I wasn't on my own.' It is little touches like this, illuminating human character, that give Ambler his special place in the thriller genre.

From time to time, in interviews and the occasional essay, Ambler has given his views on the spy novel. In his Introduction to a collection of spy stories which he edited, *To Catch a Spy* (1964), he

gave reasons for the late start of the spy novel, compared with the
detective novel. The spy has always been regarded as an unsavoury
character. He was not suitable as a hero and no-one in the last century
had considered an anti-hero as acceptable. In the spy's situation there
is an awkward contradiction: he must be a man of absolute integrity
where his employer's interests are concerned but in his professional
capacity he is *ipso facto* a liar and a thief. Politicians and generals did
not want to dirty their hands. 'We know it has to be done, but we will
not talk about it. We will give the orders if we must—though it is
better if those who do the work will write their own orders—but we
cannot participate. And we do not want to know how the results are
obtained. Our hands must be clean.' It was even difficult to use the
spy as the villain, for this would mean the hero was also involved in
some sort of secret service or counter-espionage capacity.

The most revealing interview with Ambler that I have come across
was recorded by an American journalist named Joel Hopkins, and
was published in a periodical called *Journal of Popular Culture* (Vol.
IX, No. 2, undated). Ambler said he had failed in various fields and
decided to try his hand at the spy thriller.

> The detective story genre has been worked over and worked
> over, but no-one had looked at the thriller. It was still a dirty
> word. So I decided to intellectualize it, insofar as I was able.
> It wasn't very far then, but it was sufficient. I changed the
> genre and couldn't write the books fast enough . . . Sapper
> was writing solid right wing. He was an outright fascist. He
> even had his heroes dressed in black shirts. Buchan was an
> establishment figure, so club and fuddy-duddy and I decided
> to turn that upside down and make the heroes left wing and
> popular front figures.

Note for younger readers: at the time Ambler refers to, 'left wing'
simply meant socialist and not, as it does today, the Marxist variant
or Trotskyism or even neo-fascism, or authoritarian collectivism.

The spy story flourishes most in Britain and America and the best
spy writers (I am told) are British and American. Ambler says this is
because they have suffered most from spies, through their own
societies. It is obviously easier for a Russian spy to operate in Britain
than for a British spy to operate in the Soviet Union. He doesn't think
Le Carré and Deighton write about espionage but about treachery.
Watergate is a symbolic landmark of our time and he asks darkly:

who spies on the spies? As for the setting for espionage, he is attracted by the Middle East because of its contrasts. At this point Ambler makes a revealing comment. He thinks the Middle East is a good place for character development. 'Really I am only interested in character development and to put people in settings which allows display of character.' The spy writer is inhibited by electronic developments in espionage; as Deighton flourishes Ambler finds his field narrowing. 'I think the best storytellers now happen to write what some people call spy stories. You could say Conrad's *Under Western Eyes* is a spy story, but no-one ever calls it a spy story. It's respectable.'

Hopkins referred to a reviewer in the *New York Times Book Review* who felt that the British spy novel, exemplified by Ashenden, illustrated 'the inarticulate supremacy of the English gentleman'. Ambler felt this was an odd comment, although he conceded it could be true of Fleming and Buchan. 'Since I have never been an English gentleman, I wouldn't know. I would think that with Ashenden there wasn't an English gentleman alive—no one—least of all Mr Maugham. Maugham would have been horrified to have Ashenden been called an English gentleman'. And he concluded with a kind word for Fleming.

> I liked Ian Fleming when he was alive. He was a friend. Once you stop reading Bond, however, it's hard to start again. I think it's literate. The other thing about Bond is that most people when they talk of James Bond talk of the movies and all the special effects. The books seem to be overshadowed by the movies which is an odd switch. Books usually survive movies. But Bond has been blown up by the movies with something that is more spectacular, but is somewhat inferior to the books themselves. Some of the Bond books aren't too bad. They are well written, literate, some with technical mistakes, but who cares.

Anthony Price

He's a relative late-comer who has taken on the responsibility of making and keeping the spy story intelligent. He is highly regarded by many Spy-Fi buffs and tends to be mentioned in the same breath with You-know-who and His Mate.

Colonel Butler's Wolf (1972) is not particularly outstanding, in a literary sense, yet it could stand as a landmark in the emotions surounding spy literature. It encapsulates the feelings of several other writers, including John Le Carré: a mixture of nostalgia for an honourable past, cynicism about contemporary attitudes and a growing despair concerning the country's future. Subversion is becoming a substitute for spying, although it is not always a conscious process. To subvert 'a dozen or two of tomorrow's foremost men in their fields, in industry and government and politics' will bring a better return than an expensive spy ring set up to obtain a few petty secrets. Or instead of subverting them, they could be eliminated. 'To pinpoint the best men—the coming men—and make sure they never arrived . . .' This is the new K.G.B. policy.

'What all intelligence directors dream of is getting one of their own men—not a traitor but a patriot—into the other camp. But it's almost impossible to do, because the outsiders and latecomers are always screened so carefully.' So it is necessary to slip your man in between school and university. It is a variation, and an advance, on the old Burgess/Maclean syndrome. Spy-Fi may be compared with Sci-Fi in this respect. At first neither genre is taken seriously, they are even derided, but later they are seen to be prophetic and a lot of humble, contrite praise goes their way.

What happens to patriotism in the new situation? In this novel the action takes place largely in academic circles, with several students playing important roles. Colonel Butler wants their help. 'In an earlier age he could have called on patriotism to supply all that, but that age was dead and gone. All he could rely on now was outrage and anger'. This marks another turning point in motivation. Price's Intelligence man is David Audley who is basically an academic. He is the most dislikeable, pretentious and irritating of all the literary Intelligence agents. But none of Price's characters are easy to get on with: they tend to talk in riddles and to take considerable pleasure in bewildering each other. Colonel Butler masquerades as an academic, is out of his depth, and so does little more than grunt and disapprove.

Practically everybody is pretending to be somebody else! There is layer upon layer of false identity. One has the feeling that it is too clever by half! One wonders who is outsmarting whom. 'The Russians had followed him, and Audley's men were no doubt pinpointing the Russians. It was an old game, and the trick of it was still the same: you could never be quite sure who was outsmarting whom—who was the cat, and who the mouse.'

Price is addicted to the vast consequences of minute events. He loves networks. In *October Men* (1973) Villari and Boselli follow Audley to Ostia to see who he is meeting. Ruelle is also tracking Audley. Later it is revealed that the K.G.B. have a team on the spot. In the action that follows Boselli 'didn't even know why he was fighting. Or who.' (Price doesn't build obscurity into his theme, like Deighton. It is already there.)

Italians aren't always impressed by the British, whose ideals seem muddled. Boselli disapproves of Sir Frederick Clinton, an Intelligence boss, and his team because they 'pursue truth rather than policy'. One gathers that a genuine agent doesn't go in for that sort of thing. But Price is as open to the whiff of treachery in the air as Le Carré. There is a suspicion that Audley may have defected. Richardson's mind clicks furiously like a film projector:

> Not Guy—not Guy *and* Donald!
> Surely not Kim, of all people!
> George? You don't mean George Blake?
> But Philip is the last man—
> David?

—where David is Audley.

Price's special expertise is history. Most of his novels revolve round a historical mystery or hypothesis. *October Men* doesn't but it still has its references to King Roger II of Sicily and his Italian campaign. Chapter IX begins in true Pricean style:

> 'I don't suppose—', Sir Frederick Clinton regarded Richardson with a faintly jaundiced eye, '—you are acquainted with William Pitt's Guildhall speech after Trafalgar.'

But in his next, and probably best book, *Other Paths to Glory* (1974), the historical mystery is very skilfully woven into the contemporary espionage action. The historical aspect is really no more than a sprat to catch a mackerel. Price usually has some fairly resounding generalizations to make about the spy scene. In the previous novel he had made the off-the-cuff statement that three-quarters of the men employed by the Russians in Britain are concerned more with industrial espionage than with political or military. (If true, this is a big switch from the situation as Oppenheim saw it.) In *Other Paths to Glory* Price is particularly interested in the neutral house. Whether they are big international companies or governments that are negotiating, they need privacy to work in. The curse of open diplomacy, as at summit meetings, is the TV camera and political commentator and the desire to know who wins and who loses. The hot-line was the first answer, but after that came the neutral house where there could be face-to-face discussion.

> So then they set up the neutral houses. If two countries have a problem, they just approach any third party for the key to a neutral house. No publicity, no TV, no questions asked—permanent top security guaranteed at head-of-state level. All the latest anti-bugging devices and experts from all sides can spot-check them at any time as a matter of routine. They've been in operation for five years now (1974) without a hitch.

In this novel there is a plot to blow up a neutral house when a meeting is in session. There is no indication of who the principals are, either in the discussion or the conspiracy. This suggestion by Price is similar to Braine's that agents are assassinated and all traces removed.

Our Man in Camelot (1975) is very disappointing after *Other Paths* in the previous year, which in fact won an Award. Price tries to repeat his triumph with similar ingredients, especially the interweaving of an academic problem with a contemporary political theme. Whereas the two were brilliantly integrated in the earlier novel, in this the balance is so unequal as to make the whole seem rather silly. Much of the conversation proceeds along a line of unjustified assumption. In other words, the spy (or conspiracy) story overwhelms the novel. But behind it all lies the conviction that Modern Britain is in decline. It is interesting to compare this with the similar view made by Le Carré in *Tinker, Tailor, Soldier, Spy*, which appeared the year before. The decline is summarized: 'the great war, Britain's "Finest Hour", the Anglo-American alliance, the hollow victory and the Cold War, the decline and fall of the British Empire, the decline of Britain herself . . .'

Price's originality lies in his linking of modern espionage with some aspect of historical research. His weakness as a novelist is that he cannot write a simple, flowing narration; it is constantly held up and interrupted by comment on his characters, their motivation and their concealed intentions. *War Game* (1976) is a good example:

> The Superintendent advanced towards him, but the sergeant stayed back like an obedient gun dog waiting for his signal.

Confidence tempered by caution.

'I'm sorry to have kept you waiting, Superintendent.'

'That's all right, sir. It's quite nice to have an excuse to get away from my desk for an hour or two.'

Caution plus neutrality. But no overt hostility, and in Weston's place Audley knew that he would be hopping mad behind an identical facade.

Price is in fact as complex as Deighton but more subtle.

The '44 Vintage (1978) is not an espionage novel. Indeed, it might be called a defeatist novel in the now-familiar post-Bond vein. The mission is accomplished but the rewards are nil. One of the last sentences in the book is italicized: *No winners and losers, only the survivors and the dead.* Although set in the Second World War the view is expressed that the Third has already begun. (Price's own controlled unemotionality is expressed by a quotation he makes in *Our Man in Camelot* from the C.I.A. training manual: 'When the success of a mission conflicts with the survival of an operative, no operative shall abort a mission without first having evaluated comparatively its importance against the value of the said operative . . .') A subjective judgment, certainly, but the strict disciplinarian in Price expects it. Meanwhile, his style solidifies. The whole of *The '44 Vintage* is written with immense deliberation. Every sentence must be considered, tested and weighed and finally milked for the last drop of significance. The inevitable result is a lack of flow and spontaneity.

At first sight *Tomorrow's Ghost* (1979) might be a case of Art copying Society, because Colonel Butler is under surveillance—a hot theme in the seventies. (Remember Smiley and even David Audley had been through it.) But Butler is not suspected of disloyalty or possible defection; he has enemies who oppose his promotion. It is not entirely clear who they are. There is even more opacity in this novel than usual. It can be classed as an Intelligence novel but it is unusual because it is really about politicking within the service. No other writer, apart from Le Carré, devotes so much time to it. But the style is as heavy and slow-moving as ever. He has a curious habit of combining extremely intuitive characters with heavy-handed exposition. He moves with infuriating slowness, as here. (Frances is told that her gloves have been found, which is puzzling, as she had no gloves.)

Gloves?

Those expensive gloves of yours?

Those expensive gloves of yours have been found?

'Oh—'. The white-washed wall blazed in front of her. 'Oh?'

Anyone reading Anthony Price for the first time, in the form of *Soldier No More* (1981) would soon come to the conclusion that he belongs to the intellectual wing of Spy-Fi for the following reasons. First, sex appears very late (not before page 90) and when it comes it is muted. Before that the only female is an ageing caretaker. Incidentally, Price's females are extremely immature, no matter what their age or background. Secondly, he doesn't go in for violence. Thirdly, at least one of his characters can be depended on to spout Latin. And fourthly, we will encounter an expert on a rather obscure historical period—here it is Byzantine. In a way Deighton's nameless character tries to get into this bracket through his interest in military history, but he doesn't go in deep like Price.

There is a rather startling politico-historical hypothesis in this novel. Captain Roche is a double agent, sympathetic to the Russians (the Comrades), but he forsakes this allegiance. It is 1957. He has been shocked by Suez and has a nostalgia for the good old days of Socialism—Bevin and Attlee, even Gaitskell at a pinch. He eventually decides that the Russians have been playing a very crafty game, with no concern for anything but their own narrow interests, and that Suez was virtually encouraged by them, to cover Hungary and other weaknesses in their satellite empire. This certainly illustrates Price's capacity for intellectual deviousness, if nothing else.

Noble and Ignoble

There's a kind of civil war going on in the Spy-Fi camp. It is between Colonel Russell and Charlie Muffin. The Colonel would never spit in your soup, even if you were an enemy. Charlie would spit in his best friend's.

Russell is William Haggard's Head of Security, though now retired. He and his operators are civilized men with a firm view of correct behaviour. He is a patriot of whom Hannay would have approved. On the other hand, he has always managed to get along fairly well with his opposite number in the K.G.B. This may seem surprising but even Russell has to make concessions to the unattractive period he lives in.

Haggard is one of the most thoughtful of all the spy writers. He admires mental discipline above everything else and therefore despises the emotional New Left. *Therefore*, although anti-Socialist he leans towards orthodox Communism, which he calls the Hard Right. This apparent contradiction has nothing to do with ideological content. Colonel Russell has no time for what he calls the Lunatic Left. It is said that when Krushchev came to England he was so disgusted by Labour's insistence on human rights he said that if he were English he would vote Conservative. Russell would probably have understood that, but not for the same reasons. Individual quality and respect for it are the highest values in his world. He would never subscribe to the current political practice of paying his respects to an odious person because his politics were agreeable.

I find a strong similarity between Haggard's Colonel Russell and Price's Colonel Butler. They are both upright men who would never act dishonourably on principle. (That is, they would not cheat to score a point for their country.) Their values clash stridently at times with contemporary ones. Russell is more outspoken, more bitter about the decadence of his fellow Britons. He is a greater snob than Butler, who has worked his way up from the ranks without over-compensating for his humble origins. In fact, Haggard's snobbishness is more intense than Buchan's, which is frequently commented on but not always very convincingly.

Haggard is not very happy with women in his writing. In this he does resemble Buchan. He seems to avoid young ones at all costs. In *Arena* (1961) the relationship between Walter and Cynthia resembles two old computers trying to get randy. I have already noted that Price's women tend to remain embedded in the page, rather than captivating the reader's mind with their feminine vitality.

Haggard has an irritating habit of allowing his characters to congratulate each other remorselessly. This is seen particularly in *The Unquiet Sleep* (1962), where the characters constantly tell each other that they are wonderful, understanding, intelligent, etc. (Again, it's a habit he shares with Price.) But it's a strange and unexpected habit to find in people who are represented as unsentimental characters in the field of *Realpolitik*. It is the worst of all psychological disasters, the softness of the hard man.

Russell is by no means the only incorruptible. Some of Haggard's characters are not even admirable, except for this one sturdy quality: incorruptibility. Maurice Pater in *The Bitter Harvest* (1971) is an excellent example of this type. He is ineffective as a politician, and unimaginative, but his moral backbone is unyielding. His well-balanced speeches 'never set the House on fire, nods rather than cheers were their usual meed, but somebody had to preserve his judgment, somebody sane and somebody honest, someone immune to pressure and interests.' Undoubtedly integrity was now thought old-fashioned but this didn't worry Pater. It was the quality Russell admired in him. Someone referred to him as being 'straight from the Ark'. In the political world to be honest meant 'saying a requiem mass'. In the end, even his enemies had to admit that here was a man they couldn't break. The Frenchman who was trying to compromise Pater on behalf of the Arabs knew it was not true to say that every man has his price.

The spy story has always verged, necessarily, on the political. With Haggard it becomes overtly political. A sense of reality is the most important quality a political thinker must possess. Haggard (or Russell) faces the truth: only the Superpowers count—the rest are rabbits. This is a conclusion with which John Simpson would certainly concur. But seeing the truth is one thing; maintaining the correct moral stance is another. Russell moves very carefully in the twilit moral worlds represented by both South Africa and Israel. He knows the case against both, especially South Africa, but his contempt for intellectuals (usually of the Left Wing) made it difficult for him to declare himself too emphatically. He could admit the wrongs but he couldn't join the extremists who made political capital out of them. He admired the Israeli and South African sense of conviction and their determination to support a cause wholeheartedly. And he believed, seeing the relevance very clearly, that the worst sin was self-deception.

I have already spent considerable space discussing the ignoble. The degree of ignobility varies—it ranges from the cynicism of Le Carré's Leamas to the deliberate unpleasantness of Charlie Muffin. John Gardner belongs here. Perhaps his training as a priest gave him special insight into human nastiness. He is snappy, like Deighton, but without the gadgetry and he is less fascinated by wisecracks. This is just as well because he is not very good at them. 'Outside, the rain was putting up a good imitation of a deluge.' That, I fear, is standard. Deighton can do much better. He is decidedly post-Bond and belongs to what some call the 'dark' period of spy fiction. It is interesting to find that, like Smiley, Gardner's agent in *To Run a Little Faster* has a background of domestic treachery, his wife's infidelity. This has no practical relation to the plot but seems to be a spy writer's accepted symbol of sordid reality. But Gardner goes even further: the man is divorced but his new fiancée is drowned in the course of her involvement with his activities. Incidentally, his mother is in a home, suffering from hallucinations. Simon Darrell concludes it's a dirty business and we are forced to agree with him. The end justifies the means and you are not safe even from your own side. 'In what was coming soon, it would be difficult to differentiate between villains and the law, truth and lies.' As this novel appeared in 1976, 'soon' may be upon us.

The new writers keep coming. It is hard to keep up with the output. There is also a regrettable tendency for reviewers to claim that each new arrival is taking over from Le Carré or out-shooting Deighton. In my experience this is rarely justified. I will end this section with a brief reference to Ted Allbeury whom I will allow to speak for himself. (The following statements were quoted by McCormick.) 'My inclinations have been to stick to what I know. Having been in the spy business, I know what it's like and how it all works. Anyone can mug up on the K.G.B.'s weapons or the C.I.A.'s methods, but only someone who has done it knows what it feels like to arrest a man, to shoot a man, assess a deadly opponent, chase and be chased.' We are on professional ground and there's mud in the eye for many of Allbeury's colleagues. He goes on. 'When you come out, the greatest problem is that you know too much about people because your training has been so good—it has to be, or you wouldn't survive. I still not only know when people are telling lies, I know almost before they do that that they are *going* to, and that's terrible. It was a dreadful business to stop doing this in private life. Unconsciously, you dug holes (as you traditionally did in the job) waiting for people to fall into them.'

It should be superb training for a critic.

There'll Always Be An England . . .

Spy fiction has been almost wrung dry of patrotism but there are still a few damp patches. As there are signs of a revival in patriotism, but of a quiet and thoughtful kind, spy fiction may well reflect the development. The Jubilee probably influenced this trend because numbers of people who had not been at all royalist before began asking themselves if they wanted a Hamiltonian Republic. Looking round at republican and presidential models around the world, they declined the prospect. The Falklands war, despite Mrs Thatcher, was another factor which caused some people to think that shooting down a dictator was on the right lines after the vehement attacks on Fascism that come so easily to some lips.

The leading Spy-Fi patriot is Geoffrey Household, an admirable writer who manages to be moral without being either prudish or stiff-backed. Like Ambler, he finds the Middle East (where British heroes have proliferated) a stimulating background to his work. His *Doom's Caravan* (1971) belongs to a group of novels which centre on a major obsession in English spy fiction: the possible resurgence of Islam, with or without foreign (usually German) assistance. These also include Buchan's most successful novel (in sales terms), *Greenmantle*, Ambler's best, *The Levanter*, and, coming right up to date, Quinnell's ingenious *The Mahdi*. There is no inconsistency in finding that the most English (including Buchan!) of spy writers should go to the Middle East for their subject matter.

Household's *Arabesque* (1948) is very nearly a novel of the first rank. It is only in the later stages where it occasionally descends into cliché. Its subject is loyalty. There are so many loyalties jostling with each other in this wartime tale set in Lebanon and Egypt—to the British, the Free French, the Vichy French, the Arabs and the Zionists. It is not always easy to know one's own loyalty, not to speak of others. Loujon claimed that he simply obeyed his government (Vichy) without bothering about its colour and added, 'God knows to what the rest of you will be loyal.' A British officer says he is prepared to stink so long as his country does not. But he was one of the few who managed 'to live at ease in this world of interlocking and contradictory loyalties'. There is immense confusion but it is an account of honest bewilderment and not contrived obscurity. What makes a good novel? Partly its style, but also its theme. It must have a theme that sums up a contemporary predicament. Household has seized on it here: loyalty, which divides so many modern Englishmen.

Arabesque transcends the ordinary spy genre but it contains a lot of the ingredients that go to make the spy story. They could be regarded as incidental notes to the trade. No-one really ever knows what the other person is up to. The central character is Armande, whom everyone imagines to be a spy but who says she is not, yet manages to get involved in a number of dubious security activities. It is a microcosm of the wartime situation in Lebanon, Palestine and Egypt. Captain Furney thought she might have been working for some branch of G.H.Q. which never took the trouble to let security know what they were doing. 'It seems so odd that none of these hush-hush organizations should be able to check up on each other', she says. Prayle, who she falls in love with, sums it all up in the kind of shorthand that comes naturally to him. 'Feeling your way in a mist, Armande—that's security.'

Why is Armande suspect? Rule 1 of identifying a spy: Loujon advises her to get a job. 'If a woman is not living with a husband or a lover and if she hasn't a source of income that all can see, she is suspect. And—if you really are not working for the British—you will be just as suspect to them as you were to me.' Then Rule 1 for finding an agent: 'it was obvious that a new civilian recruit for any form of Intelligence must be picked up just as she had been—watched, tested in many little conversations, and then told the minimum it was essential to know for the job in hand.' And then, what does the agent need for success? 'To be a successful security man demanded tact and mature judgment—two qualities rare in human beings and especially rare in Germans.'

Household's patriotism receives its most positive expression, but also its crudest, in *A Rough Shoot* (1951) followed by a sequel, *A Time to Kill* (1952). These are little more than adventure stories, although they have political point. The defeated Fascists of the first book become Communists (i.e., Comintern agents, in Russian pay) in the second. According to Household, this is a very easy transfer of loyalty which has been copiously illustrated in recent German history. These books are in the tradition of Buchan, being stories of agents pursuing and being pursued over quiet English countryside. The tranquillity and the violence are contrasted with a sense of incredulity. 'After all, we were in well-policed England and this time—unlike that very unpleasant night the previous autumn when I was on the run—the police would be on my side.' This was of course the side of law and order, the twin gods of English civilization. *Watcher in the Shadows* (1960) also belongs to this group. It is unmistakably English in both tone and atmosphere. The hero is an Austrian who has found sanctuary in England. It is only a spy story in so far as attempts are made to discover 'the sources of enemy intelligence.' But it is a private vendetta.

A.J. Quinnell's *The Mahdi* (1981) has an ingenious plot. The British and the Americans create a new Mahdi whom they will control and, through him, the Arab world. The Russians are at first excluded but later have to be admitted to the plot. But the ending is inconclusive and descends to mere flag-wagging, which is why I include it here. The Middle East setting is, however, another clue to the author's predilections. It cannot possibly be called a spy story but it has much in common with the genre. It is in fact very derivative, owing a great deal to Forsyth in its account of a vast master plan, which is slowly revealed in a series of short sections, jumping from place to place and character to character. The creation of a new Mahdi recalls *Greenmantle*. The Russian attempt to trap a spy with a beautiful woman recalls *From Russia with Love*. The spy novel has reached the stage where echoes and reverberations are inevitable.

I end this section with reference to an author whose hero is not really a hero at all but simply a very ordinary young Englishman. Lionel Davidson's *The Night of Wenceslas* (1960) is a delightful book which stands on its own in the field of fictional espionage in the way that *The Spy Who Sat and Waited* does, although that is roughly all they have in common. A young Englishman is tricked into spying on behalf of the Czechs. The humour is infectious. Most humour in Spy-Fi is forced—you laugh here, see? (Read Trevanian to get the idea.) The sex is invigorating. Will she go to bed with him? It is a question every young man asks himself in life but rarely in Spy-Fi, where she just goes as a matter of course. Nicholas cannot know, he just hopes. She is utterly mysterious. In the end she does. ('She' can represent more than one female.) Both Nicholas and the reader are charmed. Davidson's weakness is much the same as Household's—when the action starts the psychology is forgotten. Men and women become puppets, activated by adventure. But the quality returns at the end. This is a very neat little story. Its greatest merit is that it does not resort to obscurity to keep the interest from flagging. It is simple and very credible, partly for that reason. And, I repeat, it is very English in tone. You may feel I am putting too much stress on this point, but in fact a large area of the spy novel in this country has been colonized by the Americans.

Davidson wrote a novel called *The Sun Chemist* (1976) which has very little apparent Englishness about it, yet reveals the English obsession with the Middle East. It is intellectual in tone, with an academic background, as in Anthony Price. An attempt is made to steal a chemical formula discovered by Weizmann, the Zionist, during his early career in England as a bio-chemist. It is presumably for sale to a foreign power, which is not specified. Large historical chunks are inserted, but not very well integrated, into the fictional framework. At the end the loose strands are picked out hastily and rather clumsily tied together. In the typical spy novel the enemy is known (Fleming) but Davidson's work tends to resemble the detective novel where the enemy (or villain) is not revealed until the last chapter. Le Carré also adopts this method when looking for a mole but it is quite clear *what* we are looking for. Davidson wraps a few more layers of mystery round the action.

24: SATIRE AND SEX

In his Foreword to *Dirty Tricks* Chapman Pincher writes that none of the incidents he presents, however outrageous they seem, 'are beyond the bounds of likelihood, including those "dirty tricks" which the otherwise friendly British and American Secret Services may play on each other.' Recent history is evidence of the truth of this statement. It is no longer possible to dismiss even the most sensational of spy novels as nonsense in so far as its action is concerned. What remains, however, is the crux of all literary art, whether mainline or genre: does the author transmit the feeling of truth and reality?

It is significant that the popularity of the spy story reached its peak when schizophrenia became so widespread. With the schizophrene the real world corresponds to the individual self and the fantasy world to the false self. This is not to call the genre insane but to assert that it has a schizoid tendency. Nearly all the leading characters in modern spy fiction exhibit this psychological tension: Smiley's gloom is the result of his knowing that he is being taken over by his false self; Bond surrendered willingly to his false self; Muffin moves skilfully from one self to the other, as the situation requires.

All genres try to establish links with the traditional (and therefore respectable) heritage. Detection literature looks back to Poe and Wilkie Collins. Science fiction has an immensely long ancestry, going back to Lucian and Jonathan Swift. Spy fiction, as I have stated, cannot dig back so far, although *A Tale of Two Cities* is sometimes invoked. But some of the old pros say that the best spy book ever written was Chesterton's *The Man Who Was Thursday*. It seems at first sight a send-up of the average spy novel but for the professional agent it contains a deep-lying truth. It is that if you say quite openly that you are a spy or an anarchist, no-one will believe you and you will be able to do pretty much as you please. Attempts to hide your identity lead to suspicion, and then everyone will know you are a spy (or an anarchist). There have been some attempts, especially since the Bond era, to satirize the spy novel but most of them have been heavy-handed compared with Chesterton's little masterpiece.

McCormick actually claims that *Thursday* still provides a model for aspiring spy writers, to prevent them from 'keeling over too far in the direction of fantasy'. This is in itself a Chesterton-type paradox which means it must be treated seriously.

Hitting the Bull

There have been a few, a very few, successful attempts at parody, with consequent satirical effect.

Greene's *Our Man in Havana* is remarkable because it can be fitted into so many categories. The comic element is obvious. It is deeply tragic. It is also a superb send-up of the conventional spy novel. When Wormold is with his daughter Milly there is an ambience of combined triviality and Catholic devotion, and Wormold no doubt feels he is in the 'real' world. But 'Hawthorne, mysterious and absurd, the cruelties of police-stations and governments, the scientists who tested the new H-bomb on Christmas Island, Krushchev who wrote notes'—they were unreal. Greene is always a master of atmosphere and the atmosphere of unreality in this novel is intense. Of course, this is true of nearly every spy novel but here it is pointed by Greene's wit and professionalism. When Wormold goes to Santiago he is greeted in the reception office of the hotel 'with suspicion as though they assumed him to be a spy of one kind or another. He felt like an impostor, for this was a hotel of real spies, real police-informers and real rebel agents.' In other words, he has strayed into a book by Len Deighton (who had not yet come on the spy scene.)

The situation begins to run away with Wormold. He has set forces in motion which cannot be stopped, and they mean death to some people, including his only friend. When Hasselbacher's flat is raided Wormold knows he is guilty, though he would never have done it himself. Yet 'people similar to himself had done this, men who allowed themselves to be recruited while sitting in lavatories, who opened hotel doors with other men's keys and received instructions in secret ink and in novel uses for Lamb's *Tales from Shakespeare*.' It was a grotesque world. Why did people take it more seriously than those other worlds invented by men, fairies and science fiction?

One particular idiocy was that secret agents spend their time discovering what 'everybody knows already'. This may not be entirely true but it contains a large degree of truth. Hasselbacher tells

Wormold that They (the unknown enemy) have known about him from the beginning. They even thought he might be inventing his reports (which he was) but it seemed unlikely the British Secret Service would be so easily deceived. The explanation of how the Secret Service was in fact deceived is hilarious: Wormold's plans were never shown to experts because he worked for the Secret Service! 'We can't allow documents like that to reach anyone who really knows,' says Beatrice.

One is tempted at times to regard all Fleming's novels as a deliberate joke on the Secret Service theme. *The Man with the Golden Gun*, usually regarded as his weakest, sounds like a rather inferior imitation. James Bond's death has been announced. Someone bearing his name turns up in London, demanding to see M. Is he the genuine James Bond? The first chapter is a detailed example of the security measures adopted to establish identity, and reads like satire. The whole routine of 'clearing' is gone through. It confirms that this is James Bond; what it cannot discover is that he has been brainwashed by the Russians and has come on a mission to kill M.

This is not the only part that verges on satire. (Whether satire can ever be unconscious is another matter.) When James Bond finds himself on a locomotive that is rushing towards the body of his girlfriend, strapped across the line, it is clearly a case of melodrama not normally acceptable these days. (The fact that the body turns out to be a dummy even heightens the mockery—it merely turns shock abruptly into ridicule.) It is doubtful if any other writer could have been forgiven this. Incidentally, the spy element in this novel is extremely thin. One of the villains is a K.G.B. man but he doesn't seem to be looking for any particular information.

I have come across only two successful pieces of satire on the spy fiction genre. One is Cyril Connolly's brief extravaganza, 'Bond Strikes Camp', which appeared first in *The London Magazine* (April 1963) and was reprinted in the author's book of essays, *Previous Convictions*. This is a remarkable achievement for it is almost impossible to satirize Bond, or his kind of Spy-Fi, for reasons which I have already given. Connolly's piece is written out of an amused appreciation of Bond whereas Trevanian (for example) writes out of sourness deriving from heavy-handed scorn. Connolly's first sentence demonstrates his awareness of Fleming and his style, rather than mere flat reaction: 'Shadows of fog were tailing him through the windows of his Chelsea flat . . .' One can illustrate this sort of thing time and again: 'the blonde had left a broken rosette of lipstick . . .'; 'he nearly took the seat off a Beatnik as he swerved into Milner . . .'; 'Bond was wearing one of his many pheasant's-eye alpacas which exaggerated the new vertical line—single-breasted, narrow lapels, ton-up trousers with no turn-ups, peccary suede shoes'; 'to the taxi-driver he was one of London's many thousand fly-by-nights off to earn their lolly—yet no-one else in the great indifferent city knew his whereabouts nor what manner of man was preparing to have his way with him.'

For this is Bond's greatest test, which even M shrank from putting on him. He was required to assume drag to get his man, and flirt dangerously! Nervously M asks him if he thinks the end justifies the means. If there is one thing we can certainly say about Bond, it is that he does—but these are not the terms he uses. Is Bond patriotic? Of course he is. Will he admit it? 'I never read the small print clauses.' It is all modesty. Bond would read the clause even if it were in invisible ink. So he is 'rigged up as a moppet' and sent to a 'special sort of club' where he will be approached by General Apraxin and must be prepared to fall in with any suggestion the general may make. 'And may your patriotism be your conscience, as it is mine.' As usual, Bond visits the instructor before setting out. 'Grind yer boot down his shin and crush his instep. Wrench off his testicles with yer free hand and with the fingers held stiffly in the V sign gouge out his eyes with the other.'

The other success is *Eeny, Meeny, Miny, Mole* by someone who called himself Marcel d'Agneau. This was such a skilful parody of Le Carré's *Tinker, Tailor, Soldier, Spy* that the literary world assumed that it was by either Kingsley Amis or Anthony Burgess. In fact, the author was Sam North, a thriller writer. D'Agneau shares one quality at least with Connolly; although he can imitate his model brilliantly he also has a style of his own, which breaks through from time to time. (A satire must not be a *direct* imitation but a qualitative one.) After the suggestive title come the mock-derivative chapter headings, including 'A Small Town in East Germany'. D'Agneau, like Connolly, is witty—he doesn't thump the reader. His adoption of a French pseudonym underlines this. Most satires on Spy-Fi are feeble because there is such a strong element of caricature in the model. D'Agneau can also create character as well as projecting imitation Le Carré.

Like Le Carré, he invents his own terms and organizations. Lipsnatchers bring in the information. The Circus becomes the

Square, under the direction of the Stationmaster; the American Neighbours become the Relatives. Peter Hallam is No. 2, in place of Peter Guillam, and the Foreign Office Lacon becomes Calon. Plateau policy is the new thing, replacing Lateral. Oblique utterance and the throwaway characterize the style. But most important of all is Grimly, who has been called in from retirement to clear up the Intelligence mess. Steven, who had been put in charge, had disappeared. There had been eleven defections, but still no call for Steven. Why?

> The climb was much slower than he'd planned on. There were people ahead of him. And of that original fourteen, only three were left, only three who weren't working for the Russians. He often had to ask himself, where did he fail? What was it that he hadn't said or done that they had seen fit to leave him out? He spoke Russian, didn't he? He'd been to Eton, hadn't he? Why no secret Swiss bank account for him, or sunshine cruises on the Black Sea? His smiling picture in *Pravda's Sunday Magazine* with some glamorous blonde? It was all so unfair.

In the end Grimly pulls through, even if in hospital. He is strongly tempted to sign on for the Russians, but resists. He suddenly found himself smiling. Sussie visits him in the ward, gives him some fudge, which he enjoys, and says, 'There, I said I could make you into a smiley boy.'

Both Cornwell and his imitator adopt French *noms-de-plume*. Le Carré means Square which is the name of d'Agneau's intelligence organization. Agneau means Lamb, and in espionage parlance this means Beginner, an agent on his first job. ('The lamb run' is his first time in the field.) This novel runs parallel with *Tinker, Tailor, Soldier, Spy* in personnel, incident and surreality. Despite the joke, the total effect is defeatist. Practically the whole of Europe has surrendered to the Russians and a total of, eventually, seventy-two people involved in British Intelligence are under suspicion. The effect is compounded by some of d'Agneau's code inventions: D.B.B. is Death By Boredom and I.D.C. is Interdepartmental Chaos.

When Satire Misfires

It is extremely difficult to satirize spy fiction, because you are virtually attempting to satirize satire. To satirize Bond you might be tempted to concentrate on the snobbery, but Fleming's novels themselves are satires on snobbery, even if unaware. Only a sharp wit and a keen appreciation of stylistic nuance could manage it.

Trevanian is the pseudonym of an American Professor of English who did a sabbatical at Essex University and adopted the name of a man who escaped from Colchester Castle during the English Civil War. This may be a tenuous reason for including him in a book on British spy fiction, but he is important in other ways. To give evidence on the other side I will quote McCormick, who says he 'is a real discovery in spy fiction, composing it rather as one would expect Evelyn Waugh to have done, as a merry jape with serious undertones.' I usually respect McCormick's judgment but would feel happier if he had compared Trevanian with Emma Tennant rather than Waugh. I will not deny that he is extremely literate. His use of jargon can be delightfully inventive as when he cites, as an example of C.I.A.'s 'new-speak', to 'demote maximally' for purge by killing.

His target in *The Loo Sanction* (1974) is a broad one. He is not trying to satirize a particular author so much as spy fiction itself, including the post-Bond model. The latter, in the hands of Le Carré, Deighton, Freemantle and Gardner, could most effectively be parodied through their air of hopelessness and seediness. Trevanian never gets near this. The most he can do is introduce a character who pulls scurf out of his hair. He brings in easy sex, capture by the enemy, severe punishment, but always misses the spirit lying behind the incident. This novel has been represented as brilliant satire. In fact, it carries none of the sense of achievement, of hitting a recognizable target in the middle, which all good satire has. It is written in an unpleasant sneering tone in which the splendidly efficient American agent triumphs unerringly over the dreary yobs that have been set up for him to triumph over. If envy is a powerful motivation in art, including writing, as I believe it is, this is a good example of the academic's attempt to outwrite the more popular journalist—and, of course, missing the mark. There is also a strange alternation of apparent satire with what seems to be straightforward spy writing—but perhaps it is all intended satirically. It seems very probable that this was intended to be the *Catch 22* of spy fiction. But Heller's book was delightfully carefree and also extremely clever.

John Gardner, with his 'Boysie Oakes' Entertainments, is a marginal case. Oakes is a recognized character who has 'established' himself in this field as have, in their various ways, Richard Hannay, Bulldog Drummond, Bond, Smiley and Colonel Russell. He is said to be fundamentally a gentle person (he shrinks from cold-blooded killing) whose arteries have hardened. His great need is money, which is able to liquefy his arteries to some extent. The series is derivative. A list of jokey Acknowledgments are Deighton-inspired gimmicks, as are the chapter headings, all of which are musical terms, followed with a brief definition (*A Killer for a Song*, 1975). There is in fact a tremendous amount of influence of writer on writer (inbreeding) in the spy novel: one can, for example, trace a well defined line from Buchan through Valentine Williams to Fleming.

These novels are intended as satires on other novels in the genre, but on the whole they fail (although often very amusing) for a very familiar reason: it is almost impossible to satirize work that is already unreal or distorted. It might be fairly easy to satirize R. Wright Campbell or Lionel Davidson, but they have not the stature to invite it. Nearly everyone in the afore-mentioned novel is trying to catch Martin Bormann and Dr Mengele, the Auschwitz doctor, who, despite the combined efforts of the Spy-Fi world, are still at large. Gardner follows certain well-known James Bond conventions, such as easy sex, which has now become very boring, besides being childish, and the necessity of being captured by the enemy (often accompanied by torture) leading to a stupendous escape from the most intimidating circumstances.

The Great Spy Race (1968) by Adam Diment, tries to be terribly funny. It is so heavy-hearted that even the dumbest reader must realize it. Again, ceaseless wise-cracking and easy sex. It is a slow starter, the kind of book that makes you snarl: But what exactly is it getting at? The aim appears to be to out-Bond Bond (and to get a laugh out of him too, of course), which means it is derivative in style though not in plot. Fleming did not mystify the reader. It appears to be entirely literary—one feels that Diment knows as much about Intelligence work as Goldenballs does about Rowton Houses.

The agent MacAlpine is the least likeable I have yet come across, in a field where unlikeability is one of the major attractions. He is also boring because of his predictability. Peters is the great retired agent (another familiar figure). 'To this day I cannot remember what he really looked like. He was the real man without a face.' He had been a spy all his life, like his father and grandfather. Spying, he said, is like syphilis—heritable. He considered himself the most successful spy alive today. 'Lucy—a communist dupe, fed information like some helpless Strasbourg goose by British Intelligence. Sorge—a dedicated fanatic. No freelance spy can ever be dedicated to any political system. Most of the other great spies could not adapt to the cold war. They vanished between 1945 and '50.' The Russians and Americans have ruined spying—the Russians by insisting on doctrine, the Americans by relying on computers. Peters had many trophies hanging on his wall: the C.M.G., Order of Lenin, Purple Heart and Bar, the Croix de Guerre, several from Fascist Italy, the Knight's Cross of the Iron Cross. I will not deny that there are some shrewd hits concealed among all this but they are not firmly based enough to create viable satire.

Sex

Sex nearly always strikes a false note in the spy novel. The men may be men but most of the women are much closer to the automatic girls that used to fascinate French writers of the nineteenth century decadence than they are to the females we meet during the course of the normal day. In other words, sex is automatically treated satirically. Sometimes viciously. If a man from Mars were to visit here and then read a few dozen thrillers he would conclude that most of the authors are utterly ignorant of the real nature of women. Some writers are beginning to see how damaging this can be to the reader's acceptance of the novel as a whole. They often resort to call-girls, though usually very superior ones. The important thing is to keep the sex easy, to get on with the major lines of the story. It is obviously considered part of their job to project a false image to arouse the erotic sensibility of the reader and thus increase sales. (According to Pearson, Fleming was often irresistible to women. His letters to his future wife suggest a person capable of deep sympathy and understanding. His treatment of sex in his novels illustrates a deliberate derogation.) The publisher may well regard this as honourable conduct. In an interview with Martin Booth (*Bananas*, August 1980) George MacBeth, the poet-spy writer, said: 'With

Cadbury, I try to cross two genres—spy fiction and pornography. I take pornography seriously, as an art of arousal . . . this with spies makes a thriller, interlocking the excitements.' And so the women in these thrillers tend to resemble the vessels of Huxley's *Ape and Essence.* There are honourable exceptions and they include the ones you might expect: Le Carré and Ambler, Price and Haggard.

Snelling deals with this subject in the chapter 'His Women' in his amusing and unbuttoned book on James Bond, written by an afficianado with his tongue in his cheek. His account reveals an astonishing portrait gallery of weirdies and nymphos, nearly all of them sunk in Bondage. Fleming's *The Spy Who Loved Me* capitalizes on a favourite modern belief, that women love a killer. If she's a nice girl she prefers a legitimate killer, with a double-0 prefix. But then, not all girls are nice, nor, I would say, are they usually welcome in this genre. Bond is often quite gentlemanly but fundamentally he regards girls as cattle. In Japan he meets the Australian, Dikko Henderson (*You Only Live Twice*). They get drunk together and go to a cat-house. Next morning Henderson wonders if he had behaved badly. Bond says no, except that he hit one girl so hard on the bottom that she fell down. 'Oh that!' said Dikko Henderson with relief. 'That was just a love-pat. What's a girl's bottom for, anyway?' Then he asks Bond how he made out and said his girl looked 'pretty enthusiastic'. 'She was', says Bond. 'Good show', says Henderson. End of that conversation. Nothing dates these novels so much as the chauvinistic attitude towards women. It is like the last outburst of an expiring mode.

It is a pity because love can be an extremely potent factor in the spy's life. Burn (in *The Debatable Land*) notes that in the novel love alone (apart from fear) traditionally has power to disturb the hardened spy. 'We have seen lately that this has been true in life. We shall not often be given a pair of stories that show so unforgettably the chasm between a spy's deceit and the simplicity of love as the two books written by Philby and his third wife Eleanor.' Did he marry her on orders? Was their marriage primarily a cover? Sex can be a trap and is used to catch the unwary, but love is like a net that can snare even the most professional. Once passion has been aroused the spy is vulnerable. Or conversely, the official is caught and is transformed into a spy. In Tute's *The Resident* (1973) Dr Sergei Petrov, an oceanographer, is passionately in love with his Greek secretary. They make love in a basement room of the Royal Greek Institute of Marine

Research in Athens. It never occurred to them to look under the bed where the Greek security forces had placed a small Japanese tape-recorder, nor to examine the lapels of Dr Petrov's suit where a pinhead microphone had been put by the Russians which picked up everything within a radius of ten metres and transmitted it to a car with C.D. plates outside the Institute.

Love is the weak point, only because it can be the strongest point of contact between human beings. This is well illustrated in *The Spy Who Came in from the Cold*. Karden, who represented Mundt at the trial, interrogated Liz and got her to admit that Smiley had been watching her. 'Smiley wanted to know if Leamas had told her too much. Leamas had done the one thing British Intelligence had never expected him to do: he had taken a girl and wept on her shoulder.' He laughed and added, 'Just as Karl Riemek did. He's made the same mistake.' Liz's job was to discredit Leamas. 'It's the old principle of love on the rebound.' The plot didn't really depend on their falling in love, it was enough to bring them together and others could cook up the rest.

They merely had to be brought together and after that it was easy, they could make it look like an affair. They could call on her, send her money. It would look, to outsiders, like an infatuation. The only essential point was to make it look as if the money came from him. She said, 'I feel dirty, Alec, as if I'd been put out to stud.'

Leamas dies returning uselessly to Liz's dead body.

Many spy writers simply do dirt (to use a Lawrentian term) on sex as part of the fun. The more serious writers know that in doing dirt on love they hold the most powerful weapon in their armoury.

SELECT BIBLIOGRAPHY

Compiling a bibliography of spy fiction is a puzzling business. One man who attempted it listed 1,675 titles stretching over a period of under forty years—a period, moreover, which excluded the work of John Buchan and other early writers. I have therefore largely limited my list to titles mentioned in the text, although a few others have crept in for reasons which need not be stated. I will not pretend that I have read all the spy novels that have been published but I believe I have read most of the more interesting and more worthy ones; certainly all the influential ones. There are naturally many minor or even insignificant titles in my list but altogether they should give an accurate taste of what is on offer.

Then there is the question of relevance. When I started this study I made up my mind to be a purist and refer only to novels concerned with espionage. I soon had to discard this notion because the boundary between espionage and, say, conspiracy stories is extremely uncertain. Should one include, for example, Buchan's *Three Hostages*? Strict definition would rule it out but commonsense would urge its inclusion. How should one classify Anthony Price's excellent *Other Paths to Glory*, in which the hero is trying to discover information, yet has no idea what kind of information it might turn out to be? Frederick Forsyth presents a similar problem. In the end I had to be fairly arbitrary and decide, not whether a novel was actually concerned with espionage, but whether the reading public would in fact refer to it as a 'spy novel'.

This bibliography is divided into two sections, Fiction and Background, and the latter is divided into three subsections: Reference and Critical; Biographical; and Historical. The first two of these are necessarily short. There has been very little critical work done on spy fiction. Most writers in this genre are not written about. Thus while there are plenty of books on Somerset Maugham and several on Buchan, the rest could be counted on one's fingers. The Historical section could be greatly expanded but the books mentioned here should give sufficient background to those readers who would like to relate fiction to fact.

A: Fiction

D'AGNEAU, Marcel (pseudonym for Sam North). *Eeny, Meeny, Miny, Mole.*
  Arlington Books. 1980.
ALLBEURY, Ted. *Moscow Quadrille.* Peter Davies. 1976.
AMBLER, Eric. *The Mask of Demetrios.* Hodder & Stoughton. 1939.
  Journey Into Fear. Hodder & Stoughton. 1940
  Uncommon Danger. Hodder & Stoughton. 1941.
  Judgment on Deltchev. Hodder & Stoughton. 1951.
  The Schirmer Inheritance. Heinemann. 1953.
  The Light of Day. Heinemann. 1962.
  A Kind of Anger. Bodley Head. 1964.
  To Catch a Spy. (ed.) (Stories by Buchan, Ambler, Fleming, Gilbert,
    Greene, Mackenzie & Maugham). Bodley Head. 1964.
  Intrigue (contains *The Mask of Demetrios, Journey Into Fear* and
    Judgment on Deltchev) Hodder & Stoughton. 1965.
  The Levanter. Weidenfeld & Nicolson. 1972.
AMIS, Kingsley. *The Anti-Death League.* Gollancz. 1966. See also Markham,
  Robert.
BAGLEY, Desmond. *The Freedom Trap.* Collins. 1971.
BENNETT, Alan. *The Old Country* (play). Samuel French. 1978.
BRAINE, John. *The Pious Agent.* Eyre Methuen. 1975.
BRAND, Max. *The Phantom Spy.* (Originally published in USA by Dodd,
  Mead under title *Spy Meets Spy,* 1937).
BUCHAN, John. *The Half-Hearted.* Hodder & Stoughton. 1900.
  The Watcher by the Threshold. Blackwood, 1902.
  The Thirty-Nine Steps. Hodder & Stoughton. 1915.
  Greenmantle. Hodder & Stoughton. 1916.
  The Power-House. Blackwood. 1916.
  Mr Standfast. Hodder & Stoughton. 1919.
  The Three Hostages. Hodder & Stoughton. 1924.
  The Courts of the Morning. Hodder & Stoughton. 1929.
  The Island of Sheep. Hodder & Stoughton. 1936.
CAMPBELL, R. Wright. *The Spy Who Sat and Waited.* Weidenfeld & Nicolson.
  1975.
CHESTERTON, G.K. *The Man Who Was Thursday.* J.W. Arrowsmith. 1908.
CHEYNEY, Peter. *Dark Wanton.* Collins. 1948.
CHILDERS, Erskine. *The Riddle of the Sands.* 1903. Penguin, 1952.
COLES, Manning. *Drink to Yesterday.* Hodder & Stoughton. 1940
  They Tell No Tales. Hodder & Stoughton. 1940.
  Green Hazard. Hodder & Stoughton. 1945.
  The Fifth Man. Hodder & Stoughton. 1946.
  The Basle Express. Hodder & Stoughton. 1956.
  Death of an Ambassador. Hodder & Stoughton. 1957.

CONNOLLY, Cyril. *Previous Convictions* (contains the satire, 'Bond Strikes Camp'). Hamish Hamilton. 1963.

CONRAD, Joseph. *The Secret Agent.* Methuen. 1907.

CRISP, N.J. *The Gotland Deal.* Weidenfeld & Nicolson. 1976.

DAVIDSON, Lionel. *The Night of Wenceslas.* Gollancz. 1960.
   The Sun Chemist. Cape. 1976.

DEIGHTON, Len. *The Ipcress File.* Hodder & Stoughton. 1962.
   Horse Under Water. Cape. 1963.
   Funeral in Berlin. Cape. 1964.
   Billion-Dollar Brain. Cape. 1966.
   An Expensive Place to Die. Cape. 1967.
   Bomber. Cape. 1970.
   Close-Up. Cape. 1972.
      (Neither *Bomber* nor *Close-Up* are spy-novels but they illustrate Deighton's fictional range.)
   Spy Story. Cape. 1974.
   Yesterday's Spy. Cape. 1975.
   Twinkle, Twinkle, Little Spy. Cape. 1976.
   XPD. Hutchinson. 1981.

DIMENT, Adam. *The Great Spy Race.* Michael Joseph. 1968.

FLEMING, Ian. *Casino Royale.* Cape. 1953.
   Live and Let Die. Cape. 1954.
   Moonraker. Cape. 1955.
   Diamonds are Forever. Cape. 1956.
   From Russia, with Love. Cape. 1957.
   Dr. No. Cape. 1958.
   Goldfinger. Cape. 1959.
   For Your Eyes Only (stories). Cape. 1960.
   Thunderball. (Based on screen treatment by Kevin McClory, Jack Whittingham and Fleming). Cape. 1961.
   The Spy Who Loved Me. (with 'Vivienne Michel') Cape. 1962.
   On Her Majesty's Secret Service. Cape. 1963.
   You Only Live Twice. Cape. 1964.
   Octopussy and the Living Daylights. Cape. 1965.
   The Man with the Golden Gun. Cape. 1965.
   Omnibus edition, including *Dr No, Moonraker, Thunderball, From Russia with Love, On Her Majesty's Secret Service*, and *Goldfinger*. Heinemann, Secker & Warburg and Octopus Books. 1978.

FOLLETT, Ken. *The Shakeout.* Harwood-Smart. 1975.
   The Bear Raid. Harwood-Smart. 1976.

FORSYTH, Frederick. *The Day of the Jackal.* Hutchinson. 1971.
   The Devil's Alternative. Hutchinson. 1979.

FREEMANTLE, Brian. *Goodbye to an Old Friend.* Cape. 1973.
   Face Me When You Walk Away. Cape. 1974.

The Man Who Wanted Tomorrow. Cape. 1975.

The November Man. Cape. 1976.

Charlie Muffin. Cape. 1977.

The Inscrutable Charlie Muffin. Cape. 1979.

Charlie Muffin's Uncle Sam. Cape. 1980.

GARDNER, John. *The Liquidator.* Muller. 1964.

A Killer for a Song. Hodder & Stoughton. 1975.

To Run a Little Faster. Michael Joseph. 1976.

Licence Renewed. Cape and Hodder & Stoughton. 1981.

GIBBS, Philip. *Behind the Curtain.* Hutchinson. 1948.

GREENE, Graham. *The Confidential Agent.* Heinemann. 1939.

The Ministry of Fear. Heinemann. 1943.

Our Man in Havana. Heinemann. 1958.

The Human Factor. Bodley Head. 1978.

The Spy's Bedside Book (anthology of stories, with Hugh Greene). Hart-Davis. 1957.

HAGGARD, William. *The Arena.* Cassell. 1961.

The Unquiet Sleep. Cassell. 1962.

The Hard Sell. Cassell. 1965.

A Cool Day for Killing. Cassell. 1968.

Haggard for Your Holiday (contains *The Arena, The Unquiet Sleep* and *The Hard Sell*). Cassell. 1969.

The Hardliners. Cassell. 1970.

The Bitter Harvest. Cassell. 1971.

The Scorpion's Tail. Cassell. 1975.

Yesterday's Enemy. Cassell. 1976.

HITCHCOCK, Alfred. *Sinister Spies.* (ed.) (Includes stories by A. Conan Doyle, W. Somerset Maugham and Edgar Wallace). Max Reinhardt. 1967.

HOUSEHOLD, Geoffrey. *Arabesque.* Chatto & Windus. 1948.

A Rough Shoot. Michael Joseph. 1951.

A Time to Kill. Michael Joseph. 1952.

Watcher in the Shadows. Michael Joseph. 1960.

Doom's Caravan. Michael Joseph. 1971.

IRVING, Clive. *Axis.* Hamish Hamilton. 1980.

JANSON, Hank. *She Sleeps to Conquer.* Roberts & Winter. 1961.

KIPLING, Rudyard. *Kim.* Macmillan. 1901.

LE CARRÉ, John. *Call for the Dead.* Gollancz. 1961.

A Murder of Quality. Gollancz. 1962.

The Spy Who Came in from the Cold. Gollancz. 1963.

The Looking-Glass War. Heinemann. 1965.

A Small Town in Germany. Heinemann. 1968.

The Naive and Sentimental Lover. Hodder & Stoughton. 1971. (This is neither a spy novel nor a 'thriller'.)

Tinker, Tailor, Soldier, Spy. Hodder & Stoughton. 1974.

The Honourable Schoolboy. Hodder & Stoughton. 1977.

Smiley's People. Hodder & Stoughton. 1979.

The Quest for Karla. (Includes *Tinker, Tailor, Soldier, Spy; The Honourable Schoolboy*; and *Smiley's People*.) Hodder & Stoughton. 1982.

LE QUEUX, William. *The Great War in England in 1897.* Tower Publishing Company. 1894.

Her Majesty's Minister. Hodder & Stoughton. 1901.

Secrets of the Foreign Office. Hutchinson. 1903.

The Unknown Tomorrow. F.V. White. 1910.

Number 70, Berlin. Hodder & Stoughton. 1916.

The Luck of the Secret Service. Pearson. 1921.

Hidden Hands. Hodder & Stoughton. 1925.

MACKENZIE, Compton. *Extremes Meet.* Cassell. 1928.

The Three Couriers. Cassell. 1929.

Water on the Brain. Cassell. 1933.

MACLAREN-ROSS, Julian. *The Doomsday Book.* Hamish Hamilton. 1961.

MCNEILE, H.C. (Sapper), *The Dinner Club* (stories). Hodder & Stoughton. 1923.

Temple Tower. Hodder & Stoughton. 1929.

The Return of Bulldog Drummond. Hodder & Stoughton. 1932.

Ask for Ronald Standish (stories). Hodder & Stoughton. 1936.

MARKHAM, Robert (pseudonym for Kingsley Amis). *Colonel Sun.* Glidrose Productions. 1968.

MASTERS, John. *The Lotus and the Wind.* Michael Joseph. 1953.

MAUGHAM, W. Somerset. *Ashenden.* Heinemann. 1928.

MELVILLE-ROSS, Antony. *Tightrope.* Collins. 1981.

'MICHEL, Vivienne'. See Ian Fleming.

OPPENHEIM, E. Phillips. *Mysterious Mr Sabin.* Ward Lock. 1898. (A greatly abbreviated paperback edition was published by Digit Books, Brown, Watson. 1963).

The Great Impersonation. Hodder & Stoughton. 1920.

The Wrath to Come. Hodder & Stoughton. 1925.

Gabriel Samara. Hodder & Stoughton, 1925.

Miss Brown of X.Y.O. Hodder & Stoughton. 1927.

Matorni's Vineyard. Hodder & Stoughton. 1929.

The Secret Service Omnibus. (Contains *Miss Brown of X.Y.O., The Wrath to Come, Matorni's Vineyard, The Great Impersonation* and *Gabriel Samara*.) Hodder & Stoughton. 1932.

ORCZY, Baroness. *The Scarlet Pimpernel.* Hodder & Stoughton. 1913.

A Spy of Napoleon. Hodder & Stoughton. 1934.

PEMBERTON, Max. *The Wheels of Anarchy.* The Story of an Assassin: as Recited from the Papers and the Personal Narrative of his Secretary, Mr Bruce Ingersoll. Cassell. 1908.

PINCHER, Chapman. *The Four Horses.* Michael Joseph. 1978.
　　Dirty Tricks. Sidgwick & Jackson. 1980.
PRICE, Anthony. *The Labyrinth Makers.* Gollancz. 1970.
　　Colonel Butler's Wolf. Gollancz. 1972.
　　October Men. Gollancz. 1973.
　　Other Paths to Glory. Gollancz. 1974.
　　Our Man in Camelot. Gollancz. 1975.
　　War Game. Gollancz. 1976.
　　The '44 Vintage. Gollancz. 1978.
　　Tomorrow's Ghost. Gollancz. 1979.
　　Soldier No More. Gollancz. 1981.
PRIESTLEY, J.B. *The Shapes of Sleep.* Heinemann. 1962.
QUINNELL, A.J. *The Mahdi.* Macmillan. 1981.
'SAPPER'. See McNeile, H.C.
SIMPSON, John. *Moscow Requiem.* Robson. 1981.
SNOW, C.P. *The New Men.* Macmillan. 1954.
'TREVANIAN'. *The Loo Sanction.* Heinemann. 1974.
TUTE, Warren. *The Golden Greek.* Cassell. 1960. (Not a spy novel but useful background for Tute's work.)
　　The Powder Train. Dent. 1970.
　　The Tarnham Connection. Dent. 1971.
　　The Resident. Constable. 1973.
WAUGH, Alec. *A Spy in the Family.* W.H. Allen. 1970. (The story of a misconception, but with authentic espionage atmosphere.)
WHEATLEY, Denis. *The Sultan's Daughter.* Hutchinson. 1963. (One of a series of historical spy novels.)
WILLIAMS, Alan. *Gentleman Traitor.* Blond & Briggs. 1974.
WILLIAMS, Valentine. *The Man with the Clubfoot.* Herbert Jenkins. 1918.
　　The Return of Clubfoot. Herbert Jenkins. 1922.
　　The Crouching Beast. Hodder & Stoughton. 1928.
　　The Gold Comfit Box. Hodder & Stoughton. 1932.
　　A Clubfoot Omnibus. (Contains *The Man with the Clubfoot, The Return of Clubfoot, The Crouching Beast* and *The Gold Comfit Box.*) Hodder & Stoughton. 1936.
WODEHOUSE, P.G. *Big Money.* Herbert Jenkins. 1931. (This is certainly not a spy story. But two of its characters pretend to be in the Secret Service to win kudos with their girl-friends.)

B: Background

1: **Reference and Critical**
AMIS, Kingsley. *The James Bond Dossier*. Cape. 1965.
　　What Became of Jane Austen? (essays). Cape. 1970. (Includes 'A New
　　James Bond'.)
MCCORMICK, Donald. *Who's Who in Spy Fiction*. Elm Tree Books. 1977.
MERRY, Bruce. *Anatomy of the Spy Thriller*, Gill & Macmillan. 1977.
PEARSON, John. James Bond: the Authorized Biography of 007. A Fictional
　　Biography. Sidgwick & Jackson. 1973.
SETH, Ronald. *Encyclopaedia of Espionage*. New English Library. 1972.
SMITH, Myron J. *Cloak-and-Dagger Biography*. An Annotated Guide to
　　Spy Fiction, 1937–75. The Scarecrow Press, Metuchen, New Jersey.
　　1976.
SNELLING, O.F. *Double O Seven James Bond:* A Report. Neville Spearman.
　　1964.
USBORNE, Richard. *Clubland Heroes*. Revised edition, with Introduction.
　　Barrie & Jenkins. 1974.

2: **Biographical:** arranged alphabetically in order of subject.
Max BRAND. *Max Brand, the Big 'Westerner'*, by Robert Easton. University
　　of Oklahoma Press. 1970.
John BUCHAN. *Memory Hold-the-Door*, by John Buchan. Hodder &
　　Stoughton. 1940.
　　John Buchan: A Biography by Janet Adam-Smith. Rupert Hart-Davis.
　　1965.
　　Mr Buchan, Writer, by Arthur Turner. S.C.M. Press. 1949.
Erskine CHILDERS. *The Riddle of Erskine Childers*, by Andrew Boyle.
　　Hutchinson. 1977.
Ian FLEMING. *The Life of Ian Fleming*, by John Pearson. Cape. 1966.
　　The Wanton Chase, by Peter Quennell. Collins. 1980.
Graham GREENE. *A Sort of Life*, by Graham Greene. Bodley Head. 1971.
　　Ways of Escape, by Graham Greene. Bodley Head. 1980.
W. Somerset MAUGHAM. *The Summing Up*, by Somerset Maugham.
　　Heinemann. 1938.
　　Somerset Maugham: a Biographical and Critical Study, by Richard
　　Cordell. Heinemann. 1961.
　　Somerset and All the Maughams, by Robin Maugham. Longmans,
　　Heinemann. 1966.
　　Somerset Maugham, by Anthony Curtis. Weidenfeld & Nicolson.
　　1977 reprint.
　　Somerset Maugham, by Ted Morgan. Cape. 1980.
William LE QUEUX. *The Real Le Queux*, by N. St Barbe Sladen.
　　Nicolson & Watson. 1938.

E. Phillips OPPENHEIM. *The Pool of Memory:* Memoirs, by E. Phillips
Oppenheim. Hodder & Stoughton. 1941.
  The Prince of Storytellers, by Robert Standish. Peter Davies. 1957.

3: Historical

BOYLE, Andrew, *The Climate of Treason:* Five Who Spied for Russia.
Hutchinson. 1979.

BURN, Michael. *The Debatable Land:* a Study of the Motives of Spies in
Two Ages. Hamish Hamilton. 1970.

CALVOCORESSI, Peter. *Top Secret Ultra.* Cassell. 1980.

COMMAND. *Security Procedures in the Public Service* (Lord Ratcliffe)
H.M.S.O. 1978.

FITZGIBBON, Constantine. *Secret Intelligence in the Twentieth Century.*
Hart-Davis. 1976.

HYDE, H. Montgomery. *The Atom Bomb Spies.* Hamish Hamilton. 1980.

PHILBY, Kim. *My Silent War.* Introduction by Graham Greene. MacGibbon
& Kee. 1968.

PINCHER, Chapman. *Their Trade is Treachery.* Sidgwick & Jackson. 1981.

NEWMAN, Bernard. *The World of Espionage.* Souvenir Press. 1962.

SEARLE, Patrick and MCCONVILLE, Maureen. *Philby: the Long Road to
Moscow.* Hamish Hamilton. 1973.

WISE, David and ROSS, Thomas B. *The Espionage Establishment.* Cape. 1968.

INDEX

Note: fictional characters have been put between inverted commas, to distinguish them from living people. This includes the Secret Service, which does not exist under that name.